THE LONG WALK TO FREEDOM

THE LONG WALK TO FREEDOM

Runaway Slave Narratives

Edited and with Introductions by

DEVON W. CARBADO
AND DONALD WEISE

Beacon Press

BOSTON

BEACON PRESS
25 Beacon Street
Boston, Massachusetts 02108-2892
www.beacon.org

Beacon Press books
are published under the auspices of
the Unitarian Universalist Association of Congregations.

15   14   13   12   8   7   6   5   4   3   2   1

Text design and composition by Wilsted & Taylor Publishing Services

A version of the historical afterword was previously published as "From Bondage to
Freedom: Slavery in America," in Larry Gara, Brenda E. Stevenson, and C. Peter Ripley,
Underground Railroad: An Epic in United States History (Washington, DC: U.S. Department
of the Interior, National Park Service, 1998). Reprinted here with permission.

The runaway slave narratives in this book were taken from
archival sources and transcriptions on the University of North Carolina's
website *Documenting the American South*. Some errors in grammar,
punctuation, and spelling have been corrected.

Library of Congress Cataloging-in-Publication Data
The long walk to freedom : runaway slave narratives /
edited and with introductions by Devon W. Carbado and Donald Weise.
p. cm.
Includes bibliographical references.
ISBN 978-0-8070-6912-7 (hardcover: alk. paper)
1. Fugitive slaves—United States—Biography. 2. Slaves' writings, American.
3. Slavery—United States—History—19th century—Sources. 4. Underground
Railroad—Sources. I. Carbado, Devon W. II. Weise, Donald.
E450.L83 2012
306.3'62092—dc23   2012004905

CONTENTS

———

.

"I Will Run Away"

"God, deliver me! Let me be free! Is there any God? Why am I a slave?
I will run away. I will not stand it. Get caught, or get clear,
I'll try it. I had as well die with ague as the fever. I have only one life
to lose. I had as well be killed running as die standing."

FREDERICK DOUGLASS, *NARRATIVE OF*
THE LIFE OF FREDERICK DOUGLASS

A decade ago, John Hope Franklin and Loren Schweninger published *Runaway Slaves: Rebels on the Plantation.* The book was part of a much broader literature that challenged the idea that slaves were generally pliant and resigned to their roles as human chattel. While W. E. B. Du Bois, in *Black Reconstruction in America,* had argued vociferously against the idea of slaves as docile and pliant, Franklin and Schweninger's book, among other works, helped to solidify the idea. Far from passively acquiescing to what was euphemistically referred to as "the South's peculiar institution," slaves rebelled against their masters and ran away whenever they could. That they risked life and limb to do so was itself an indication of the brutality of slavery.

Runaway Slaves was successful—both in commercial terms and with respect to the critical acclaim the book received. But despite its success, since then only a few texts focusing solely on runaway slaves have been published. To be sure, dozens of books of slave narratives are already on the market; the autobiographies of Frederick Douglass and Sojourner Truth, for example, can be found readily. Indeed, slave narratives remain one of the most enduring genres of African American literature.

The Long Walk to Freedom contains the first-ever collection of *fugitive* slave narratives, presented as a unique genre, not simply as slave narratives more generally. The twelve narratives collectively span approximately seventy-six years. Excerpts from the best-known book-length narratives—including those by Douglass, Nat Turner, Harriet Jacobs, William and Ellen Craft—stand alongside narratives that haven't been published in more than a hundred years.

Although most slave narratives were written or recorded after Abolition, the most widely read—even today—are antebellum fugitive accounts. Unlike the narratives of ex-slaves who had purchased their freedom prior to the Civil War or were emancipated afterward, fugitives' stories offer dramatic exploits that overcome staid polemics. Here, one finds patrols of slave catchers and their hounds in relentless pursuit of runaways, wild animals on the attack, intrigue on the Underground Railroad, slaves dangerously masquerading as freed people—sometimes disguised as the opposite sex—in order to pass. The runaway narrative of William Craft, for example, describes how he and his wife, neither of whom was literate, employed public transportation to make their way from Georgia to Pennsylvania. To do so, Ellen Craft disguised herself as a white man traveling with her slave companion.

One finds in these narratives romantic elements as well—slaves running hundreds, if not thousands, of miles to be reunited at all costs with a loved one—that help establish emotional connections between the author and reader, much as if one were reading a novel.

But these are not works of fiction.[1] Cumulatively, these narratives are a useful window on a specific form of black resistance to slavery. The existence of these narratives makes clear that the limited number of large-scale slave revolts does not mean that slaves acquiesced in or were content with their status as slaves. Far from being passive objects of property, slaves resisted—often in incremental and pragmatic ways.

For example, Isaac D. Williams's story conveys the strong, rebellious, and persistent spirit that many slaves possessed in order to run away. In his flight north, Williams was initially pursued by bloodhounds, which he was able to kill. But he was eventually caught and shot, his body riddled with bullets. Nevertheless, Williams survived, managed to escape jail, and fled north again, continuing to defy the dangers of nature and the numerous police and slave owners he encountered along the way.

Slaves ran away for various reasons, among them brutal treatment; confrontations with an owner or overseer; the opportunity to escape; the fear of being sold or transferred, particularly away from one's family; and the fundamental desire to be free. Moses Roper's narrative documents the severe floggings he received from several different slave owners, five hundred lashes at the worst. His repeated attempts to escape, at the risk of again being flogged, no doubt were spurred by these acts of violence, which over time quite literally broke slaves down. "My natural elasticity was crushed," wrote Frederick Douglass in his narrative on the impact of being repeatedly beaten. "[M]y intellect languished, the disposition to read departed . . . the dark night of slavery closed in upon me; and behold a man transformed into a brute!"

According to most historians, "the dark night of slavery" traces back to the first African people brought to British America in August 1619 and sold to English colonizers in Jamestown, Virginia. Some of the relatively small number of Africans in the colonies during this period likely worked as indentured servants side-by-side with white indentured servants who had fled the economic hardships of Europe. Others worked as slaves. As slaves did, white indentured servants often ran away and were punished harshly upon return. Thus, it was not uncommon to see advertisements in local newspapers for both black and white fugitives. For example, the September 26, 1751, edition of the *Pennsylvania Journal* sought the return of "an Irish Servant

Man, Named Christopher Cooney, of Short Stature, pale Complex-ion, short brown Hair."[2] But because whiteness carried with it the presumption of freedom and blackness the presumption of slavery, indentured whites had an easier time escaping their servitude than did blacks.

In 1775, on the eve of the Revolutionary War, slavery in the thirteen Colonies was more than 150 years old and had become part of the legal and racial caste system. But the revolutionary fervor of the time made the institution of slavery more vulnerable than it had ever been. The ideals of the colonists—freedom from English oppression, and self-determination—were at least somewhat, if not thoroughly, inconsis-tent with the idea of slavery.

Other factors also helped to delegitimize the institution. One was economic: the tobacco market had crashed, and the wheat crops that replaced tobacco did not require the same kind of labor-intensive work, reducing the demand for slave workers. Compounding matters was a general recession, which found many slave owners unable to feed and support their unpaid labor force.

Religion also generated abolitionist ideas. The Great Awakening— a movement that reinvigorated Christianity by encouraging an emotional engagement with religion, a sense of personal spiritual commitment, and feelings of guilt for one's moral transgressions— particularly motivated Baptists and Methodists to save the souls of black folks.

Moreover, Lord Dunmore, the dethroned governor of Virginia, to cite one example, "issued a proclamation of freedom to all slaves who would fight for the king."[3] This invitation also undermined slavery, and many slaves ran away in search of that promised freedom.

Finally, the Revolutionary War itself weakened the institution of slavery by creating runaway opportunities through general upheaval (for example, slave masters fled war-torn territories along with their slaves) and because the significant number of white men who left their plantations to join the Patriot Army created an absence that the slaves could and did exploit. More than twenty thousand slaves, many runaways, ended up under the authority of the British military during this time.

Even for the blacks who remained in slavery during the Revolutionary War period, change seemed to be on the way. Because the war had further diminished the already dwindling tobacco economy, reducing the demand for slave labor, slaves had greater freedom to pursue more skilled occupations. Indeed, slave owners permitted their more trusted slaves to lease themselves out to other owners. This transaction was risky for both the slave owner and the slave. The owner never knew whether his "property" would be returned "intact," and the slave never knew the conditions under which he (and it was mostly men who could lease themselves out) could be forced to work in a new setting. Nevertheless, the practice of leasing enabled slaves to visit relatives and friends, and to forge relationships with whites outside of the plantation economy. Leasing also provided a means by which slaves could run away. It is unclear how many slaves exploited that limited opportunity, though, since free blacks could still be captured and re-enslaved, as Robert the Hermit's runaway narrative attests. Robert Voorhis persuaded "a friend" to pay his master 50 pounds for his freedom. Voorhis rejoiced in the promise of his future when the payment occurred, but then quickly learned that his status as a slave would not be shed so easily. His friend, James Bevens or Bivens, sold him into the Southern market, and Voorhis was taken onto a schooner and chained there. He was subsequently sold at a public auction in South Carolina.

Still, other anti-slavery currents flowed from the federal government. The Continental Congress passed a resolution opposing slavery as well as the Northwest Ordinance, which prohibited slavery in what is today Indiana, Illinois, Michigan, Wisconsin, and parts of Minnesota. There was reason to be at least cautiously optimistic about the dismantling of slavery as the Revolutionary War came to an end.

But there were early signs that slavery might have a postwar life. In the heady rhetoric of the Declaration of Independence and a successful resolution to war, the fledgling United States of America embarked upon the hard work of nation building. The drafters of the Constitution took a sober look at the rhetoric of radical egalitarianism in the Declaration, and they blinked. The adoption of the Constitution in 1787, and its ratification one year later, depended on a compromise, one that integrated slavery into the Constitution.

Yet, even with the constitutionalization of slavery in our "Founding Document," there was reason to be somewhat hopeful. In Maryland and Virginia, the legislatures openly debated antislavery proposals and passed laws making manumission—the ability of slave owners to free their slaves—easier. Several other states passed similar measures that encouraged some owners to immediately free their slaves and others, including George Washington, to do so in their wills. Between 1782 and 1790, more than ten thousand slaves were freed. Northern legislatures were even more aggressive. Some, such as Vermont, abolished the institution outright. Others, including New York, promulgated gradual emancipation acts, freeing people born into slavery upon becoming young adults. An anti-slavery mood, however slight, could be felt nationally.

But this abolitionist mood soon waned. Precipitating this change was the shift in agriculture from tobacco and rice to cotton. Eli Whitney's cotton gin, invented in 1793, made it possible for plantations to mass produce cotton and sell it for commercial profit. Profits soared. By 1800, the United States was producing around 40 million pounds of cotton, and slavery's main center became the Deep South, the home of cotton production.

This revised system of slavery was brutal. But it did not yet compel most slaves to venture north, even though several Northern states had abolished slavery by the mid-1800s. In fact, many runaway slaves travelled only relatively short distances within the South in part because they were trying not to permanently escape from slavery but rather to temporarily withhold their labor as a form of economic negotiation with their slave owners. Slavery involved a constant process of negotiation, as slaves bargained over the pace of work, free time, monetary rewards, and the freedom to practice burials, marriages, and religious ceremonies away from white oversight. Running away was a part of this negotiation process.

However, some slaves did attempt to escape slavery permanently. While the idea of escaping slavery may bring to mind the Underground Railroad that carried slaves to the free Northern states, in reality more than half of these long-distance runaways headed to Southern cities, where they hoped to blend into free black populations. This fact should not obscure the importance of the Underground Railroad, which at its height in the 1850s, facilitated the escape of approximately one thousand people per year from Southern slave states to the North. Blacks played a crucial role in organizing and effectuating this abolitionist activity. Many slaves who had escaped to the North risked their lives and freedom returning to the South to help others escape. Harriet Tubman, for example, made nineteen trips back into slave country and helped at least three hundred enslaved people escape. Blacks in the North also formed vigilance committees, which helped board and lodge escaped slaves, gave them money, educated them as to their legal rights, and helped them find jobs.

The community around the Underground Railroad proved particularly ripe for the production of slave narratives. Abolitionists were convinced that the eyewitness testimony of former slaves against slavery would touch the hearts and minds of many in the Northern population who were either ignorant of or indifferent to the plight of African Americans in the South. The most popular antebellum narratives, by authors such as Frederick Douglass, William Wells Brown, and Harriet Jacobs, stressed how African Americans survived in slavery, resisting exploitation, occasionally fighting back, and escaping in search of better prospects elsewhere in the North and in Canada. Tens of thousands of copies of these narratives were made available to the American public—and never before had the words of enslaved blacks reached such wide audiences. In time, the approximately seventy testimonies published prior to the end of the Civil War played an instrumental role in dismantling slavery.

For those slaves who attempted to escape permanently, the ob-

stacles in their path were so enormous that the majority were apprehended long before they ever reached free soil. Slaves were usually
illiterate and could not read signs or maps. Generally, they lacked sufficient food, water, and access to transportation. Moreover, their raw
cotton clothing was often a conspicuous marker of their slave status,
further increasing the likelihood that the runaway would be recaptured, as most ultimately were.

Suspicious whites were a constant threat to runaways. And some
runaway slaves were more "suspicious" to them than others. Light-
skinned blacks had an easier time escaping than did their darker-
skinned counterparts. But even light-skinned blacks were vulnerable
to capture. Indeed, many runaway advertisements specifically indicated that the sought-after slave might try to pass as white. One, for
example, noted that the owner's runaway, Guy, would "no doubt en-
deavor to pass himself as a white man." Another indicated that his runaway was "remarkably white for a slave" and that the runaway could
"pass for a white man."[4] In this sense, not even light-skinned blacks
who made it to free territories were guaranteed sanctuary. Runaways
were routinely seized out of state by professional slave hunters, local
authorities, and sometimes even their own masters, who would travel
considerable distances to claim their "property."

James Curry's narrative is instructive on this point. It reveals the
vulnerability of runaways to being re-enslaved. Curry recounts escaping and making his way to Pennsylvania. There, thinking he was
now free, he stopped to work for a white man. However, Curry
was informed by a "colored woman" in the house that if he did not
have free papers he would likely be forced back into slavery. Worried
about this eventuality, Curry left and continued on to Canada.

Curry had reason to worry. In 1842, in *Prigg v. Pennsylvania,* the
Supreme Court strengthened the Fugitive Slave Act of 1793, which
required free states to return fugitive slaves to their masters. Because
the act said very little about the process by which slaves would be returned, or of the burden of proof required to sustain a claim of ownership, "slave traders would knowingly target free blacks and then

submit forged affidavits to the court" claiming ownership.[5] This led states like Pennsylvania to enact anti-kidnapping statutes, requiring slave catchers to seek judicial authorization before removing slaves from the state's jurisdiction. The Supreme Court declared Pennsylvania's law unconstitutional, ruling that it obstructed the rights of slave owners to reclaim their property—fugitive slaves. The *Prigg* opinion, and the right of recapture that it created for slave owners, made running away all the more precarious.

Thirteen years after *Prigg,* the Supreme Court again weighed in on the question of slavery in *Dred Scott v. Sandford,* which declared that blacks, whether slave or free, were not citizens and that "the black man had no rights that that white man had to respect."[6] *Dred Scott* also decided that the Missouri Compromise was null, putting an end to the check on the growth of slavery. Abolitionists were infuriated by this opinion, and it recommitted them to their anti-slavery cause.

While the *Dred Scott* case boded well for the Southern states, the impending election of Abraham Lincoln caused slave owners to worry. In his presidential campaign, Lincoln had indicated that he would curtail the extension of slavery, even though he did not call for its complete abolition. Upon Lincoln's election, seven Southern states seceded from the Union. Many contend that Lincoln's sole goal from then on was to save the Union, with the abolition of slavery becoming a secondary goal or merely an incidental benefit, should it even happen. Lincoln himself said, "What I do about slavery, and the colored race, I do because it helps to save the Union, and what I forbear, I forbear because I do not believe it would help save the Union."[7]

The Civil War began in 1861 when Confederate forces attacked a military installation at Fort Sumter in South Carolina. While many enslaved people fought for the South, many more escaped to the North to fight in the Union armies. In 1862, Congress passed an act prohibiting the use of military force to return escaped slaves.[8] Shortly thereafter, slavery was abolished in Washington, DC, and by June 19, 1862, it was abolished in all the territories. President Lincoln's Emancipation Proclamation now officially allowed blacks to enlist in the military, although for far less pay than whites received, and with shoddy equipment and medical care. To keep up the fight against the Union forces, the South began to promote emancipation and to use blacks as soldiers for their side. But, on April 9, 1865, the South was defeated, and the Civil War was over.[9]

The First Reconstruction began during the war, in 1863, and persisted until 1877. During this period, various pockets of people in many states, including Southern states, advocated for abolition and a reorganization of government. To ensure the end of slavery, free blacks advocated for much more. This advocacy helped to establish the Freedmen's Bureau, which met some of the basic needs of formerly enslaved people, such as the distribution of clothing and food.[10] However, the bureau was never able to follow through with the distribution of land to free blacks.[11]

The moment carried with it radical possibilities nonetheless. Congress passed the Thirteenth, Fourteenth, and Fifteenth amendments and the Civil Rights Act of 1875, which outlawed the exclusion of blacks from public accommodations. Moreover, numerous blacks were elected to Southern state legislatures, and, after 1869, two blacks were elected to the U.S. Senate. Additionally, by 1876, seventy thousand black children were going to school when none had formally attended before.

Yet, at the end of the Civil War, nineteen out of the twenty-four Northern states did not allow blacks to vote, and, soon thereafter, all the Southern states wrote disfranchisement provisions into law. Additionally, the 1860s and '70s saw the formation of the Ku Klux Klan, which organized raids, lynchings, and the burnings of blacks.[12] This was the beginning of Jim Crow, a system that, as a matter of constitutional law, was not significantly undermined until the Supreme Court ruled on *Brown v. Board of Education,* in 1954.

In the meantime, Emancipation was the former slaves' new reality, and they employed this reality as a time to reflect on their slavery experiences. The testimonials they gave differed somewhat from earlier accounts. While the experiences of slavery continued to figure prominently in fugitive narratives, themes of racial uplift became more salient. Taking racism as a given, many of these narratives reflected the idea that black collective action and institution building was a necessary precondition to full citizenship. At the same time, the narratives made clear that blacks were deserving of and capable of handling full citizenship—their resistance to slavery had helped make them political actors who could decide their own destiny.

Finally, runaway slave narratives helped to establish a tradition of protest writing within the African American community. Running away, though enormously difficult and courageous, was a more realizable political activity than organized slave revolts. While mass-organized slave revolts did occur, they were not the dominant form of slave resistance. This is not to say that there were no efforts of mass resistance. Indeed, according to Herbert Aptheker, more than 250 slave revolts occurred in America between 1619 and 1865.[13] While scholars continue to debate the accuracy of this number, most agree that "[n]othing in the South remotely resembled the Haitian insurrection in which slaves took advantage of the French revolution to wage a triumphant revolutionary war of their own."[14] Much more frequent were slaves' "daily micro aggressions"—breaking tools, feigning illness, destroying crops, arson, avoiding work, impeding the work of others, poisoning their owners—and running away. By bringing these everyday protests to the attention of a larger audience, runaway narratives and slave narratives more generally opened the door to the protest writings of Ida B. Wells, W. E. B. Du Bois, Richard Wright, Martin Luther King Jr., James Baldwin, Malcolm X, Amiri Baraka, Audre Lorde, Angela Davis, Alice Walker, Toni Morrison, and Ishmael Reed, among many other African American firebrand authors. Protest is a significant part of the African American literary tradition—and that tradition has at least part of its roots in runaway slave narratives.

To highlight particular dimensions of the runaway experience, *The Long Walk to Freedom* is organized into four parts. Part 1, "Running to

Be Free," highlights narratives whose authors seem to be particularly driven by a desire to be free. Moses Roper's narrative, for example, chronicles his early years, including his childhood and sale to the merciless Mr. Gooch, a cotton planter in Cashaw County, South Carolina, and the most severe of Roper's many owners. These experiences made Roper yearn for freedom, which he sought to achieve by running away. Frederick Douglass, too, was motivated by a desire to be free—and he was willing to risk his life for. As Douglass put it, "I have only one life to lose. I had as well be killed running as die standing."

The narratives in part 2, "Running Because of Family," reveal the vulnerability, fragility, and strength of the slave family. Slavery tore families apart. Children were separated from parents and husbands from wives, as Isaac Johnson's runaway narrative reveals. Johnson was born to and grew up with a white man and a black woman. On Johnson's seventh birthday, his white father sold Isaac, his mother, and his three other brothers into slavery. Each was purchased by a different family. Isaac never saw any of his family members again.

Part 3, "Running Inspired by Religion," captures how deeply religion shaped the runaway slave experience. Christianity engendered not only a spiritual awakening in slaves, but a political awakening as well. Solomon Bayley's narrative conveys his strong faith and belief in God, and his reliance upon religion to provide him with the strength to continue to struggle for his freedom. Religion also influenced one of the most important uprisings in the nineteenth century, Nat Turner's rebellion. Turner used religion and preaching to encourage eighty other enslaved people to revolt, which resulted in the runaways' killing of fifty-seven whites. Turner's narrative tells of a spirit that appeared before him urging him to await a sign for the moment in which he should rise and fight the "Serpent." Two days into the revolt, the escaped blacks were defeated, and a large number of those who participated were executed, including Nat Turner.[15] This rebellion shocked whites in the South and fueled hysteria, with the constant fear that rebellion was always lurking around the corner.

Part 4, "Running by Any Means Necessary," is a window onto

the obstacles slaves had to overcome to run away, the means they employed to do so, and the lengths to which slaves would go to conceal their identities as runaways. Take the narrative of Harriet Jacobs, the remarkable survival story of a woman who hid herself in a seven-by-nine-foot crawlspace on her master's property to avoid the sexual advances and physical abuses her master inflicted. Consider as well the narrative of Henry "Box" Brown. Brown's narrative tells the triumphant story of how he sealed himself in a box, posed as dry goods, and had himself delivered to the Pennsylvania Anti-Slavery Society in Philadelphia. Brown endured twenty-seven hours in that box, including considerable amounts of time on his head, but was successful in reaching Philadelphia. Those, like Brown, who successfully escaped from slavery and lived to write about it have fascinated and inspired readers ever since. Part 4 brings into sharp relief the extreme measures slaves undertook to run away.

In organizing *The Long Walk to Freedom* along the foregoing lines, our hope is to capture the many dimensions of the runaway phenomenon—why slaves ran away, how they did so, what happened to them while on the run, the places they fled to, their survival strategies, the extent to which they found freedom, how long they remained in hiding, their reliance on white abolitionists, their sense of political agency, their interaction with other runaways, and the help they received from freed blacks. Yet, *The Long Walk to Freedom* does not purport to fully capture the runaway experience. No single text could. What this book does is provide an account of the runaway experience in which the fugitive slaves speak in their own voices and on their own terms.

The voices of the fugitive slaves reflected in these narratives become even more compelling against a background understanding of slavery. While this introduction references some of the broader historical developments of slavery, our analysis focuses mostly on the runaway phenomenon. For readers who want a broader sense of the history of slavery, we have included as a historical afterword an essay by Brenda Stevenson, professor of history at the University of

California at Los Angeles, who, in 1996, published one of the most definitive books on slave families, *Life in Black and White: Family and Community in the Slave South.* While any attempt to provide a history of slavery in a few pages is necessarily incomplete, hers is a concise, careful, and cogently written account that further contextualizes the runaway slave phenomenon.

NOTES

1. Scholars continue to debate the authenticity of some slave narratives. While it is reasonable to raise questions about the veracity or accuracy of any particular runaway narrative, cumulatively, they reflect a historical phenomenon.
2. Kolchin, *American Slavery,* 13.
3. Hartgrove, "The Negro Soldier in the American Revolution." 110, 115.
4. Franklin and Schweninger, *Runaway Slaves,* 215.
5. Sullivan, "Classical Racialism, Justice Story, and Margaret Morgan's Journey from Freedom to Slavery," 65.
6. Dred Scott v. Sandford, 60 U.S. (19 How.) 393 (1857).
7. Foner, *History of Black Americans: From the Emergence of the Cotton Kingdom to the Eve of the Compromise of 1850,* 343.
8. Boles, *Black Southerners,* 189, n. 4.
9. Ibid., 198.
10. Foner, *History of Black Americans: From the Emergence of the Cotton Kingdom to the Eve of the Compromise of 1850,* 31, n. 8.
11. Ibid.
12. Ibid., 243.
13. Aptheker, *American Negro Slave Revolts.*
14. Kolchin, *American Slavery,* 156.
15. Aptheker, *American Negro Slave Revolts,* 54–55, n. 14.

PART ONE

Running to Be Free

*Mr. Anderson attempting to shoot Moses Roper. According to the law,
after telling a slave to stop three times, slaveholders were allowed to shoot.
From* A Narrative of the Adventures and Escape of Moses Roper, from
American Slavery. *Image courtesy of* Documenting the American South,
the University of North Carolina at Chapel Hill Libraries.

ONE

From *A Narrative of the Adventures and Escape of Moses Roper, from American Slavery. With an Appendix, Containing a List of Places Visited by the Author in Great Britain and Ireland and the British Isles; and Other Matter.*

The autobiography of Moses Roper stands as one of the most important early narratives to expose the horrors of slavery. Published in 1848, his book-length narrative recalls in unflinching detail the extreme brutality that Roper, a habitual runaway, and fellow slaves experienced at the hands of sixteen masters before his final escape from slavery in 1834.

Born around 1815 to a half-white slave mother and her master, Roper was nearly murdered with a knife at birth by his father's wife— Roper's mother's mistress—when the family resemblance and infidelity were brought to light. Only the intercession of Roper's grandmother prevented his death. He was raised as a domestic until about age seven, when his master (and father) traded his mother and him for new slaves.

In these chapters, the author chronicles his early years, including his childhood and sale to the merciless Mr. Gooch, a cotton planter in

Originally published: Berwick-upon-Tweed: Published for the author and printed at the Warder Office, 1848.

Editors' note: Subsequent footnotes in this section are from Moses Roper's original document.

Cashaw County, South Carolina, and the most severe of Roper's many owners. In so doing, Roper helps lay to rest prevailing and romantic notions about the realities of slave life and the unwillingness of some blacks to submit to it, even on penalty of death.

CHAPTER I.

Birth-place of the Author.—The first time he was sold from his Mother, and passed through several other hands.

I was born in North Carolina, in Caswell County, I am not able to tell in what month or year. What I shall now relate, is what was told me by my mother and grandmother. A few months before I was born, my father married my mother's young mistress. As soon as my father's wife heard of my birth, she sent one of my mother's sisters to see whether I was white or black, and when my aunt had seen me, she returned back as soon as she could, and told her mistress that I was white, and resembled Mr. Roper very much. Mr. Roper's wife not being pleased with this report, she got a large club-stick and knife, and hastened to the place in which my mother was confined. She went into my mother's room with a full intention to murder me with her knife and club, but as she was going to stick the knife into me, my grandmother happening to come in, caught the knife and saved my life. But as well as I can recollect from what my mother told me, my father sold her and myself, soon after her confinement. I cannot recollect anything that is worth notice till I was six or seven years of age. My mother being half white, and my father a white man, I was at that time very white. Soon after I was six or seven years of age, my mother's old master died, that is, my father's wife's father. All his slaves had to be divided among the children.[1]

---

1. Slaves are usually a part of the marriage portion, but lent rather than given, to be returned to the estate at the decease of the father, in order that they may be divided equally among his children.

I have mentioned before of my father disposing of me; I am not sure whether he exchanged me and my mother for another slave or not, but think it very likely he did exchange me with one of his wife's brothers or sisters, because I remember when my mother's old master died, I was living with my father's wife's brother-in-law, whose name was Mr. Durham. My mother was drawn with the other slaves.

The way they divide their slaves is this: they write the names of different slaves on a small piece of paper, and put it into a box, and let them all draw. I think that Mr. Durham drew my mother, and Mr. Fowler drew me, so we were separated a considerable distance, I cannot say how far. My resembling my father so much, and being whiter than the other slaves, caused me to be soon sold to what they call a negro trader, who took me to the Southern States of America, several hundred miles from my mother. As well as I can recollect I was then about six years old. The trader, Mr. Mitchell, after travelling several hundred miles, and selling a good many of his slaves, found he could not sell me very well, (as I was so much whiter than other slaves were) for he had been trying several months—left me with a Mr. Sneed, who kept a large boarding-house, who took me to wait at table, and sell me if he could. I think I stayed with Mr. Sneed about a year, but he could not sell me. When Mr. Mitchell had sold his slaves, he went to the north, and brought up another drove, and returned to the south with them, and sent his son-in-law into Washington, in Georgia, after me; so he came and took me from Mr. Sneed, and met his father-in-law with me, in a town called Lancaster, with his drove of slaves. We stayed in Lancaster a week, because it was court week, and there were a great many people there, and it was a good opportunity for selling the slaves; and there he was enabled to sell me to a gentleman, Dr. Jones, who was both a Doctor and a Cotton Planter. He took me into his shop to beat up and mix medicines, which was not a very hard employment, but I did not keep it long, as the Doctor soon sent me to his cotton plantation, that I might be burnt darker by the sun. He sent me to be with a tailor to learn the trade, but the journeymen being white men, Mr. Bryant, the tailor, did not let me work in the shop; I cannot say whether it was the prejudice of his men in not wanting me to sit in the shop with them, or whether Mr. Bryant wanted to keep me about the house to do the domestic work, instead of teaching me the trade. After several months, my master came to know how I got on with the trade: I am not able to tell Mr. Bryant's answer, but it was either that I could not learn, or that his journeymen were unwilling that I should sit in the shop with them. I was only once in the shop all the time I was there, and then only for an hour or two before his wife called me out to do some other work. So my master took me home, and as he was going to send a load of cotton to Camden, about forty miles distance, he sent me with the bales of cotton to be sold with it, where I was sold to a gentleman, named Allen; but Mr. Allen soon exchanged me for a female slave to please his wife. The traders who bought me, were named Cooper and Lindsey, who took me for sale, but could not sell me, people objecting to my being rather white. They then took me to the city of Fayetteville, North Carolina, where he swopt me for a boy, that was blacker than me, to Mr. Smith, who lived several miles off.

I was with Mr. Smith nearly a year. I arrived at the first knowledge of my age when I lived with him. I was then between twelve and thirteen years old; it was when President Jackson was elected the first time, and he has been President eight years, so I must be nearly twenty-one years of age. At this time I was quite a small boy, and was sold to Mr. Hodge, a negro trader. Here I began to enter into hardships.

CHAPTER II.

The Author's being sold to Mr. J. Gooch.—The cruel treatment he both received and witnessed while on his estate.—Repeated attempts at running away.—Escapes to his mother after being absent from her about ten years.—Meets with his sister, whom he had never seen before, on the road, who conducted him to his mother.

After travelling several hundred miles, Mr. Hodge sold me to Mr. Gooch, the Cotton Planter, Cashaw County, South Carolina; he purchased me at a town called Liberty Hill, about three miles from his home. As soon as he got home, he immediately put me on his cotton plantation to work, and put me under overseers, gave me an allowance of meat and bread with the other slaves, which was not half enough for me to live upon, and very laborious work; here my heart was almost broke with grief at leaving my fellow-slaves. Mr. Gooch did not mind my grief, for he flogged me nearly every day, and very severely. Mr. Gooch bought me for his son-in-low, Mr. Hammans, about five miles distance from his residence. This man had but two slaves besides myself; he treated me very kindly for a week or two, but in summer, when cotton was ready to hoe, he gave me task work, connected with this department, which I could not get done, not having worked on cotton farms before. When I failed in my task he commenced flogging me, and set me to work without any shirt, in the cotton field, in a very hot sun, in the month of July. In August, Mr. Condell, his overseer, gave me a task at pulling fodder; having finished my task before night, I left the field, the rain came on which soaked the fodder; on discovering this, he threatened to flog me for not getting in the fodder before the rain came. I attempted to run away, knowing that I should get a flogging. I was then between thirteen and fourteen years of age; I ran away to the woods half naked; I was caught by a slave-holder who put me in Lancaster Gaol. When they put slaves in gaol, they advertise for their masters to own them; but if the master does not claim his slave in six months from the time of imprisonment, the slave is sold for gaol fees. When the slave runs away, the master always adopts a more rigorous system of flogging; this was the case in the present instance. After this, having determined from my youth to gain my freedom, I made several attempts, was caught, and got a severe flogging of one hundred lashes, each time. Mr. Hammans was a very severe and cruel master, and his wife still worse; she used to tie me up and flog me while naked.

After Mr. Hammans saw that I was determined to die in the woods, and not live with him, he tried to obtain a piece of land from his father-in-law, Mr. Gooch: not having the means of purchasing it, he exchanged me for the land.

As soon as Mr. Gooch had possession of me again, knowing that I was averse to going back to him, he chained me by the neck to his chaise. In this manner he took me to his home at Mac Daniels Ferry, in the County of Chester, a distance of fifteen miles. After which, he put me into a swamp to cut trees, the heaviest work, which men of twenty-five or thirty years of age have to do, I being but sixteen. Here I was on very short allowance of food, and having heavy work, was too weak to fulfil my tasks. For this, I got many severe floggings: and, after I had got my irons off, I made another attempt at running away. He took my irons off, in the full anticipation that I could never get across the Catarba River, even when at liberty. On this, I procured a small Indian canoe, which was tied to a tree, and ultimately got across the river in it. I then wandered through the wilderness for several days without any food, and but a drop of water to allay my thirst, till I become so starved, that I was obliged to go to a house to beg for something to eat, when I was captured, and again imprisoned.

Mr. Gooch having heard of me through an advertisement, sent his son after me; he tied me up, and took me back to his father. Mr. Gooch then obtained the assistance of another slaveholder, and tied me up in his blacksmith's shop, and gave me fifty lashes with a cow-hide. He then put a log chain, weighing twenty-five pounds, round my neck, and sent me into a field, into which he followed me with a cow-hide, intending to set his slaves to flog me again. Knowing this, and dreading to suffer again in this way, I gave him the slip, and got out of his sight, he having stopped to speak with the other slaveholder.

I got to a canal on the Catarba River, on the banks of which, and near to a loch, I procured a stone and a piece of iron, with which I forced the ring off my chain, and got it off, and then crossed the river, and walked about twenty miles, when I fell in with a slave-holder, named Ballad, who had married the sister of Mr. Hammans. I knew that he was not so cruel as Mr. Gooch, and therefore begged of him to buy me. Mr. Ballad, who was one of the best planters in the neighbourhood, said that he was not able to buy me, and stated that he was obliged to take me back to my master, on account of the heavy fine attaching to a man harbouring a slave. Mr. Ballad proceeded to take me back; as we came in sight of Mr. Gooch's all the treatment that I had met with there, came forcibly upon my mind, the powerful influence of which is beyond description. On my knees, with tears in my eyes, with terror in my countenance, and fervency in all my features, I implored Mr. Ballad to buy me, but he again refused, and I was taken back to my dreaded and cruel master. Having reached Mr. Gooch's he proceeded to punish me. This he did, by first tying my wrists together and placing them over the knees, he then put a stick through, under my knees and over my arms, and having thus secured my arms, he proceeded to flog me, and gave me five hundred lashes on my bare back. This may appear incredible, but the marks which they left at present remain on my body, a standing testimony to the truth of this statement of his severity. He then chained me down in a log-pen with a forty pounds chain, and made me lie on the damp earth all night. In the morning, after his breakfast, he came to me, and without giving me any breakfast, tied me to a large heavy harrow, which is usually drawn by a horse, and made me drag it to the cotton field for the horse to use in the field. Thus, the reader will see, that it was of no possible use to my master to make me drag it to the cotton field and not through it; his cruelty went so far, as actually to make me the slave of his horse, and thus to degrade me. He then flogged me again, and set me to work in the cotton field the whole of that day, and at night chained me down in the log-pen as before. The next morning he took me to the cotton field, and gave me a third flogging, and sent me to hoe cotton. At this time I was dreadfully sore and weak with the repeated floggings and cruel treatment I had endured. He put me under a black man, with orders, that if I did not keep up my row in hoeing with this man, he was to flog me. The reader must recollect here, that not being used to this kind of work, having been a domestic slave, it was impossible for me to keep up with him, and therefore I was repeatedly flogged during the day.

Mr. Gooch had a female servant about eighteen years old, who had also been a domestic slave, and, through not being able to fulfil her task, had run away: which slave he was at this time punishing for that offence. On the third day, he chained me to this female slave, with a large chain of forty pounds[2] weight round my neck.

It was most harrowing to my feelings thus to be chained to a young female slave, for whom I would rather have suffered one hundred lashes than she should have been thus treated; he kept me chained to her during the week, and repeatedly flogged us both, while thus chained together, and forced us to keep up with the other slaves, although retarded by the heavy weight of the log-chain.

Here again, words cannot describe the misery which possessed both body and mind whilst under this treatment, and which was most dreadfully increased by the sympathy which I felt for my poor, degraded fellow-sufferer. On the Friday morning, I entreated my master to set me free from my chains, and promised him to do the task which was given me, and more if possible, if he would desist from flogging me. This he refused to do until Saturday night, when he did set me free.—This must rather be ascribed to his own interest in preserving me from death, as it was very evident I could no longer have survived under such treatment.

After this, though still determined in my own mind to escape, I stayed with him some months, during which he frequently flogged me, but not so severely as before related.—During this time, I had opportunity for recovering my health, and using means to heal my wounds. My master's cruelty was not confined to me, it was his general conduct to all his slaves. I might relate many instances to substantiate this, but will confine myself to one or two. Mr. Gooch, it is proper to observe, was a member of a Baptist Church, called Black Jack Meeting House, in Cashaw County, which church I attended for several years, but was never inside. This is accounted for by the fact, that the coloured population are not permitted to mix with the white population. In the Roman Catholic Church no distinction is made.

---

2. This was a chain that they used to draw logs with from the woods, when they clear their land.

Mr. Gooch had a slave named Phil, who was a member of a Methodist Church; this man was between seventy and eighty years of age; he was so feeble that he could not accomplish his tasks, for which his master used to chain him round the neck, and run him down a steep hill; this treatment he never relinquished to the time of his death. Another case was that of a slave, named Peter, who, for not doing his task, he flogged nearly to death, and afterwards pulled out his pistol to shoot him, but his (Mr. Gooch's) daughter snatched the pistol from his hand. Another mode of punishment which this man adopted, was that of using iron horns, with bells, attached to the back of the slave's neck. . . .

This instrument he used to prevent the negroes running away, being a very ponderous machine, several feet in height, and the cross pieces being two feet four, and six feet in length. This custom is generally adopted among the slave-holders in South Carolina, and other slave States. One morning, about an hour before day break, I was going on an errand for my master; having proceeded about a quarter of a mile, I came up to a man named King, (Mr. Sumlin's overseer,) who had caught a young girl that had run away with the above machine on her. She had proceeded four miles from her station, with the intention of getting into the hands of a more humane master. She came up with this overseer nearly dead, and could get no farther; he immediately secured her, and took her back to her master, a Mr. Johnson.

Having been in the habit of going over many slave States with my master, I had good opportunities of witnessing the harsh treatment which was adopted by masters towards their slaves. As I have never heard or read anything connected with slavery, so cruel as what I have myself witnessed, it will be as well to mention a case or two.

A large farmer, Colonel McQuiller in Cashaw county, South Carolina, was in the habit of driving nails into a hogshead so as to leave the point of the nail just protruding in the inside of the cask; into this, he used to put his slaves for punishment, and roll them down a very long and steep hill. I have heard from several slaves, (though I had no means of ascertaining the truth of this statement,) that in this way he had killed six or seven of his slaves. This plan was first adopted by a Mr. Perry, who lived on the Catarba River, and has since been adopted by several planters. Another was that of a young lad, who had been hired by Mr. Bell, a member of a holding church, to hoc three-quarters of an acre of cotton per day. Having been brought up as a domestic slave, he was not able to accomplish the task assigned to him. On the Saturday night, he left three or four rows to do on the Sunday; on the same night it rained very hard, by which the master could tell that he had done some of the rows on the Sunday; on Monday, his master took and tied him up to a tree in the field, and kept him there the whole of that day and flogged him at intervals. At night, when he was taken down, he was so weak that he could not get home, having a mile to go. Two white men who were employed by Mr. Bell, put him on a horse, took him home, and threw him, down on the kitchen floor, while they proceeded to their supper. In a little while, they heard some deep groans proceeding from the kitchen; they went to see him die; he had groaned his last. Thus, Mr. Bell flogged the poor boy, even to death, for what? For breaking the Sabbath, when he (his master) had set him a task, on Saturday, which it was not possible for him to do, and which, if he did not do, no mercy would be extended towards him! The general custom in this respect is, that if a man kills his own slave, no notice is taken of it by the civil functionaries; but if a man kills a slave belonging to another master, he is compelled to pay the worth of the slave. In this case, a jury met, returned a verdict of "Wilful Murder" against this man, and ordered him to pay the value. Mr. Bell was unable to do this, but a Mr. Cunningham paid the debt, and took this Mr. Bell, with this recommendation for cruelty, to be his overseer.

It will be observed that most of the cases here cited, are those in respect to males. Many instances, however, in respect to females, might be mentioned, but are too disgusting to appear in this narrative. The cases here brought forward are not rare, but the continued feature of slavery. But I must now follow up the narrative as regards myself in peculiar. I stayed with this master for several months, during which time we went on very well in general. In August, 1831 (this was my first acquaintance with any date), I happened to hear a man mention this date, and, as it excited my curiosity, I asked what it meant; they told me it was the number of the year from the birth of Christ. On this date, August 1831, some cows broke into a crib where the corn is kept, and ate a great deal. For this, his slaves were tied up, and received several floggings: but myself and another man, hearing the groans of those who were being flogged, stayed back in the field, and would not come up. Upon this, I thought to escape punishment. On the Monday morning, however, I heard my master flogging the other man who was in the field; he could not see me, it being a field of Indian corn, which grows to a great height. Being afraid that he would catch me, and dreading a flogging more than many other, I determined to run for it; and, after travelling forty miles, I arrived at the estate of Mr. Crawford, in North Carolina, Mecklinburgh county. Having formerly heard people talk about the Free States, I determined upon going thither, and, if possible, in my way to find out my poor mother, who was in slavery, several hundred miles from Chester; but the hope of doing the latter was very faint, and, even if I did, it was not likely that she would know me, having been separated from her when between five and six years old.

The first night I slept in a barn, upon Mr. Crawford's estate, and, having overslept myself, was awoke by Mr. Crawford's overseer, upon which I was dreadfully frightened; he asked me what I was doing there? I made no reply to him then; and he making sure that he had secured a runaway slave, did not press me for an answer. On my way to his house, however, I made up the following story, which I told him in the presence of his wife:—I said that I had been bound to a very cruel master when I was a little boy, and that having been treated very badly I wanted to get home to see my mother. This statement may appear to some to be untrue, but as I understood the word *bound,* I considered it to apply to my case, having been sold to him, and thereby bound to serve him; though still, I did rather hope that he would understand it, that I was bound when a boy till twenty-one years of age. Though I was white at that time, he would not believe my story, on account of my hair being curly and wooly, which led him to conclude I was possessed of enslaved blood. The overseer's wife, however, who seemed much interested in me, said she did not think I was of the African origin, and that she had seen white men still darker than me; her persuasion prevailed; and after the overseer had given me as much butter-milk as I could drink, and something to eat, which was very acceptable, having had nothing for two days, I set off for Charlotte, in North Carolina, the largest town in the county. I went on very quickly the whole of that day, fearful of being pursued. The trees were thick on each side of the road, and only a few houses, at the distance of two or three miles apart; as I proceeded, I turned round in all directions to see if I was pursued, and if I caught a glimpse of any one coming along the road, I immediately rushed into the thickest part of the wood, to elude the grasp of what, I was afraid, might be my master. I went on in this way the whole day; at night, I came up with two wagons, they had been to market; the regular road wagons do not generally put up at inns, but encamp in the roads and fields. When I came to them, I told them the same story I had told Mr. Crawford's overseer, with the assurance that the statement would meet the same success. After they had heard me, they gave me something to eat, and also a lodging in the camp with them.

I then went on with them about five miles, and they agreed to take me with them as far as they went, if I would assist them. This I promised to do. In the morning, however, I was much frightened by one of the men putting several questions to me—we were then about three miles from Charlotte. When within a mile of the town, we stopped at a brook to water the horses; while stopping there I saw the men whispering, and fancying I overheard them say they would put me in Charlotte gaol when they got there, I made my escape into the woods, pretending to be looking after something till I got out of their sight. I then ran on as fast I could, but did not go through the town of Charlotte, as had been my intention; being a large town I was fearful it might prove fatal to my escape. Here I was at a loss how to get on, as houses were not very distant from each other for nearly two hundred miles.

While thinking what I should do, I observed some waggons before me, which I determined to keep behind, and never go nearer to them than a quarter of a mile—in this way I travelled till I got to Salisbury.

If I happened to meet any person on the road, I was afraid they would take me up, I asked them how far the waggons had gone on before me? to make them suppose I belonged to the waggons. At night, I slept on the ground in the woods, some little distance from the waggons, but not near enough to be seen by the men belonging to them. All this time, I had but little food, principally fruit, which I found on the road. On Thursday night, I got into Salisbury, having left Chester on the Monday preceding. After this, being afraid my master was in pursuit of me, I left the usual line of road, and took another direction, through Huntsville and Salem, principally through fields and woods; on my way to Caswell Court-House, a distance of nearly two hundred miles from Salisbury,[3] I was stopped by a white man, to whom I told my old story, and again succeeded in my escape.

I also came up with a small cart, driven by a poor man, who had been moving into some of the western territories, and was going back to Virginia, to move some more of his luggage. On this I told him I was going the same way to Hilton, thirteen miles from Caswell Court-House; he took me up in his cart, and went to the Red House, two miles from Milton, the place where Mr. Mitchell took me from, when six years old, to go to the Southern States. This was a very providential circumstance, for it happened, that at the time I had to pass through Caswell Court-house, a fair or election was going on, which caused the place to be much crowded with people, and rendered it more dangerous for me to pass through.

At the Red House I left the cart, and wandered about a long time, not knowing which way to go and find my mother. After some time, I took the road leading over Ikeo Creek. I shortly came up with a little girl, about six years old, and asked her where she was going; she said, to her mother's, pointing to a house on a hill, half a mile off. She had been at the overseer's house, and was returning to her mother. I then felt some emotions arising in my breast, which I cannot describe, but will be explained in the sequel. I told her I was very thirsty, and would

---

3. The distance from Salisbury to Caswell Court-House is not so far, but I had to go a round-about way.

go with her to get something to drink. On our way I asked her several questions, such as her name, that of her mother; she said hers was Maria, and that of her mother's Nancy. I inquired, if her mother had any more children? She said five besides herself, and that they had been sold, that one had been sold when a little boy. I then asked the name of this child? She said it was Moses. These answers, as we approached the house, led me nearer and nearer to the finding out the object of my pursuit, and of recognising in the little girl the person of my own sister.

CHAPTER III.

*An account of the Author's meeting with his Mother,
who did not know him, but was with her a very short time
before he was taken by armed men, and imprisoned for
thirty-one days, and then taken back to his master.*

At last I got to my mother's house! My mother was at home. I asked her if she knew me? She said, no. Her master was having a house built close by, and as the men were digging a well, she supposed that I was one of the diggers. I told her, I knew her very well, and thought that if she looked at me a little, she would know me, but this had no effect. I then asked her if she had any sons? She said, yes; but none so large as me. I then waited a few minutes, and narrated some circumstances to her, attending my being sold into slavery, and how she grieved at my loss. Here the mother's feelings on that dire occasion, and which a mother can only know, rushed to her mind; she saw her own son before her, for whom she had so often wept; and, in an instant, we were clasped in each other's arms, amidst the ardent interchange of caresses and tears of joy. Ten years had elapsed since I had seen my dear mother. My own feelings, and the circumstances attending my coming home, have been often brought to mind since, on a perusal of the 42d, 43d, 44th, and 45th chapters of Genesis. What could picture my feelings so well, as I once more beheld the mother who had brought me into the world, and had nourished me, not with the anticipation of my being torn from her maternal care, when only six years old, to become the prey of a mercenary and blood-stained slave-holder: I say, what picture so vivid in description of this part of my tale, as the 7th and 8th verses of the 42d chapter of Genesis, "And Joseph saw his brethren, and he knew them, but made himself strange unto them. And Joseph knew his brethren, but they knew not him." After the first emotion of the mother, on recognising her first-born, had somewhat subsided, could the reader not fancy the little one, my sister, as she told her simple tale of meeting with me to her mother, how she would say, while the parent listened with intense interest: "The man asked me straitly of our state and our kindred, saying, is your father yet alive, and have ye another brother." Or, when at last, I could no longer refrain from making myself known, I say I was ready to burst into a frenzy of joy. How applicable the 1st, 2d, and 3d verses of the 45th chapter, "Then Joseph could not refrain himself before all that stood by him, and he wept aloud, and said unto his brethren, I am Joseph, doth my father still live." Then when the mother knew her son, when the brothers and sisters owned their brother; "he kissed all his brethren and wept over them, and after that his brethren talked with him," 15th verse. At night my mother's husband, a blacksmith, belonging to Mr. Jefferson at the Red House, came home; he was surprised to see me with the family, not knowing who I was. He had been married to my mother, when I was a babe, and had always been very fond of me. After the same tale had been told him, and the same emotions filled his soul, he again kissed the object of his early affection. The next morning I wanted to go on my journey, in order to make sure of my escape to the Free States. But as might be expected, my mother, father, brothers, and sisters, could ill part with their long lost one; and persuaded me to go into the woods in the day time, and at night come home and sleep there. This I did for about a week; on the next Sunday night, I laid me down to sleep between my two brothers, on a pallet, which my mother had prepared for me; about twelve o'clock I was suddenly awoke, and found my bed surrounded by twelve slaveholders with pistols in hand, who took me away (not allowing me to bid farewell to those I loved so dearly) to the Red House, where they confined me in a room the rest of the night, and in the morning lodged me in the gaol of Caswell Court-House.

What was the scene at home, what sorrow possessed their hearts, I am unable to describe, as I never after saw any of them more. I heard, however, that my mother was, soon after I left, confined, and was very long before she recovered the effects of this disaster.[4]

I was told afterwards, that some of those men who took me were professing Christians, but, to me, they did not seem to live up to what they professed; they did not seem, by their practice, at least, to recognise that God as their God, who hath said, "thou shalt not deliver unto his master, the servant which is escaped from his master unto thee, he shall dwell with thee, even among you, in that place which he shall choose, in one of thy gates, where it liketh him best; thou shalt not oppress him."—Deut. xxiii, 15, 16.

I was confined here in a dungeon under ground, the grating of which looked to the door of the gaoler's house. His wife had a great antipathy to me. She was Mr. Roper's wife's cousin. My grandmother used to come to me nearly every day, and bring me something to eat, besides the regular gaol allowance, by which my sufferings were somewhat decreased. Whenever the gaoler went out, which he often did, his wife used to come to my dungeon, and shut the wooden door over the grating, by which I was nearly suffocated, the place being very damp and noisome. My master did not hear of my being in gaol for thirty-one days after I had been placed there. He immediately sent his son, and son-in-law, Mr. Anderson, after me. They came in a horse and chaise, took me from the gaol to a blacksmith's shop, and got an iron collar fitted round my neck, with a heavy chain attached, then tied my hands, and fastened the other end of the chain on a horse, and put me on its back. Just before we started, my grandmother came to bid me farewell;

---

4. My mother had seven children living when I last saw her, and the above one was born soon after I left, made the eighth, and they are now all in slavery except myself.

I gave her my hand as well as I could, and she having given me two or three presents, we parted. I had felt enough, far too much, for the weak state I was in; but how shall I describe my feeling, upon parting with the *last* relative that I *ever saw.* The reader must judge by what would be his own feelings under similar circumstances. We then went on for fifty miles; I was very weak and could hardly sit on the horse. Having been in prison so long, I had lost the southern tan; and as the people could not see my hair, having my hat on, they thought I was a white man—a criminal—and asked me what crime I had committed. We arrived late at night, at the house of Mr. Britton. I shall never forget the journey that night. The thunder was one continued roar, and the lightning blazing all around. I expected every minute that my iron collar would attract it, and I should be knocked off the horse, and dragged along the ground. This gentleman, a year or two before, had liberated his slaves, and sent them into Ohio, having joined the Society of Friends, which society does not allow the holding of slaves. I was, therefore, treated very well there, and they gave me a very hearty supper, which did me much good in my weak state.

They secured me in the night by locking me to the post of the bed on which they slept. The next morning, we went on to Salisbury. At that place we stopped to water the horses; they chained me to a tree in the yard, by the side of their chaise. On my horse they put the saddle bags which contained the provisions. As I was in the yard, a black man came and asked me what I had been doing; I told him that I had run away from my master, after which he told me several tales about the slaves, and among them he mentioned the case of a Quaker, who was then in prison, waiting to be hung, for giving a free passage to a slave. I had been considering all the way how I could escape from my horse, and once had an idea of cutting his head off, but thought it too cruel: and at last thought of trying to get a rasp and cut the chain by which I was fastened to the horse. As they often let me get on a quarter of a mile before them, I thought I should have a good opportunity of doing this without being seen. The black man procured me a rasp, and I put it into the saddle-bags which contained the provisions. We then went on our journey, and one of the sons asked me if I wanted anything to eat; I answered no, though very hungry at the time, as I was afraid of their going to the bags and discovering the rasp. However, they had not had their own meal at the inn as I had supposed, and went to the bags to supply themselves, where they found the rasp. Upon this, they fastened my horse beside the horse in their chaise, and kept a stricter watch over me. Nothing remarkable occurred till we got within eight miles of Mr. Gooch's, where we stopped a short time; and, taking advantage of their absence, I broke a switch from some boughs above my head, lashed my horse and set off at full speed. I had got about a quarter of a mile before they could get their horse loose from their chaise; one then rode the horse, and the other ran as fast as he could after me. When I caught sight of them, I turned off the main road into the woods, hoping to escape their sight; their horse, however, being much swifter than mine, they soon got within a short distance of me. I then came to a rail fence, which I found it very difficult to get over, but breaking several rails away, I effected my object. They then called me upon to stop more than three times; and I not doing so, they fired after me, but the pistol only snapped.

This is according to law; after three calls they may shoot a runaway slave. Soon after the one on the horse came up with me, and catching hold of the bridle of my horse, pushed the pistol to my side; the other soon came up, and breaking off several stout branches from the trees, they gave me about one hundred blows. This they did very near to a planter's house. The gentleman was not at home, but his wife came out and begged them not to *kill me so near the house;* they took no notice of this, but kept on beating me. They then fastened me to the axle tree of their chaise. One of them got into the chaise, the other took my horse, and they ran me all the eight miles as fast as they could; the one on my horse going behind to guard me.

CHAPTER IV.

*The Author is Flogged and Punished in various ways, but still
perseveres in his attempts to Escape, till he was sold to Mr. Wilson.*

In this way we came to my old master, Mr. Gooch. The first person I saw was himself; he unchained me from the chaise, and at first seemed to treat me very gently, asking me where I had been, &c. The first thing the sons did was to show the rasp which I had got to cut my chain. My master gave me a hearty dinner, the best he ever did give me; but it was to keep me from dying before he had given me all the flogging he intended. After dinner he took me to a log-house, stripped me quite naked, fastened a rail up very high, tied my hands to the rail, fastened my feet together, put a rail between my feet, and stood on one end of it to hold me down; the two sons then gave me fifty lashes each, the son-in-law another fifty, and Mr. Gooch himself fifty more.

While doing this his wife came out, and begged him not to kill me, the first act of sympathy I ever noticed in her. When I called for water, they brought a pail-full and threw it over my back ploughed up by the lashes. After this, they took me to the blacksmith's shop, got *two large bars of iron,* which they bent round my feet, each bar *weighing twenty pounds,* and put a heavy log-chain on my neck. This was on Saturday. On the Monday, he chained me to the same female slave as before. As he had to go out that day, he did not give me the punishment which he intended to give me every day, but at night when he came home, he made us walk round his estate, and by all the houses of the slaves, for them to taunt us; when we came home he told us we must be up very early in the morning, and go to the field before the other slaves. We were up at day-break, but we could not get on fast, on account of the heavy irons on my feet. It may be necessary to state that these irons were first made red hot and bent in a circle, so as just to allow of my feet going through; it having been cooled, and my leg with the iron on lifted up to an anvil, it was made secure round my ancles. When I walked with these irons on, I used to hold them up with my hands by means of a cord. We walked *about a mile in two hours,* but knowing the punishment he was going to inflict on us, we made up our minds to escape into the woods, and secrete ourselves. This we did, and he not being able to find us, which they could not do; and about twelve o'clock, when we thought they would give up looking for us at that time, we went on, and came to the banks of the Catarba. Here I got a stone, and opened the ring of the chain on her neck, and got it off; and the chain round my neck was only passed through a ring; as soon as I got hers off, I slipped the chain through my ring, and got it off my own neck.[5]

We then went on by the banks of the river for some distance, and found a little canoe about two feet wide. I managed to get in, although the irons on my feet made it very dangerous, for if I had upset the canoe, I could not swim. The female got in after me, and gave me the paddles, by which we got some distance down the river. The current being very strong, it drove us against a small island; we paddled round the island to the other side, and then made towards the opposite bank. Here again we were stopped by the current, and made up to a large rock in the river, between the island and the opposite shore. As the weather was very rough we landed on the rock, and secured the canoe, as it was not possible to get back to the island. It was a very dark night and rained tremendously; and, as the water was rising rapidly towards the top of the rock, we gave all up for lost, and sometimes hoped, and sometimes feared to hope, that we should never see the morning. But Providence was moved in our favour; the rain ceased, the water reached the edge of the rock, then receded, and we were out of danger from this cause. We remained all night upon the rock, and in the morning reached the opposite shore, and then made our way through the woods till we came to a field of Indian corn, where we plucked some of the green ears and ate them, having had nothing for two days and nights. We came to the estate of—, where we met with a coloured man who knew me, and having run away himself from a bad master, he gave us some food, and told us we might sleep in the barn that night. Being very fatigued, we overslept ourselves; the proprietor came to the barn, but as I was in one corner under some Indian corn tops, and she in another, he did not perceive us, and we did not leave the barn before night, (Wednesday.) We then

---

5. It may be well to state here, that the ring which fastened the log-chain together round the female's neck, was an open ring, similar to those used at the end of a watch chain.

went out, got something to eat, and strayed about the estate till Sunday. On that day, I met with some men, one of whom had irons on the same as me; he told me that his master was going out to see his friends, and that he would try and get my feet loose; for this purpose I parted with this female, fearing, that if she were caught with me, she would be forced to tell who took my irons off. The man tried some time without effect, he then gave me a file and I tried myself, but was disappointed on account of their thickness.

On the Monday I went on towards Lancaster, and got within three miles of it that night; and went towards the plantation of Mr. Crockett, as I knew some of his slaves, and hoped to get some food given me. When I got there, however, the dogs smelt me out and barked; upon which, Mr. Crockett came out, followed me with his rifle, and came up with me. He put me on a horse's back, which put me to extreme pain, from the great weight hanging at my feet. We reached Lancaster gaol that night, and he lodged me there. I was placed in the next dungeon to a man who was going to be hung. I shall never forget his cries and groans, as he prayed all night for the mercy of God. Mr. Gooch did not hear of me for several weeks; when he did, he sent his son-in-law, Mr. Anderson, after me. Mr. Gooch himself came within a mile of Lancaster, and waited until Mr. Anderson brought me. At this time I had but one of the irons on my feet, having got so thin round my ancles that I had slipped one off while in gaol. His son-in-law tied my hands, and made me walk along till we came to Mr. Gooch. As soon as we arrived at McDaniel's Ford, two miles above the ferry, on the Catarba river, they made me wade across, themselves going on horseback. The water was very deep, and having irons on one foot and round my neck. I could not keep a footing. They dragged me along by my chain on the top of the water. It was as much as they could do to hold me by the chain, the current being very strong. They then took me home, flogged me, put extra irons on my neck and feet, and put me under the driver, with more work than ever I had before. He did not flog me so severely as before, but continued it every day. Among the instruments of torture employed, I here describe one:—This is a

machine used for packing and pressing cotton. By it he hung me up
by the hands at letter *a*, a horse, and at times, a man moving round
the screw *e*, and carrying it up and down, and pressing the block *c*
into a box *d*, into which the cotton is put. At this time he hung me up
for a quarter of an hour. I was carried up ten feet from the ground,
when Mr. Gooch asked me if I was tired? He then let me rest for five
minutes, then carried me round again, after which, he let me down
and put me into the box *d*, and shut me down in it for about ten minutes. After this torture, I stayed with him several months, and did my
work very well. It was about the beginning of 1832, when he took off
my irons, and being in dread of him, he having threatened me with
more punishment, I attempted again to escape from him. At this time
I got into North Carolina: but a reward having been offered for me, a
Mr. Robinson caught me, and chained me to a chair, upon which he
sat up with me all night, and next day proceeded home with me. This
was Saturday. Mr. Gooch had gone to church, several miles from his
house. When he came back, the first thing he did was to pour some
tar upon my head, then rubbed it all over my face, took a torch with
pitch on, and set it on fire; he put it out before it did me very great
injury, but the pain which I endured was most excruciating, nearly all
my hair having been burnt off. On Monday, he put irons on me again,
weighing nearly fifty pounds. He threatened me again on the Sunday
with another flogging; and on the Monday morning, before daybreak,
I got away again, with my irons on, and was about three hours going a
distance of two miles.[6] . . . I had gone a good distance, when I met
with a coloured man, who got some wedges, and took my irons off.
However, I was caught again, and put into prison in Charlotte, where
Mr. Gooch came, and took me back to Chester. He asked me how I got
my irons off. They having been got off by a slave, I would not answer
his question, for fear of getting the man punished. Upon this he put

---

6. It must be recollected, that when a person is two miles from a house, in that part
of the country, he can hide himself in the woods for weeks, and I knew a slave who was
hid for six months without discovery, the trees being so thick.

the fingers of my hands into a vice, and squeezed all my nails off. He then had my feet put on an anvil, and ordered a man to beat my toes, till he smashed some of my nails off. The marks of this treatment still remain upon me, some of my nails never having grown perfect since. He inflicted this punishment, in order to get out of me how I got my irons off, but never succeeded. After this, he hardly knew what to do with me; the whole stock of his cruelties seemed to be exhausted. He chained me down in the log-house. Soon after this, he sent a female slave to see if I was safe. Mr. Gooch had not secured me as he thought: but had only run my chain through the ring, without locking it. This I observed; and while the slave was coming, I was employed in loosening the chain with the hand that was not wounded. As soon as I observed her coming, I drew the chain up tight, and she observing that I seemed fast, went away and told her master, who was in the field ordering the slaves. When she was gone, I drew the chain through the ring, escaped under the flooring of the log-house, and went on under it, till I came out at the other side and ran on; but, being sore and weak, I had not got a mile before I was caught, and again carried back. He tied me up to a tree in the woods at night, and made his slaves flog me. I cannot say how many lashes I received; but it was the worst flogging I ever had, and the last which Mr. Gooch ever gave me.

TWO

From *Narrative of James Curry,*
A Fugitive Slave.

1840

James Curry was born to a freed black man and a slave mother in North Carolina near the Virginia state border in 1815. Curry's narrative opens with a brief outline describing his family's history as runaways, including two separate but unsuccessful attempts by his mother, who, after raising her children, no longer attempted to escape. Yet, as the author assures the reader in his concise but dramatic narrative, freedom among slaves was a "constant theme."

In this excerpt, Curry documents a yearning to be free at all costs that began for him as a child. Although he implies that his master, Moses Chambers, was less severe, relatively speaking, than other slave owners ("he seldom whipped his slaves cruelly"), Curry is determined to escape. The opportunity arrives in 1837 when, at age twenty-two, he sets off with his wife, a freed woman, and his two brothers. In rendering this vivid portrait, Curry effectively describes the enormous obstacles faced by all fugitives and why the likelihood of attaining freedom involved extreme odds.

Originally published: *The Liberator,* January 10, 1840.

From my childhood, the desire for freedom reigned predominant in my breast, and I resolved, if I was ever whipped after I became a man, I would no longer be a slave. When I was a lad, my master's uncle came one day to see him, and as I was passing near them, the old man took hold of me and asked my master if this was one of Lucy's boys. Being told that I was, he said, "Well, his father was a free man and perhaps when he gets to be a man, he'll be wanting to be free too." Thinks I to myself, indeed I shall. But if he had asked me if I wanted to be free, I should have answered, "No, Sir." Of course, no slave would dare to say, in the presence of a white man, that he wished for freedom. But among themselves, it is their constant theme. No slaves think they were made to be slaves. Let them keep them ever so ignorant, it is impossible to beat it into them that they were made to be slaves. I have heard some of the most ignorant I ever saw, say "it will not always be so, God *will* bring them to an account." I used to wonder why it was that our people were kept in slavery. I would look at the birds as they flew over my head or sung their free songs upon the trees, and think it strange, that, of all God's creatures, the poor negro only was held in bondage. I knew there were free states, but I thought the people there did not know how we were treated. I had heard of England, and that *there,* there were no slaves; and I thought if I could only get there and tell my story, there would immediately be something done which would bring freedom to the slave.

The slaves, altho' kept in the lowest ignorance in which it is possible to keep them, are, nevertheless, far more intelligent than they are usually represented, or than they ever appear to white people. (Of course, in this and every thing else, I speak only so far as my knowledge extends.) The few faculties they are allowed to cultivate are continually exercised, and therefore greatly strengthened; for instance, that of providing comforts for themselves and those they love, by extra work, and little trade. Then they are generally brought together from distant places and communicate to each other all the knowledge they possess. The slaves also from neighboring plantations hold frequent intercourse with each other, and then they cannot help learning white people talk. For instance, just before the last presidential election, there came a report from a neighboring plantation, that, if Van Buren was elected, he was going to give all the slaves their freedom. It spread rapidly among all the slaves in the neighborhood, and great, very great was the rejoicing. One old man, who was a Christian, came and told us, that now, all we had got to do, was, as Moses commanded the children of Israel on the shore of the Red Sea, "to stand still and see the salvation of God." Mr. Van Buren was elected, but he gave no freedom to the slaves. My master was not a cruel master, only at times. He was considered a good man among slaveholders. But he was a narrow-minded, covetous, unfeeling man. His own house bore witness to his parsimony. Indeed, you would be astonished to go into many of the slaveholders' houses in that part of the country. You would know by looking into them that their hearts were not liberal enough to feed their slaves. Why, the poorest people here, into whose houses I have been, have more furniture than my master's house contained, and yet he was supposed to be worth about $50,000.

His slaves suffered more from his covetous, avaricious disposition, than from cruel punishment. His son gave one time two little pigs to my mother, which were so sickly that he despaired of raising them. They ran about the kitchen yard, and she fed them with the slops which would otherwise have been thrown away, until they got to be nice large hogs. Then my master had them put into his pen, and fatted for his own use. A deaf and dumb miller, who ground my master's wheat, gave me one time when I went to mill, two nice little pigs, which I fatted on the produce of my little patch of ground. When they were ready, I killed one of them, and presented my master with a nice piece for his family. In a few days, he ordered me to kill the other and salt it down in his barrel. I did so, but cut out a small piece for my own use, not privately for I considered it mine, and carried it to our cabin, where we cooked and ate it at night. The next day, my master gave me a whipping for doing it, and my mother for allowing me to do it. I afterwards bought one, and was fattening it for sale, when, one time, when I was not present, he ordered it put into his pen. When I was told of it, I resolved that I would take the worth of it from him; but my mother had taught me not to steal, and I never could bring my mind to fulfill my resolution. Such things as these we constantly suffered, and yet many of the slaves in the neighborhood would have rejoiced to belong to him, but for the circumstance that he was a regular slave-trader, making it a business to buy up slaves, and drive them away to the south; and they would be in constant fear of being sold. Yet, although he seldom whipped his slaves cruelly, at times, when he began to whip a slave, it seemed as though he never knew when to stop. He usually was drunk as often as once a week, and then, if any thing occurred to enrage him, there was no limit to his fury.

One time, a slave, about forty years old, had bought some wheat of some of the neighbor's boys, which he had stolen from his master. My master's son-in-law, Lewis Morgan, had told this slave, that, if he would buy all the wheat he could of the neighbor's slaves, he would take it of him and give him a profit. One overseer detected him with it on the way to Lewis Morgan's and he confessed how he came by it. The overseer then took him to the master, and they went with him to the plantation where the wheat belonged, and as they passed through the field where we were at work, they took me and another slave along with them. The thief was called up, and they wore both taken to the woods, where they were stripped and tied each to a fallen tree, extended upon it face downwards, with their feet and hands tied under it. The two masters commenced beating them at 8 o'clock in the morning, the overseer relieving either when he was tired. They beat them with willow sticks, from five to six feet in length, tied together in bunches of from three to five, according to their size, and they continued beating them until one o'clock in the afternoon, having a bottle of rum and a pail of water standing by to drink from. Their passions seemed to rise and fall like the waves of the sea, and the poor creatures suffered accordingly. My master whipped at this time by far the most cruelly. He would require the poor slave to confess the truth, and then to deny it, and then back again, and so on, beating him from truth to lie, and from a lie to the truth, over and over again. (Of course, he did not tell, except to his fellow sufferers, that Lewis Morgan was concerned in the transaction, as this would only have increased his punishment.) His flesh, at length, would draw and quiver all over his body, like newly killed beef, and finally it appeared as though it was dead. The poor creature was all the time shrieking, and begging, and pleading for mercy; but it had no more effect upon them than would the squealing of a hog they had been killing. At one o'clock, they were released, but my poor fellow-slave was confined to his cabin two weeks before his terrible wounds were healed sufficiently for him to return to his labor. And during most of that time, whenever he was moved, you might hear him scream at a great distance. My master, as soon as this unmerciful torture was completed, went directly to the tavern, where he had a drove of slaves ready to start, and set off for Alabama. I wish some of your people could see a drove of men, women and children driven away to the south. Husbands and wives, parents and children torn from each other. Oh! the weeping, the most dreadful weeping and howling! and it has no effect at all upon the hearts of the oppressors. They will only curse them, and whip them to make them still. When thus driven away, chained together in pairs, no attention is paid to the decency of their appearance. They go bare-headed and bare-footed, with any rag they can themselves find wrapped around their bodies. But the driver has clothing prepared for them to put on, just before they reach the market, and they are forced to array themselves with studied nicety for their exposure at public sale.

I could relate many instances of extreme cruelty practised upon plantations in our neighborhood, instances of *woman* laying heavy stripes upon the back of *woman,* even under circumstances which should have removed every feeling but that of sympathy from the heart of *woman,* and which was sometimes attended with effects most shocking; of men stripped, and their flesh most terribly lacerated by the loaded whip, the sound of which might be heard on a still evening, as it fell on the naked back of the sufferer, at a great distance; of age and disease put out of the way by avarice and cruelty; but as I was not an eye-witness, and only knew them from the relations of those who did witness them, although I have myself no doubt of their truth, I forbear; assuring all, however, who may read this narrative, that *there is no sin which man can commit, that those slaveholders are not guilty of.*

One circumstance I may relate, which was so publicly known that nobody would think of disputing it, as it proves how entirely devoid of sympathy is the mind of a slaveholder with the victims of his cupidity and avarice. A slave in our neighborhood, who was a pious man, was, for some offence, threatened with whipping by his overseer. He refused to submit, and the overseer went after the master to assist him. He ran for the woods. They immediately followed and set the hounds after him. They run him until he got to the mill-pond, into a bend of which they drove him, where there was no turning to the right or left. He had never swam, but the hounds were behind him, and he plunged in, swam to the middle of the pond, and sank to rise no more. A fellow slave on hearing of it, went and inquired where he sank, and swam in, and diving to the bottom, he found him, took hold of his clothes with his teeth, and brought him to the shore, and he and his companions buried him. The master told them that he would give any slave a hundred lashes, who should be known to shed a tear, and several of them were whipped cruelly for this tribute of sorrow over their released fellow-sufferer. This master was the same Thomas Maguhee whom I have mentioned before.

I have been told that Paul Cammon, son of Judge Cammon, who owned a plantation out of the town where he lived, used to go out once in two or three weeks, and while there, have one or two slaves tied and whip them unmercifully, for no offence, but merely, as he said, *to let them know he was their master.*

But, to return to myself. When in my twentieth year, I became attached to a free colored girl, who lived about two miles from our plantation. When I asked my master's consent to our marriage, he refused to give it, and swore that he would cut my throat from ear to ear, before I should marry a free nigger; and with thus he left me. I did not expect him to consent, but I had determined to do in this as I pleased; I knew he would not kill me, because I was money to him, and all the time keeping freedom in my view, I knew I could run away if he punished me. And so we were married. We did not dare to have any even of the trifling ceremony allowed to the slaves, but God married us. It was about two months before he said any thing to me about it. He then attacked me one Sabbath morning, and told me I had broken his orders. He said I should not have my free wife, for he would separate us, as far as there was land to carry me. I told him if I was separated from her, I should choose to be sent away. He then told me that she was a bad girl, and endeavored by his falsehoods to make me believe it. My indignation was roused, I forgot whom I was talking to, and was on the point of giving him the lie, when I recollected myself and smothered my feelings. He then again said he would cut my throat from ear to ear, and if he had his pen-knife, he would do it now. I told him he might kill me if he chose, I had rather die than be separated from my wife. A man with whom he had been negotiating for overseer, was standing by, and he said to my master, I would not do that; you know what the Scripture says about separating man and wife; and he soon desisted and never said any more about it.

But notwithstanding my union with the object of my affection, and the comparatively good treatment I received, I still cherished the longing for liberty, which, from my childhood, had been the prevailing desire of my heart. Hitherto, my attachment to my relations, to my mother in particular, had determined me to remain as long as a strict performance of my allotted labors saved me from being whipped; but the time came, when, having obtained a knowledge of the course which would carry me to Pennsylvania, I only waited for an occasion to escape. It is very common for slaves, when whipped or threatened with a whipping, to run into the woods, and after a short time, when subdued by hunger, not knowing whither to flee for relief, to return and throw themselves upon the mercy of their masters. Therefore, when a slave runs away, on such an occasion, it is expected that he will soon return, and little trouble is taken about it for some days. For such an occasion I now waited, and it was not long before it came without my seeking it. In May, 1837, just after I was 22 years old, the overseer sent a boy to me one evening, with a horse, bidding me go with him to feed him. It was then between nine and ten o'clock at night. I had toiled through the day for my master, had just got my dinner, and was on my way to the hatter's shop for my night's work, when the boy came to me. I did not think it necessary for me to go with him, so I told him where to put the horse, and that the feed was all ready and he might throw it in; and then I went to my work at the shop, where I was allowed to make hats, using nothing of my master's, except tools and the dye, which would be thrown away after my uncle had done with it. In a few minutes, the overseer came in and asked me why I did not go with the boy. I began to reply, by telling him that I thought he did not care if the horse was but fed, and the boy could just as well do it alone; he said he would let me know that I should obey my orders, and if I did not move and feed the horse, he would thrush me as long as he could find me. I went to the house to obey him, and he followed me; but the horse was fed when I got there. He then swore that he would flog me because I had not obeyed his orders. He took a hickory rod and struck me some thirty or forty strokes, over my clothes. My first impulse was to take the stick out of his hand, for I was much stronger than he. But I recollected that my master was in the house, and if I did so, he would be called, and probably I should be stripped and tied, and instead of thirty or forty, should receive hundreds of stripes. I therefore concluded it was wisest to take quietly whatever he chose to inflict, but as the strokes fell upon my back, I firmly resolved that I would no longer be a slave. I would now escape or die in the attempt. They might shoot me down if they chose, but I would not live a slave.

The next morning, I decided, that, as my master was preparing for one of his slave-driving expeditions to Alabama, I would wait until he was gone; that when he was fairly started on his journey, I would start on mine, he for the south, and I for the north. In the meantime, I instructed my two younger brothers in my plans. It happened that on the afternoon of the 14th of June, about three weeks after the whipping I received, and just after my master had set off for Alabama, as we were going to the field after breakfast, to ploughing, the overseer got very angry with me and my two brothers, and threatened to whip us before night. He said that as he could not do it himself, there were men in the neighborhood he could get to help him, and then he walked away. This was our opportunity. We took our horses round to the road fence and hitched them, and ran for my wife's house. There I changed my clothes, and took my leave of her, with the hope of being soon able to send for her from a land of freedom, and left her in a state of distress which I cannot describe. We started without money and without clothes, except what we wore (not daring to carry a bundle), but with our hearts full of hope.

We travelled by night, and slept in the woods during the day. After travelling two or three nights, we got alarmed and turned out of the road, and before we turned into it again, it had separated, and we took the wrong road. It was cloudy for two or three days, and after travelling three nights, we found ourselves just where we were three days before, and almost home again. We were sadly disappointed, but not discouraged; and so, turning our faces again northward, we went on. I should have said before, that I knew the way to Petersburgh, Va. having been several times sent there by my master with a team. Near Petersburgh, we passed a neat farm-house, with every thing around it in perfect order, which had once been shown to me by a slave, as I was driving my master's team to the city. "That," said he, "belongs to a Friend; they never hold slaves." Now I was strongly tempted to stop there, and ask instruction in my northward course, as I knew the way no farther; but I dared not. So, not knowing the north star, we took the two lower stars of the great bear for our guide, and putting our trust in God, we passed Petersburgh. We suffered much from hunger. There was no fruit and no grain to be found at that season, and we sometimes went two days, and sometimes three, without tasting food, as we did not dare to ask, except when we found a slave's, or free colored person's house remote from any other, and then we were never refused, if they had food to give. Thus we came on, until about forty-five miles from Washington, when, having in the night obtained some meal, and having then been three days without food, my poor brothers begged me to go out of the woods in the day time, and get some fire in order to bake us some bread. I went to a house, got some and returned to the woods. We made a fire in the hollow stump of a tree, mixed our meal with water, which we found near, and wrapping it in leaves, threw it in and baked it.

After eating heartily, we began to bake some to carry with us, when, hearing a noise in the bushes, we looked up, and beheld dogs coming towards us, and behind them several white men, who called out, "O! you rascals, what are you doing there? Catch him! catch him!" The dogs sprang towards us. My feelings I cannot describe, as I started, and ran with all my might. My brothers, having taken off their coats and hats, stopped to pick them up, and then ran off in another direction, and the dogs followed them, while I escaped, and never saw them more. I heard the dogs barking after them, when I had got as much as a mile from where we started. Oh! then I was most miserable, left alone, a poor hunted stranger in a strange land—my brothers gone. I know not how to express the feelings of that moment. After listening awhile, I went forward. I had lost my way, and knew not where I was, but I looked at the sun, and as near as I could, pursued a northward course. In that afternoon I was attacked by a wild beast. I knew not what it was. I thought, surely I am beset this day, but unlike the men, more ferocious than wild beasts, I succeeded in driving him away, and that night crossed a branch of the Potomac. Just before I reached the town of Dumfries, I came across an old horse in a field with a bell on his neck. I had been warned by a colored man, a few nights before, to beware of Dumfries. I was worn out with running, and I took the bell off the horse's neck, took the bell collar for a whip, and putting a hickory bark round his head for a bridle, I jumped on his back, and thus mounted, I rode through Dumfries. The bull-dogs lay along the street, ready to seize the poor night traveller, but, being on horseback, they did not molest me. I have no doubt that I should have been taken up, if I had been on foot. When I got through the town, I dismounted, and said to my horse, "go back to your master, I did not mean to injure him, and hope we will get you again, but you have done me a great deal of good." And then I hastened on, and got as far from him as I could before morning.

At Alexandria, I crossed the Potomac river, and came to Washington, where I made friends with a colored family, with whom I rested eight days. I then took the Montgomery road, but, wishing to escape Baltimore, I turned off, and it being cloudy, I lost my course, and fell back again upon the Potomac river, and travelled on the tow path of the canal from Friday night until Sunday morning, when I lay down and slept a little, and then, having no place to hide for the day, I determined to go on until I could find a place of safety. I soon saw a man riding towards me on horse-back. As he came near, he put his eyes upon me, and I felt sure that he intended to question me. I fell to praying to God to protect me, and so begging and praying fervently, I went forward. When he met me, he stopped his horse, leaned forward and looked at me, and then, without speaking, rode on again. I still fully believe it was at first his intention to question me. I soon entered a colored person's house on the side of the canal, where they gave me breakfast and treated me very kindly. I travelled on through Williamsport and Hagerstown, in Maryland, and, on the 19th day of July, about two hours before day. I crossed the line into Pennsylvania, with a heart full of gratitude to God, believing that I was indeed a free man, and that now, under the protection of law, there was "none who could molest me or make me afraid." In the course of the morning, I was spoken to by a man, sitting at the window of a house in Chambersburg, who asked me if I wanted a job of work. I replied that I did, and he took me into his garden, and set me to work. When the job there was done, he told me I might clean his carriage. At dinner, I ate in the kitchen with a colored woman. She inquired where I came from, I told her the name of the town in Pennsylvania. Said she, "I didn't know but you came from Virginia, or Maryland, and sometimes, some of our colored friends come from there hither, and think they are free, but the people about here are very ugly, and they take them and carry them back; and if you haven't sufficient free papers, I would advise you not to stay here to-night." This was enough for me. I had discovered that the man was very curious about me, and seemed disposed to keep me at work upon little jobs until night. I went out, and jumped over the garden wall, and was soon on the turnpike road. I was very fearful, and came on tremblingly; but near Philadelphia, I fell in with members of the Society of Friends, whom I never feared to trust, who "took in the stranger," and I worked for them until Christmas.

After finding, to my great disappointment, that I was now a free man, and that I could not send for my wife from here, I determined to go to Canada. But the situation of that country at that time was such, that my friends thought it not best for me to go immediately, and advised me to come into the State of Massachusetts, as the safest place for me until the difficulties in Canada were passed away. I was taken by kind friends to New York, from whence the Abolitionists sent me to Massachusetts, and here I have found a resting place, and have met with friends who have freely administered to my necessities, and whose kindness to the poor fugitive I shall ever remember with emotions of heartfelt gratitude. And here I have fulfilled the promise made in slavery to my Maker, that I would acknowledge him before men, when I came into a land of freedom. And although I have suffered much, very much in my escape, and have not here found that perfect freedom which I anticipated, yet I have never for one moment regretted that I thus sought my liberty.

In a few days I start for Canada, fully believing that he who has thus far protected me, will guide me safely, where, under the free government of Queen Victoria, I may feel myself a man. I trust in God.

THREE

From *Narrative of the Life of Frederick Douglass, An American Slave. Written by Himself.*

*W*hen the twenty-seven-year-old fugitive slave known as Frederick Douglass published his autobiography in 1845, he became the best-selling author of what in time would become the most famous slave narrative ever written. Indeed, he became the most famous African American of the nineteenth century, if not of all time up to that point. As a leading abolitionist, celebrated author, commanding orator, and lifelong civil rights activist, Douglass is a giant in American history.

Born Frederick Augustus Washington Bailey to a slave mother, Harriet Bailey, and a white father whom Douglass never met but suspected had been his mother's master, the author grew up in Talbot County, Maryland. When he was eight, he was taken from his family and sent to Baltimore to work for his master's relatives, ship carpenter Hugh Auld and his wife. There his well-intentioned mistress taught him the alphabet until her husband found out and ordered the lessons stopped. No matter that Douglass had lost his tutor: the encounter forever changed his life. Literacy became for him the first step on the path to freedom.

Originally published: Boston: Anti-Slavery Office, 1845.

One of the most harrowing sections of Narrative of the Life of Frederick Douglass *is the author's account of his years spent under the mercilessly brutal supervision of farmer Edward Covey, a noted "slave-breaker." Here the reader finds in unsparing but eloquent detail the horrors of slavery and one slave's determination to flee from it at the risk of his own life. Douglass's first attempted escape came in 1836, but his plans were exposed and foiled. Undaunted, he disguised himself as a sailor and fled two years later to New York, where he changed his name from Bailey to Douglass as a means of concealing his identity. Once settled in Massachusetts, he joined the abolitionist movement, becoming one of its most ardent spokespeople until his death in 1895.*

———

CHAPTER X.

I left Master Thomas's house, and went to live with Mr. Covey, on the 1st of January, 1833. I was now, for the first time in my life, a field hand. In my new employment, I found myself even more awkward than a country boy appeared to be in a large city. I had been at my new home but one week before Mr. Covey gave me a very severe whipping, cutting my back, causing the blood to run, and raising ridges on my flesh as large as my little finger. The details of this affair are as follows: Mr. Covey sent me, very early in the morning of one of our coldest days in the month of January, to the woods, to get a load of wood. He gave me a team of unbroken oxen. He told me which was the in-hand ox, and which the off-hand one. He then tied the end of a large rope around the horns of the in-hand ox, and gave me the other end of it, and told me, if the oxen started to run, that I must hold on upon the rope. I had never driven oxen before, and of course I was very awkward. I, however, succeeded in getting to the edge of the woods with little difficulty; but I had got a very few rods into the woods, when the oxen took fright, and started full tilt, carrying the cart against trees, and over stumps, in the most frightful manner. I expected every moment that my brains would be dashed out against the trees. After running thus for a considerable distance, they finally upset the cart, dashing it with great force against a tree, and threw themselves into it dense thicket. How I escaped death, I do not know. There I was, entirely alone, in a thick wood, in a place new to me. My cart was upset and shattered, my oxen were entangled among the young trees, and there was none to help me. After a long spell of effort, I succeeded in getting my cart righted, my oxen disentangled, and again yoked to the cart. I now proceeded with my team to the place where I had, the day before, been chopping wood, and loaded my cart pretty heavily, thinking in this way to tame my oxen. I then proceeded on my way home. I had now consumed one half of the day. I got out of the woods safely, and now felt out of danger, I stopped my oxen to open the woods gate; and just as I did so, before I could get hold of my ox-rope, the oxen again started, rushed through the gate, catching it between the wheel and the body of the cart, tearing it to pieces, and coming within a few inches of crushing me against the gate-post. Thus twice, in one short day, I escaped death by the merest chance. On my return, I told Mr. Covey what had happened, and how it happened. He ordered me to return to the woods again immediately. I did so, and he followed on after me. Just as I got into the woods, he came up and told me to stop my cart, and that he would teach me how to trifle away my time, and break gates. He then went to a large gum-tree, and with his axe cut three large switches, and, after trimming them up neatly with his pocket-knife, he ordered me to take off my clothes. I made him no answer, but stood with my clothes on. He repeated his order. I still made him no answer, nor did I move to strip myself. Upon this he rushed at me with the fierceness of a tiger, tore off my clothes, and lashed me till he had worn out his switches, cutting me so savagely as to leave the marks visible for a long time after. This whipping was the first of a number just like it, and for similar offences.

I lived with Mr. Covey one year. During the first six months, of that year, scarce a week passed without his whipping me. I was seldom free from a sore back. My awkwardness was almost always his excuse for whipping me. We were worked fully up to the point of endurance. Long before day we were up, our horses fed, and by the first approach of day we were off to the field with our hoes and ploughing teams. Mr. Covey gave us enough to eat, but scarce time to eat it. We were often less than five minutes taking our meals. We were often in the field from the first approach of day till its last lingering ray had left us; and at saving-fodder time, midnight often caught us in the field binding blades.

Covey would be out with us. The way he used to stand it, was this. He would spend the most of his afternoons in bed. He would then come out fresh in the evening, ready to urge us on with his words, example, and frequently with the whip. Mr. Covey was one of the few slaveholders who could and did work with his hands. He was a hard-working man. He knew by himself just what a man or a boy could do. There was no deceiving him. His work went on in his absence almost as well as in his presence; and he had the faculty of making us feel that he was ever present with us. This he did by surprising us. He seldom approached the spot where we were at work openly, if he could do it secretly. He always aimed at taking us by surprise. Such was his cunning, that we used to call him, among ourselves, "the snake." When we were at work in the cornfield, he would sometimes crawl on his hands and knees to avoid detection, and all at once he would rise nearly in our midst, and scream out, "Ha, ha! Come, come! Dash on, dash on!" This being his mode of attack, it was never safe to stop a single minute. His comings were like a thief in the night. He appeared to us as being ever at hand. He was under every tree, behind every stump, in every bush, and at every window, on the plantation. He would sometimes mount his horse, as if bound to St. Michael's, a distance of seven miles, and in half an hour afterwards you would see him coiled up in the corner of the wood-fence, watching every motion of the slaves. He would, for this purpose, leave his horse tied up in the woods. Again, he would sometimes walk up to us, and give us orders as though he was upon the point of starting on a long journey, turn his back upon us, and make as though he was going to the house to get ready; and, before he would get half way thither, he would turn short and crawl into a fence-corner, or behind some tree, and there watch us till the going down of the sun.

Mr. Covey's *forte* consisted in his power to deceive. His life was devoted to planning and perpetrating the grossest deceptions. Every thing he possessed in the shape of learning or religion, he made con-form to his disposition to deceive. He seemed to think himself equal to deceiving the Almighty. He would make a short prayer in the morning, and a long prayer at night; and, strange as it may seem, few men would at times appear more devotional than he. The exercises of his family devotions were always commenced with singing; and, as he was a very poor singer himself, the duty of raising the hymn generally came upon me. He would read his hymn, and nod at me to commence. I would at times do so; at others, I would not. My non-compliance would almost always produce much confusion. To show himself independent of me, he would start and stagger through with his hymn in the most discor-dant manner. In this state of mind, he prayed with more than ordinary spirit. Poor man! Such was his disposition, and success at deceiving, I do verily believe that he sometimes deceived himself into the solemn belief, that he was a sincere worshipper of the most high God; and this, too, at a time when he may be said to have been guilty of compel-ling his woman slave to commit the sin of adultery. The facts in the case are these: Mr. Covey was a poor man; he was just commencing in life; he was only able to buy one slave; and, shocking as is the fact, he bought her, as he said, for *a breeder.* This woman was named Caroline. Mr. Covey bought her from Mr. Thomas Lowe, about six miles from St. Michael's. She was a large, able-bodied woman, about twenty years old. She had already given birth to one child, which proved her to be just what he wanted. After buying her, he hired a married man of Mr. Samuel Harrison, to live with him one year; and him he used to fasten up with her every night! The result was, that, at the end of the year, the miserable woman gave birth to twins. At this result Mr. Covey seemed to be highly pleased, both with the man and the wretched woman. Such was his joy, and that of his wife, that nothing they could do for

Caroline during her confinement was too good, or too hard, to be done. The children were regarded as being quite an addition to his wealth.

If at any one time of my life more than another, I was made to drink the bitterest dregs of slavery, that time was during the first six months of my stay with Mr. Covey. We were worked in all weathers. It was never too hot or too cold; it could never rain, blow, hail, or snow, too hard for us to work in the field. Work, work, work, was scarcely more the order of the day than of the night. The longest days were too short for him, and the shortest nights too long for him. I was somewhat unmanageable when I first went there, but a few months of this discipline tamed me. Mr. Covey succeeded in breaking me. I was broken in body, soul, and spirit. My natural elasticity was crushed, my intellect languished, the disposition to read departed, the cheerful spark that lingered about my eye died; the dark night of slavery closed in upon me; and behold a man transformed into a brute!

Sunday was my only leisure time. I spent this in a sort of beast-like stupor, between sleep and wake, under some large tree. At times I would rise up, a flash of energetic freedom would dart through my soul, accompanied with a faint beam of hope, that flickered for a moment, and then vanished. I sank down again, mourning over my wretched condition. I was sometimes prompted to take my life, and that of Covey, but was prevented by a combination of hope and fear. My sufferings on this plantation seem now like a dream rather than a stern reality.

Our house stood within a few rods of the Chesapeake Bay, whose broad bosom was ever white with sails from every quarter of the habitable globe. Those beautiful vessels, robed in purest white, so delightful to the eye of freemen, were to me so many shrouded ghosts, to terrify and torment me with thoughts of my wretched condition. I have often, in the deep stillness of a summer's Sabbath, stood all alone upon the lofty banks of that noble bay, and traced, with saddened heart and tearful eye, the countless number of sails moving off to the mighty ocean. The sight of these always affected me powerfully. My thoughts would compel utterance; and there, with no audience but the Almighty, I would pour out my soul's complaint, in my rude way, with an apostrophe to the moving multitude of ships:—

"You are loosed from your moorings, and are free; I am fast in my chains, and am a slave! You move merrily before the gentle gale, and I sadly before the bloody whip! You are freedom's swift-winged angels, that fly round the world; I am confined in bands of iron! O that I were free! O, that I were on one of your gallant decks, and under your protecting wing! Alas! betwixt me and you, the turbid waters roll. Go on, go on. O that I could also go! Could I but swim! If I could fly! O, why was I born a man, of whom to make a brute. The glad ship is gone; she hides in the dim distance. I am left in the hottest hell of unending slavery. O God, save me! God, deliver me! Let me be free! Is there any God? Why am I a slave? I will run away. I will not stand it. Get caught, or get clear, I'll try it. I had as well die with ague as the fever. I have only one life to lose. I had as well be killed running as die standing. Only think of it; one hundred miles straight north, and I am free! Try it? Yes! God helping me, I will. It cannot be that I shall live and die a slave. I will take to the water. This very bay shall yet bear me into freedom. The steamboats steered in a north-east course from North Point. I will do the same; and when I get to the head of the bay, I will turn my canoe adrift, and walk straight through Delaware into Pennsylvania. When I get there, I shall not be required to have a pass; I can travel without being disturbed. Let but the first opportunity offer, and, come what will, I am off. Meanwhile, I will try to bear up under the yoke. I am not the only slave in the world. Why should I fret? I can bear as much as any of them. Besides, I am but a boy, and all boys are bound to some one. It may be that my misery in slavery will only increase my happiness when I get free. There is a better day coming."

Thus I used to think, and thus I used to speak to myself; goaded almost to madness at one moment, and at the next reconciling myself to my wretched lot.

I have already intimated that my condition was much worse, during the first six months of my stay at Mr. Covey's, than in the last six. The circumstances leading to the change in Mr. Covey's course toward me form an epoch in my humble history. You have seen how a man was made a slave; you shall see how a slave was made a man. On one of the hottest days of the month of August, 1833, Bill Smith, William Hughes, a slave named Eli, and myself, were engaged in fanning wheat. Hughes was clearing the fanned wheat from before the fan, Eli was turning, Smith was feeding, and I was carrying wheat to the fan. The work was simple, requiring strength rather than intellect; yet, to one entirely unused to such work, it came very hard. About three o'clock of that day, I broke down; my strength failed me; I was seized with a violent aching of the head, attended with extreme dizziness; I trembled in every limb. Finding what was coming, I nerved myself up, feeling it would never do to stop work. I stood as long as I could stagger to the hopper with grain. When I could stand no longer, I fell, and felt as held down by an immense weight. The fan of course stopped; every one had his own work to do; and no one could do the work of the other, and have his own go on at the same time.

Mr. Covey was at the house, about one hundred yards from the treading-yard where we were fanning. On hearing the fan stop, he left immediately, and came to the spot where we were. He hastily inquired what the matter was. Bill answered that I was sick, and there was no one to bring wheat to the fan. I had by this time crawled away under the side of the post and rail-fence by which the yard was enclosed, hoping to find relief by getting out of the sun. He then asked where I was. He was told by one of the hands. He came to the spot, and, after looking at me awhile, asked me what was the matter. I told him as well as I could, for I scarce had strength to speak. He then gave me a savage kick in the side, and told me to get up. I tried to do so, but fell back in the attempt. He gave me another kick, and again told me to rise. I again tried, and succeeded in gaining my feet; but, stooping to get the tub with which I was feeding the fan, I again staggered and fell. While down in this situation, Mr. Covey took up the hickory slat with which Hughes had been striking off the half-bushel measure, and with it gave me a heavy blow upon the head, making a large wound, and the blood ran freely; and with this again told me to get up. I made no effort to comply, having now made up my mind to let him do his worst. In a short time after receiving this blow, my head grew better. Mr. Covey had now left me to my fate. At this moment I resolved, for the first time, to go to my master, enter a complaint, and ask his protection. In order to this, I must that afternoon walk seven miles; and this, under the circumstances, was truly a severe undertaking. I was exceedingly feeble; made so as much by the kicks and blows which I received, as by the severe fit of sickness to which I had been subjected. I, however, watched my chance, while Covey was looking in an opposite direction, and started for St. Michael's. I succeeded in getting a considerable distance on my way to the woods, when Covey discovered me, and called after me to come back, threatening what he would do if I did not come. I, disregarded both his calls and his threats, and made my way to the woods as fast as my feeble state would allow; and thinking I might be overhauled by him if I kept the road, I walked through the woods, keeping far enough from the road to avoid detection, and near enough to prevent losing my way. I had not gone far before my little strength again failed me. I could go no farther. I fell down, and lay for a considerable time. The blood was yet oozing from the wound on my head. For a time I thought I should bleed to death; and think now that I should have done so, but that the blood so matted my hair as to stop the wound. After lying there about three quarters of an hour, I nerved myself up again, and started on my way, through bogs and briers, barefooted and bareheaded, tearing my feet sometimes at nearly every step; and after a journey of about seven miles, occupying some five hours to perform it, I arrived at master's store. I then presented an appearance enough to affect any but a heart of iron. From the crown of my head to my feet, I was covered with blood. My hair was all clotted with dust and blood; my shirt was stiff with blood. My legs and feet were torn in sundry places with briers and thorns, and were also covered with blood. I suppose I looked like a man who had escaped a den of wild beasts, and barely escaped them. In this state I appeared before my master, humbly entreating him to interpose his authority for my protection. I told him all the circumstances as well as I could, and it seemed, as I spoke, at times to affect him. He would then walk the floor, and seek to justify Covey by saying he expected I deserved it. He asked me what I wanted. I told him, to let me get a new home; that as sure as I lived with Mr. Covey again, I should live with but to die with him; that Covey would surely kill me; he was in a fair way for it. Master Thomas ridiculed the idea that there was any danger of Mr. Covey's killing me, and said that he knew Mr. Covey; that he was a good man, and that he could not think of taking me from him; that, should he do so, he would lose the whole year's wages; that I belonged to Mr. Covey for one year, and that I must go back to him, come what might; and that I must not trouble him with any more stories, or that he would himself *get hold of me*. After threatening me thus, he gave me a very large dose of salts, telling me that I might remain in St. Michael's that night, (it being quite late,) but that I must be off back to Mr. Covey's early in the morning; and that if I did not, he would *get hold of me,* which meant that he would whip me. I remained all night, and, according to his orders, I started off to Covey's in the morning, (Saturday morning,) wearied in body and broken in spirit. I got no supper that night, or breakfast that morning. I reached Covey's about nine o'clock; and just as I was getting over the fence that divided Mrs. Kemp's fields from ours, out ran Covey with his cowskin, to give me another whipping. Before he could reach me, I succeeded in getting to the cornfield; and as the corn was very high, it afforded me the means of hiding. He seemed very angry, and searched for me a long time. My behavior was altogether unaccountable. He finally gave up the chase, thinking, I suppose, that I must come home for something to eat; he would give himself no further trouble in looking for me. I spent that day mostly in the woods, having the alternative before me,—to go home and be whipped to death, or stay in the woods and be starved to death. That night, I fell in with Sandy Jenkins, a slave with whom I was some- what acquainted. Sandy had a free wife who lived about four miles from Mr. Covey's; and it being Saturday, he was on his way to see her.

I told him my circumstances, and he very kindly invited me to go home with him. I went home with him, and talked this whole matter over, and got his advice as to what course it was best for me to pursue. I found Sandy an old adviser. He told me, with great solemnity, I must go back to Covey; but that before I went, I must go with him into another part of the woods, where there was a certain *root,* which, if I would take some of it with me, carrying it *always on my right side,* would render it impossible for Mr. Covey, or any other white man, to whip me. He said he had carried it for years; and since he had done so, he had never received a blow, and never expected to while he carried it. I at first rejected the idea, that the simple carrying of a root in my pocket would have any such effect as he had said, and was not disposed to take it; but Sandy impressed the necessity with much earnestness, telling me it could do no harm, if it did no good. To please him, I at length took the root, and, according to his direction, carried it upon my right side. This was Sunday morning. I immediately started for home; and upon entering the yard gate, out came Mr. Covey on his way to meeting. He spoke, to me very kindly, bade me drive the pigs from a lot near by, and passed on towards the church. Now, this singular conduct of Mr. Covey really made me begin to think that there was something in the *root* which Sandy, had given me; and had it been on any other day than Sunday, I could have attributed the conduct to no other cause than the influence of that root, and as it was, I was half inclined to think the *root* to be something more than I at first had taken it to be. All went well till Monday morning. On this morning, the virtue of the *root* was fully tested. Long before daylight I was called to go and rub, curry, and feed, the horses. I obeyed, and was glad to obey. But whilst thus engaged, whilst in the act of throwing down some blades from the loft, Mr. Covey entered the stable with a long rope; and just as I was half out of the loft, he caught hold of my legs, and was about tying me. As soon as I found what he was up to, I gave a sudden spring, and as I did so, he holding to my legs, I was brought sprawling on the stable floor. Mr. Covey seemed now to think he had me, and could do what he pleased; but at this moment—from whence came the spirit I don't know—I resolved to fight; and, suiting my action to the resolution, I seized Covey hard by the throat; and, as I did so, I rose. He held onto me, and I to him. My resistance was so entirely unexpected, that Covey seemed taken all aback. He trembled like a leaf. This gave me assurance, and I held him uneasy, causing the blood to run where I touched him with the ends of my fingers. Mr. Covey soon called out to Hughes for help. Hughes came, and, while Covey held me, attempted to tie my right hand. While he was in the act of doing so, I watched my chance, and gave him a heavy kick close under the ribs. This kick fairly sickened Hughes, so that he left me in the hands of Mr. Covey. This kick had the effect of not only weakening Hughes, but Covey also. When he saw Hughes bending over with pain, his courage quailed. He asked me if I meant to persist in my resistance. I told him I did, come what might; that he had used me like a brute for six months, and that I was determined to be used so no longer. With that, he strove to drag me to a stick that was lying just out of the stable door. He meant to knock me down. But just as he was leaning over to get the stick, I seized him with both hands by his collar, and brought him by a sudden snatch to the ground. By this time, Bill came. Covey called upon him for assistance. Bill wanted to know what he could do. Covey said, "Take hold of him, take hold of him!" Bill said his master hired him out to work, and not to help to whip me; so he left Covey and myself to fight our own battle out. We were at it for nearly two hours. Covey at length let me go, puffing and blowing at a great rate, saying that if I had not resisted, he would not have whipped me half so much. The truth was, that he had not whipped me at all. I considered him as getting entirely the worst end of the bargain; for he had drawn no blood from me, but I had from him. The whole six months afterwards, that I spent with Mr. Covey, he never laid the weight of his finger upon me in anger. He would occasionally say, he didn't want to get hold of me again. "No," thought I, "you need not; for you will come off worse than you did before."

This battle with Mr. Covey was the turning-point in my career as a slave. It rekindled the few expiring embers of freedom, and revived within me a sense of my own manhood. It recalled the departed self-confidence, and inspired me again with a determination to be free. The gratification afforded by the triumph was a full compensation for whatever else might follow, even death itself. He only can understand the deep satisfaction which I experienced, who has himself repelled by force the bloody arm of slavery. I felt as I never felt before. It was a glorious resurrection, from the tomb of slavery, to the heaven of freedom. My long-crushed spirit rose, cowardice departed, bold defiance took its place; and I now resolved that, however long I might remain a slave in form, the day had passed forever when I could be a slave in fact. I did not hesitate to let it be known of me, that the white man who expected to succeed in whipping, must also succeed in killing me.

From this time I was never again what might be called fairly whipped, though I remained a slave four years afterwards. I had several fights, but was never whipped.

It was for a long time a matter of surprise to me why Mr. Covey did not immediately have me taken by the constable to the whipping-post, and there regularly whipped for the crime of raising my hand against a white man in defence of myself. And the only explanation I can now think of does not entirely satisfy me; but such as it is, I will give it. Mr. Covey enjoyed the most unbounded reputation for being a first-rate overseer and negro-breaker. It was of considerable importance to him. That reputation was at stake; and had he sent me—a boy about sixteen years old—to the public whipping-post, his reputation would have been lost; so, to save his reputation, he suffered me to go unpunished.

My term of actual service to Mr. Edward Covey ended on Christmas day, 1833. The days between Christmas and New Year's day are allowed as holidays; and, accordingly, we were not required to perform any labor, more than to feed and take care of the stock. This time we regarded as our own, by the grace of our masters; and we therefore used or abused it nearly as we pleased. Those of us who had families at a distance, were generally allowed to spend the whole six days in their society. This time, however, was spent in various ways. The staid, sober, thinking and industrious ones of our number would employ themselves in making corn-brooms, mats, horse-collars, and baskets; and another class of us would spend the time in hunting opossums, hares, and coons. But by far the larger part engaged in such sports and merriments as playing ball, wrestling, running foot-races, fiddling, dancing, and drinking whisky; and this latter mode of spending the time was by far the most agreeable to the feelings of our masters. A slave who would work during the holidays was considered by our masters as scarcely deserving them. He was regarded as one who rejected the favor of his master. It was deemed a disgrace not to get drunk at Christmas; and he was regarded as lazy indeed, who had not provided himself with the necessary means, during the year, to get whisky enough to last him through Christmas.

From what I know of the effect of these holidays upon the slave, I believe them to be among the most effective means in the hands of the slaveholder in keeping down the spirit of insurrection. Were the slaveholders at once to abandon this practice, I have not the slightest doubt it would lead to an immediate insurrection among the slaves. These holidays serve as conductors, or safety-valves, to carry off the rebellious spirit of enslaved humanity. But for these, the slave would be forced up to the wildest desperation; and woe betide the slaveholder, the day he ventures to remove or hinder the operation of those conductors! I warn him that, in such an event, a spirit will go forth in their midst, more to be dreaded than the most appalling earthquake.

The holidays are part and parcel of the gross fraud, wrong, and inhumanity of slavery. They are professedly a custom established by the benevolence of the slaveholders; but I undertake to say, it is the result of selfishness, and one of the grossest frauds committed upon the down-trodden slave. They do not give the slaves this time because they would not like to have their work during its continuance, but because they know it would be unsafe to deprive them of it. This will be seen by the fact, that the slaveholders like to have their slaves spend those days just in such a manner as to make them as glad of their ending as of their beginning. Their object seems to be, to disgust their slaves with freedom, by plunging them into the lowest depths of dissipation. For instance, the slaveholders not only like to see the slave drink of his own accord, but will adopt various plans to make him drunk. One plan is, to make bets on their slaves, as to who can drink the most whisky without getting drunk; and in this way they succeed in getting whole multitudes to drink to excess. Thus, when the slave asks for virtuous freedom, the cunning slaveholder, knowing his ignorance, cheats him with a dose of vicious dissipation, artfully labelled with the name of liberty. The most of us used to drink it down, and the result was just what might be supposed: many of us were led to think that there was little to choose between liberty and slavery. We felt, and very properly too, that we had almost as well be slaves to man as to rum. So, when the holidays ended, we staggered up from the filth of our wallowing, took a long breath, and marched to the field,—feeling, upon the whole, rather glad to go, from what our master had deceived us into a belief was freedom, back to the arms of slavery. . . .

On the first of January, 1834, I left Mr. Covey, and went to live with Mr. William Freeland, who lived about three miles from St. Michael's. I soon found Mr. Freeland a very different man from Mr. Covey. Though not rich, he was what would be called an educated southern gentleman. Mr. Covey, as I have shown, was a well-trained negro-breaker and slave-driver. The former (slaveholder though he was) seemed to possess some regard for honor, some reverence for justice and some respect for humanity. The latter seemed totally insensible to all such sentiments. Mr. Freeland had many of the faults peculiar to slaveholders, such as being very passionate and fretful; but I must do him the justice to say, that he was exceedingly free from those degrading vices to which Mr. Covey was constantly addicted. The one was open and frank, and we always knew where to find him. The other was a most artful deceiver, and could be understood only by such as were skilful enough to detect his cunningly-devised frauds. Another advantage I gained in my new master was, he made no pretensions to, or profession of, religion; and this, in my opinion, was truly a great advantage. I assert most unhesitatingly, that the religion of the south is a mere covering for the most horrid crimes,—a justifier of the most appalling barbarity,—a sanctifier of the most hateful frauds,— and a dark shelter under, which the darkest, foulest, grossest, and most infernal deeds of slaveholders find the strongest protection. . . .

The year passed off smoothly. It seemed only about half as long as the year which preceded it. I went through it without receiving a single blow. I will give Mr. Freeland the credit of being the best master I ever had, *till I became my own master.* For the ease with which I passed the year, I was, however, somewhat indebted to the society of my fellow-slaves. They were noble souls; they not only possessed loving hearts, but brave ones. We were linked and inter-linked with each other. I loved them with a love stronger than any thing I have experienced since. It is sometimes said that we slaves do not love and confide in each other. In answer to this assertion, I can say, I never loved any or confided in any people more than my fellow-slaves, and especially those with whom I lived at Mr. Freeland's. I believe we would have died for each other. We never undertook to do any thing, of any importance, without a mutual consultation. We never moved separately. We were one; and as much so by our tempers and dispositions, as by the mutual hardships to which we were necessarily subjected by our condition as slaves.

At the close of the year 1834, Mr. Freeland again hired me of my master, for the year 1835. But, by this time, I began to want to live *upon free land* as well as *with Freeland;* and I was no longer content, therefore, to live with him or any other slaveholder. I began, with the commencement of the year, to prepare myself for a final struggle, which should decide my fate one way or the other. My tendency was upward. I was fast approaching manhood, and year after year had passed, and I was still a slave. These thoughts roused me—I must do something. I therefore resolved that 1835 should not pass without witnessing an attempt, on my part, to secure my liberty. But I was not willing to cherish this determination alone. My fellow-slaves were dear to me. I was anxious to have them participate with me in this, my life-giving determination. I therefore, though with great prudence, commenced early to ascertain their views and feelings in regard to their condition, and to imbue their minds with thoughts of freedom. I bent myself to devising ways and means for our escape, and meanwhile strove, on all fitting occasions, to impress them with the gross fraud and inhumanity of slavery. I went first to Henry, next to John, then to the others. I found, in them all, warm hearts and noble spirits. They were ready to hear, and ready to act when a feasible plan should be proposed. This was what I wanted. I talked to them of our want of manhood, if we submitted to our enslavement without at least one noble effort to be free. We met often, and consulted frequently, and told our hopes and fears, recounted the difficulties, real and imagined, which we should be called on to meet. At times we were almost disposed to give up, and try to content ourselves with our wretched lot; at others, we were firm and unbending in our determination to go. Whenever we suggested any plan, there was shrinking—the odds were fearful. Our path was beset with the greatest obstacles; and if we succeeded in gaining the end of it, our right to be free was yet questionable—we were yet liable to be returned to bondage. We could see no spot, this side of the ocean, where we could be free. We knew nothing about Canada. Our knowledge of the north did not extend farther than New York; and to go there, and be forever harassed with the frightful liability of being returned to slavery—with the certainty of being treated tenfold worse than before—the thought was truly a horrible one, and one which it was not easy to overcome. The case sometimes stood thus: At every gate through which we were to pass, we saw a watchman—at every ferry a guard—on every bridge a sentinel—and in every wood a patrol. We were hemmed in upon every side. Here were the difficulties, real or imagined—the good to be sought, and the evil to be shunned. On the one hand, there stood slavery, a stern reality, glaring frightfully upon us,—its robes already crimsoned with the blood of millions, and even now feasting itself greedily upon our own flesh.

On the other hand, away back in the dim distance, under the flickering light of the north star, behind some craggy hill or snow-covered mountain, stood a doubtful freedom—half frozen—beckoning us to come and share its hospitality. This in itself was sometimes enough to stagger us; but when we permitted ourselves to survey the road, we were frequently appalled. Upon either side we saw grim death, assuming the most horrid shapes. Now it was starvation, causing us to eat our own flesh;—now we were contending with the waves, and were drowned;—now we were overtaken, and torn to pieces by the fangs of the terrible bloodhound. We were stung by scorpions, chased by wild beasts, bitten by snakes, and finally, after having nearly reached the desired spot,—after swimming rivers, encountering wild beasts, sleeping in the woods, suffering hunger and nakedness,—we were overtaken by our pursuers, and, in our resistance, we were shot dead upon the spot! I say, this picture sometimes appalled us, and made us

"rather bear those ills we had,
Than fly to others, that we knew not of."

In coming to a fixed determination to run away, we did more than Patrick Henry, when he resolved upon liberty or death. With us it was a doubtful liberty at most, and almost certain death if we failed. For my part, I should prefer death to hopeless bondage.

Sandy, one of our number, gave up the notion, but still encouraged us. Our company then consisted of Henry Harris, John Harris, Henry Bailey, Charles Roberts, and myself. Henry Bailey was my uncle, and belonged to my master. Charles married my aunt: he belonged to my master's father-in-law, Mr. William Hamilton.

The plan we finally concluded upon was, to get a large canoe belonging to Mr. Hamilton, and upon the Saturday night previous to Easter holidays, paddle directly up the Chesapeake Bay. On our arrival at the head of the bay, a distance of seventy or eighty miles from where we lived, it was our purpose to turn our canoe adrift, and follow the guidance of the north star till we got beyond the limits of Maryland. Our reason for taking the water route was, that we were less liable to be suspected as runaways; we hoped to be regarded as fishermen; whereas, if we should take the land route, we should be subjected to interruptions of almost every kind. Any one having a white face, and being so disposed, could stop us, and subject us to examination.

The week before our intended start, I wrote several protections, one for each of us. As well as I can remember, they were in the following words, to wit:—

"THIS is to certify that I, the undersigned, have given the bearer, my servant, full liberty to go to Baltimore, and spend the Easter holidays. Written with mine own hand, &c., 1835.
"WILLIAM HAMILTON,
"Near St. Michael's, in Talbot county, Maryland."

We were not going to Baltimore; but, in going up the bay, we went toward Baltimore, and these protections were only intended to protect us while on the bay.

As the time drew near for our departure, our anxiety became more and more intense. It was truly a matter of life and death with us. The strength of our determination was about to be fully tested. At this time, I was very active in explaining every difficulty, removing every doubt, dispelling every fear, and inspiring all with the firmness indispensable to success in our undertaking; assuring them that half was gained the instant we made the move; we had talked long enough; we were now ready to move; if not now, we never should be; and if we did not intend to move now, we had as well fold our arms, sit down, and acknowledge ourselves fit only to be slaves. This, none of us were prepared to acknowledge. Every man stood firm; and at our last meeting we pledged ourselves afresh, in the most solemn manner, that, at the time appointed, we would certainly start in pursuit of freedom. This was in the middle of the week, at the end of which we were to be off. We went, as usual, to our several fields of labor, but with bosoms highly agitated with thoughts of our truly hazardous undertaking. We tried to conceal our feelings as much as possible; and I think we succeeded very well.

After a painful waiting, the Saturday morning, whose night was to witness our departure, came. I hailed it with joy, bring what of sadness it might. Friday night was a sleepless one for me. I probably felt more anxious than the rest, because I was, by common consent, at the head of the whole affair. The responsibility of success or failure lay heavily upon me. The glory of the one, and the confusion of the other, were alike mine. The first two hours of that morning were such as I never experienced before, and hope never to again. Early in the morning, we went, as usual, to the field. We were spreading manure; and all at once, while thus engaged, I was overwhelmed with an indescribable feeling, in the fullness of which I turned to Sandy, who was near by, and said, "We are betrayed!" "Well," said he, "that thought has this moment struck me." We said no more. I was never more certain of any thing.

The horn was blown as usual, and we went up from the field to the house for breakfast. I went for the form, more than for want of any thing to eat that morning. Just as I got to the house, in looking, out at the lane gate, I saw four white men, with two colored men. The white men were on horseback, and the colored ones were walking behind, as if tied. I watched them a few moments till they got up to our lane gate. Here they halted, and tied the colored men to the gate-post. I was not yet certain as to what the matter was. In a few moments, in rode Mr. Hamilton, with a speed betokening great excitement. He came to the door, and inquired if Master William was in. He was told he was at the barn. Mr. Hamilton, without dismounting, rode up to the barn with extraordinary speed. In a few moments, he and Mr. Freeland returned to the house. By this time, the three constables rode up, and in great haste dismounted, tied their horses, and met Master William and Mr. Hamilton returning from the barn; and after talking awhile, they all walked up to the kitchen door. There was no one in the kitchen but myself and John. Henry and Sandy were up at the barn. Mr. Freeland put his head in at the door, and called me by name, saying, there were some gentlemen at the door who wished to see me. I stepped to the door, and inquired what they wanted. They at once seized me, and, without giving me any satisfaction, tied me—lashing my hands closely together. I insisted upon knowing what the matter was. They at length said, that they had learned I had been in a "scrape," and that I was to be examined before my master; and if their information proved false, I should not be hurt.

In a few moments, they succeeded in tying John. They then turned to Henry, who had by this time returned, and commanded him to cross his hands. "I won't!" said Henry, in a firm tone, indicating his readiness to meet the consequences of his refusal. "Won't you?" said Tom Graham, the constable. "No, I won't!" said Henry, in a still stronger tone. With this, two of the constables pulled out their shining pistols, and swore, by their Creator, that they would make him cross his hands or kill him. Each cocked his pistol, and, with fingers on the trigger, walked up to Henry, saying, at the same time, if he did not cross his hands, they would blow his damned heart out. "Shoot me, shoot me!" said Henry; "you can't kill me but once. Shoot, shoot,—and be damned! *I won't be tied!*" This he said in a tone of loud defiance; and at the same time, with a motion as quick as lightning, he with one single stroke dashed the pistols from the hand of each constable. As he did this, all hands fell upon him, and, after beating him some time, they finally overpowered him, and got him tied.

During the scuffle, I managed, I know not how, to get my pass out, and, without being discovered, put it into the fire. We were all now tied; and just as we were to leave for Easton jail, Betsy Freeland, mother of William Freeland, came to the door with her hands full of biscuits, and divided them between Henry and John. She then delivered herself of a speech, to the following effect:—addressing herself to me, she said, "*You devil! You yellow devil!* it was you that put it into the heads of Henry and John to run away. But for you, you long-legged mulatto devil! Henry nor John would never have thought of such a thing." I made no reply, and was immediately hurried off towards St. Michael's. Just a moment previous to the scuffle with Henry, Mr. Hamilton suggested the propriety of making a search for the protections which he had understood Frederick had written for himself and the rest. But, just at the moment he was about carrying his proposal into effect, his aid was needed in helping to tie Henry; and the excitement attending the scuffle caused them either to forget, or to deem it unsafe, under the circumstances, to search. So we were not yet convicted of the intention to run away.

When we got about half way to St. Michael's, while the constables having us in charge were looking ahead, Henry inquired of me what he should do with his pass. I told him to eat it with his biscuit, and own nothing; and we passed the word around, *"Own nothing;"* and *"Own nothing!"* said we all. Our confidence in each other was unshaken. We were resolved to succeed or fail together, after the calamity had befallen us as much as before. We were now prepared for any thing. We were to be dragged that morning fifteen miles behind horses, and then to be placed in the Easton jail. When we reached St. Michael's, we underwent a sort of examination. We all denied that we ever intended to run away. We did this more to bring out the evidence against us, than from any hope of getting clear of being sold; for, as I have said, we were ready for that. The fact was, we cared but little where we went, so we went together. Our greatest concern was about separation. We dreaded that more than any thing this side of death. We found the evidence against us to be the testimony of one person; our master would not tell who it was; but we came to a unanimous decision among ourselves as to who their informant was. We were sent off to the jail at Easton. When we got there, we were delivered up to the sheriff, Mr. Joseph Graham, and by him placed in jail. Henry, John, and myself, were placed in one room together—Charles, and Henry Bailey, in another. Their object in separating us was to hinder concert.

We had been in jail scarcely twenty minutes, when a swarm of slave traders, and agents for slave traders, flocked into jail to look at us, and to ascertain if we were for sale. Such a set of beings I never saw before! I felt myself surrounded by so many fiends from perdition. A band of pirates never looked more like their father, the devil. They laughed and grinned over us, saying, "Ah, my boys! we have got you, haven't we?" And after taunting us in various ways, they one by one went into an examination of us, with intent to ascertain our value. They would impudently ask us if we would not like to have them for our masters. We would make them no answer, and leave them to find out as best they could. Then they would curse and swear at us, telling us that they could take the devil out of us in a very little while, if we were only in their hands.

While in jail, we found ourselves in much more comfortable quarters, than we expected when we went there. We did not get much to eat, nor that which was very good; but we had a good clean room, from the windows of which we could see what was going on in the street, which was very much better than though we had been placed in one of the dark, damp cells. Upon the whole, we got along very well, so far as the jail and its keeper were concerned. Immediately after the holidays were over, contrary to all our expectations, Mr. Hamilton and Mr. Freeland came up to Easton, and took Charles, the two Henrys, and John, out of jail, and carried them home, leaving me alone. I regarded this separation as a final one. It caused me more pain than any thing else in the whole transaction. I was ready for any thing rather than separation. I supposed that they had consulted together, and had decided that, as I was the whole cause of the intention of the others to run away, it was hard to make the innocent suffer with the guilty; and that they had, therefore, concluded to take the others home, and sell me, as a warning to the others that remained. It is due to the noble Henry to say, he seemed almost as reluctant at leaving the prison as at leaving home to come to the prison. But we knew we should, in all probability, be separated, if we were sold; and since he was in their hands, he concluded to go peaceably home.

I was now left to my fate. I was all alone, and within the walls of a stone prison. But a few days before, and I was full of hope. I expected to have been safe in a land of freedom; but now I was covered with gloom, sunk down to the utmost despair. I thought the possibility of freedom was gone. I was kept in this way about one week, at the end of which, Captain Auld, my master, to my surprise and utter astonishment, came up, and took me out, with the intention of sending me, with a gentleman of his acquaintance, into Alabama. But, from some cause or other, he did not send me to Alabama, but concluded to send me back to Baltimore, to live again with his brother Hugh, and to learn a trade.

Thus, after an absence of three years and one month, I was once more permitted to return to my old home at Baltimore. My master sent me away, because there existed against me a very great prejudice in the community, and he feared I might be killed.

In a few weeks after I went to Baltimore, Master Hugh hired me to Mr. William Gardner, an extensive ship-builder, on Fell's Point. I was put there to learn how to calk. It, however, proved a very unfavorable place for the accomplishment of this object. Mr. Gardner was engaged that spring in building two large man-of-war brigs, professedly for the Mexican government. The vessels were to be launched in the July of that year, and in failure thereof, Mr. Gardner was to lose a considerable sum; so that when I entered, all was hurry. There was no time to learn any thing. Every man had to do that which he knew how to do. In entering the ship-yard, my orders from Mr. Gardner were, to do whatever the carpenters commanded me to do. This was placing me at the beck and call of about seventy-five men. I was to regard all these as masters. Their word was to be my law. My situation was a most trying one. At times I needed a dozen pair of hands. I was called a dozen ways in the space of a single minute. Three or four voices would strike my ear at the same moment. It was—"Fred, come help me to cant this timber here."—"Fred, come carry this timber yonder."—"Fred, bring that roller here."—"Fred, go get a fresh can of water."—"Fred, come help saw off the end of this timber."—"Fred, go quick, and get the crowbar."—"Fred, hold on the end of this fall."—"Fred, go to the black-smith's shop, and get a new punch."—"Hurra, Fred! Run and bring me a cold chisel."—"I say, Fred, bear a hand, and get up a fire as quick as lightning under that steam-box."—"Halloo, nigger! Come, turn this grindstone."—"Come, come! Move, move! And *bowse* this timber forward."—"I say, darky, blast your eyes, why don't you heat up some pitch?"—"Halloo! Halloo! Halloo!" (Three voices at the same time.) "Come here!—Go there!—Hold on where you are! Damn you, if you move, I'll knock your brains out!"

This was my school for eight months; and I might have remained there longer, but for a most horrid fight I had with four of the white apprentices, in which my left eye was nearly knocked out, and I was horribly mangled in other respects. The facts in the case were these: Until a very little while after I went there, white and black ship-carpenters worked side by side, and no one seemed to see any impropriety in it. All hands seemed to be very well satisfied. Many of the black carpenters were freemen. Things seemed to be going on very well. All at once, the white carpenters knocked off, and said they would not work with free colored workmen. Their reason for this, as alleged, was, that if free colored carpenters were encouraged, they would soon take the trade into their own hands, and poor white men would be thrown out of employment. They therefore felt called upon at once to put a stop to it. And, taking advantage of Mr. Gardner's necessities, they broke off, swearing they would work no longer, unless he would discharge his black carpenters. Now, though this did not extend to me in form, it did reach me in fact. My fellow-apprentices very soon began to feel it degrading to them to work with me. They began to put on airs, and talk about the "niggers" taking the country, saying we all ought to be killed; and, being encouraged by the journeymen, they commenced making my condition as hard as they could, by hectoring me around, and sometimes striking me. I, of course, kept the vow I made after the fight with Mr. Covey, and struck back again, regardless of consequences; and while I kept them from combining, I succeeded very well; for I could whip the whole of them, taking them separately. They, however, at length combined, and came upon me, armed with sticks, stones, and heavy handspikes. One came in front with a half brick. There was one at each side of me, and one behind me. While I was attending to those in front, and on either side, the one behind ran up with the handspike, and struck me a heavy blow upon the head. It stunned me. I fell, and with this they all ran upon me, and fell to beating me with their fists. I let them lay on for a while, gathering strength. In an instant, I gave a sudden surge, and rose to my hands and knees. Just

as I did that, one of their number gave me, with his heavy boot, a powerful kick in the left eye. My eyeball seemed to have burst. When they
saw my eye closed, and badly swollen, they left me. With this I seized
the handspike, and for a time pursued them. But here the carpenters
interfered, and I thought I might as well give it up. It was impossible to stand my hand against so many. All this took place in sight of
not less than fifty white ship-carpenters, and not one interposed a
friendly word; but some cried, "Kill the damned nigger! Kill him!
Kill him! He struck a white person." I found my only chance for life
was in flight. I succeeded in getting away without an additional blow,
and barely so; for to strike a white man is death by Lynch law—and
that was the law in Mr. Gardner's ship-yard; nor is there much of
any other out of Mr. Gardner's ship-yard.

I went directly home, and told the story of my wrongs to Master
Hugh; and I am happy to say of him, irreligious as he was, his conduct was heavenly, compared with that of his brother Thomas under
similar circumstances. He listened attentively to my narration of the
circumstances leading to the savage outrage, and gave many proofs of
his strong indignation at it. The heart of my once overkind mistress
was again melted into pity. My puffed-out eye and blood-covered face
moved her to tears. She took a chair by me, washed the blood from my
face, and, with a mother's tenderness, bound up my head, covering
the wounded eye with a lean piece of fresh beef. It was almost compensation for my suffering to witness, once more, a manifestation of
kindness from this, my once affectionate old mistress. Master Hugh
was very much enraged. He gave expression to his feelings by pouring out curses upon the heads of those who did the deed. As soon as
I got a little the better of my bruises, he took me with him to Esquire
Watson's, on Bond Street, to see what could be done about the matter.
Mr. Watson inquired who saw the assault committed. Master Hugh
told him it was done in Mr. Gardner's ship-yard, at midday, where
there were a large company of men at work. "As to that," he said, "the
deed was done, and there was no question as to who did it." His answer was, he could do nothing in the case, unless some white man

would come forward and testify. He could issue no warrant on my word. If I had been killed in the presence of a thousand colored people, their testimony combined would have been insufficient to have arrested one of the murderers. Master Hugh, for once, was compelled to say this state of things was too bad. Of course, it was impossible to get any white man to volunteer his testimony in my behalf, and against the white young men. Even those who may have sympathized with me were not prepared to do this. It required a degree of courage unknown to them to do so; for just at that time, the slightest manifestation of humanity toward a colored person was denounced as abolitionism, and that name subjected its bearer to frightful liabilities. The watchwords of the bloody-minded in that region, and in those days, were, "Damn the abolitionists!" and "Damn the niggers!" There was nothing done, and probably nothing would have been done if I had been killed. Such was, and such remains, the state of things in the Christian city of Baltimore.

Master Hugh, finding he could get no redress, refused to let me go back again to Mr. Gardner. He kept me himself, and his wife dressed my wound till I was again restored to health. He then took me into the ship-yard of which he was foreman, in the employment of Mr. Walter Price. There I was immediately set to calking, and very soon learned the art of using my mallet and irons. In the course of one year from the time I left Mr. Gardner's, I was able to command the highest wages given to the most experienced calkers. I was now of some importance to my master. I was bringing him from six to seven dollars per week. I sometimes brought him nine dollars per week: my wages were a dollar and a half a day. After learning how to calk, I sought my own employment, made my own contracts, and collected the money which I earned. My pathway became much more smooth than before; my condition was now much more comfortable. When I could get no calking to do, I did nothing. During these leisure times, those old notions about freedom would steal over me again. When in Mr. Gardner's employment, I was kept in such a perpetual whirl of excitement, I could think of nothing, scarcely, but my life; and in thinking of my life, I almost forgot my liberty. I have observed this in my experience of slavery,—that whenever my condition was improved, instead of its increasing my contentment, it only increased my desire to be free, and set me to thinking of plans to gain my freedom. I have found that, to make a contented slave, it is necessary to make a thoughtless one. It is necessary to darken his moral and mental vision, and, as far as possible, to annihilate the power of reason. He must be able to detect no inconsistencies in slavery; he must be made to feel that slavery is right; and he can be brought to that only when be ceases to be a man.

I was now getting, as I have said, one dollar and fifty cents per day. I contracted for it; I earned it; it was paid to me; it was rightfully my own; yet, upon each returning Saturday night, I was compelled to deliver every cent of that money to Master Hugh. And why? Not because he earned it,—not because he had any hand in earning it,—not because I owed it to him,—nor because he possessed the slightest shadow of a right to it; but solely because he had the power to compel me to give it up. The right of the grim-visaged pirate upon the high seas is exactly the same.

PART TWO

Running Because of Family

The master mounted on his horse driving John before him.
From Isaac T. Hopper, Narrative of the Life of Thomas Cooper
(New York: Published by Isaac T. Hopper, 1832).
Image courtesy of Documenting the American South,
University of North Carolina at Chapel Hill Libraries.

FOUR

From *Slavery Days in Old Kentucky.*
A True Story of a Father Who Sold
His Wife and Four Children.
By One of the Children.

A fine example of a narrative that calls attention to the harsh reali-
ties of slavery decades after slavery was abolished, Slavery Days in Old
Kentucky *was published in 1901 at the request of individuals who had*
inquired about the author's experiences in bondage. In fact, the book
was undertaken by its author, Isaac Johnson, as a potent reminder to
the "present generation [that] knows but little of actual slavery." Writ-
ing in the preface, Johnson added, "Attempts are sometimes made to
color the Institution to make it appear as though the old days of Ameri-
can slavery were patriarchal days to be desired, to surround the Insti-
tution with a glamour as though it possessed great intrinsic merits of
value to both races." Johnson's narrative therefore gives "to the world a
knowledge of the subject that no eloquence may ever make the same thing
again possible."

Unlike most slaves, Johnson grew up, until the age of seven, secluded
from racial hostilities. His mother lived openly as the wife of her white
master, who sired four sons with her. In his powerful narrative, the

Originally published: Ogdensburg, NY: *Republican & Journal Print*, 1901.

author recalls his family existing peacefully on a tobacco farm, until neighbors began questioning their controversial living arrangement. In a sudden turn of events, Johnson's father sold all of his possessions— including his wife and children—and left Kentucky. Among the most moving episodes of this autobiography is the slave auction of Johnson's mother, siblings, and himself. However, equally terrifying are his recollections as a fugitive slave—and the chilling consequences meted out by whites to those who were caught.

CHAPTER I.
IN THE BEGINNING.

So many people have inquired as to the particulars of my slave life and seemingly listened to the same with interest, that I have concluded to give the story in this form.

I was born in the State of Kentucky in 1844. When I first came to a knowledge of myself I was a child living with my parents on a farm located on the banks of Green river in my native State. The family at that time consisted of my father, Richard Yeager, my mother, Jane, an older brother, Louis, a younger brother, Ambrose, and later on another brother, Eddie. I was next to Louis in age. Here we lived a happy and contented family, and prosperous beyond most of the farmers in that section of the State. For reasons that will appear before the end is reached my surname is the maiden name of my mother. As I look back to my boyhood days I can see that my mother was an intelligent woman, considering her station in life, and it is from her, and my paternal uncles in after years, I learned as to my ancestry.

My grandfather was an Irishman, named Griffin Yeager, and his brothers were engaged in the villainous vocation of the Slave Trade. Their business was to steal negroes from Africa or wherever they could get them and sell them as slaves in the United States. My mother was stolen by these people from the island of Madagascar in the year

1840. She was brought to America and given to my grandfather who concluded she would make a good servant. He gave her the name of Jane and kept her till he died, which was soon after.

By the terms of grandfather's will, Jane was bequeathed to his eldest son Richard, commonly known as Dick Yeager. Dick also received by the will other personal property, and, equipped with cows, sheep, horses and some farming utensils, he took Jane and moved onto the farm referred to on Green river. He used Jane in all respects as a wife and she, in her innocence, supposed she was such. I well remember their little house. It was about twenty feet by sixteen with a nine foot ceiling. It had only one outside door and two windows. The house was divided into two rooms, a kitchen and bed room. A fireplace occupied a part of one end, the foundation being large flat stones on which the cooking was done. Their furniture was limited as well as their cooking utensils, but these were sufficient for their wants, and on the whole it was a happy home. They at first had no neighbors nearer than ten miles. They worked together in harmony, she taking the lead in the house and he in the field, where she often assisted him. The first year they raised such vegetables as they needed but these brought no money. They then commenced raising tobacco and hogs. Their first crop of tobacco brought them $1600 in cash, but the hogs all died. They were so encouraged by the tobacco crop that they devoted all their energy to this product thereafter, and in time they became the leading tobacco growers. Other people soon came as neighbors, none of whom owned slaves. The new comers disapproved of and freely talked about Yeager and his manner of living with a slave and raising children by her. This talk resulted in social ostracism of the Yeager family notwithstanding he was more prosperous than any of them. Yeager felt the social cut keenly and concluded to sell out and leave that part of the country. He accordingly advertised his farm and stock for sale. At this time his children were aged as follows: Louis was nine years of age, Isaac (myself) was seven, Ambrose five and Eddie was two. The sale took place. He retained the horses which were taken to the New Orleans market, leaving the family during his absence. Here we remained waiting patiently his return, till about two months thereafter, when the sheriff came and took us all to Bardstown in Nelson county, about two days journey eastward, and here we were placed in the negro pen for the night.

CHAPTER II.

THE AUCTION SALE.

The next morning, to our astonishment, a crowd gathered and took turns examining us. What it all meant we could not imagine till Louis was led out about ten o'clock, placed on the auction block and the auctioneer cried out: "How much do I hear for this nigger?" Allow me to say here, it was only the vulgar and low whites who used the term "nigger," the better classes always spoke of us as negroes or colored folks. The auctioneer continued his cry for bids and Louis was at last sold for eight hundred dollars. By this time we had taken in the situation, and it seemed as though my mother's heart would break. Such despair I hope I may never again witness. We children knew something terrible was being done, but were not old enough to fully understand.

Then the auctioneer called for Isaac and I was led out, the auctioneer saying, "Time is precious, gentlemen, I must sell them all before night; how much do I hear for this nigger?" We were instructed beforehand that we must answer all questions put to us by "Yes, sir," and "No, sir." I was asked if I had ever been whipped, or sick, or had had the toothache, and similar questions to all of which I answered. He then cried for bids. The first bid was four hundred dollars. This was gradually raised until I was struck off for seven hundred dollars, and sold to William Madinglay, who came forward and said: "Come along with me, boy, you belong to me." I said to him: "Let me go and see my mother." He answered me crossly: "Come along with me, I will train you without your mother's help." I was taken one side and chained to a post as though I had been a horse. I remained hitched to this post till late in the afternoon.

The next one sold was Ambrose. I could not see him, but I could hear the auctioneer crying for bids and my little four year old brother was sold for five hundred dollars to William Murphy.

The next to be set up was my mother and our little baby boy Eddie. To the cry for bids no one responded for some time and it looked for awhile that they were to escape being sold. But some one called out: "Put them up separately." Then the cry was: "How much do I hear for the woman without the baby?" The first bid was eight hundred dollars, and this was gradually raised till she was sold for eleven hundred dollars.

The next sale was of Eddie, my little brother whom we all loved so much, he was sold for two hundred dollars, to one John Hunter. Thus, in a very short time, our happy family was scattered, without even the privilege of saying "Good by" to each other, and never again to be seen, at least so far as I was concerned.

CHAPTER III.
MY NEW HOME.

Late in the afternoon my new master put me into a wagon and took me over very rough and hilly roads to his home about five miles distant, on a farm located on the bank of Beech Fork river. We reached this home of William Madinglay about ten o'clock at night. His wife, one child, and Peter, a slave, constituted his family, and I made one more.

On reaching the place, Madinglay called loudly: "Peter!" This individual soon appeared, saying: "Yes, sir, Master!" He was then asked:

"Have you put in feed for the horses?"

"Yes, sir, Master!"

Turning to me he said: "Come along with me."

We went to the kitchen and there we met his wife at the door when she asked: "What have you there, William?"

His answer was: "Oh, I have a little boy here for you."

"Indeed, you have a bright little fellow," she replied.

He then said: "This is one of the Yeager niggers we saw advertised for sale at auction."

"I declare he is not a very dark colored one."

"No, wife, he isn't, you see he is one of those pumpkin seed niggers from the mountains."

"Oh Bill! What makes you talk that way? I think he will make a good servant."

His reply was: "I reckon he will when he gets that black snake around him a couple of times." (He referred to the raw hide whip.)

"William, I hope he will not need that at all, I don't think he is as stupid as Peter."

"Oh well, Margaret, I don't mind if he is stupid, I can train him, there is nothing like the black snake for stupidness."

I had never heard such talk before, and I hung my head and began to cry when she said: Oh Bill, don't scare the boy to death, I think he will be a good boy.

Master then commanded: "Stand up there and straighten up, let your Mistress see what kind of a boy you are, she hasn't half seen you yet."

She brought a lamp from the shelf and carefully looked me over, after which she said: "Oh what a nice little lad, and what a nice suit he has on!"

"Oh yes, wife, up on the mountains they don't know how to work the niggers, but I will teach him how to work. The idea of a nigger with a suit on him like that! Wait till I get a suit on him, I'll show him how to work."

She then asked: "What is your name?"

"Isaac," I answered.

"That's a nice little name. Take off your hat, put it on the chair and sit down in the corner."

I took off my hat and coat and looked for a place to hang them, as I had been accustomed to do in our old home, but found none. I laid them on the little bundle I had with me and walked over to the corner of the fireplace and sat on the floor. Peter came in and Master asked: "Have you got your chores all done?"

"Yes, sir, Master."

"Did you go to the mill to-day?"

"Yes, sir, Master."

"Did you bring a load of meal home!"

"Yes, sir, Master."

"Is there plenty of wood at the still?"

"Yes, sir, Master."

"Do you know if they are going to grind tomorrow?"

"Yes, sir, Master, dey's going to grind tomorrow."

After Master and his wife had eaten their supper, which consisted of mush and milk, she brought us a pan of the same for our supper, after which Master said: "Peter, this is a little nigger who is to help you in your work, he is green, but you must teach him."

Mistress then brought an old quilt saying: "This is a quilt for your bed tonight, you and Peter can sleep together, he will show you."

Peter also had an old quilt, we laid one down and took the other for a cover, our bed being the floor.

Oh, what a change! The sight of Peter set me nearly crazy. All he wore was a long tow shirt, a cloth cap and no shoes. It did not take him long to turn in as he had nothing to take off. I took off my shoes, socks, pants and coat, and then looked around to see what he had for a pillow and found he had none, but was curled up like a snake. I sat there for hours thinking of my mother, brothers and father until I was nearly wild with the change that had come, changed from a happy home to be used like a dog, and a pretty mean one at that. I wondered if I should ever see my people again. I little dreamed then what I afterwards learned, that my own father had brought all this change to us, that we were sold by his orders and the three thousand three hundred dollars we were sold for went into his pockets less the expenses of the sale. He had sold his own flesh and blood. That is what American slavery made possible. That is the "Divine institution" we have heard so much about, the cornerstone of the proposed Confederacy. Is it any wonder the Southerners were defeated with such an incubus around their necks, dragging them down to a condition lower than their slaves, making them human demons! Do you wonder that when freedom came to me I preferred the maiden name of my sainted mother to the name of my father? In my ignorance of the true situation I mourned for him in common with my mother and brothers, and sat through that night bewildered, until tired nature forced me to lie down. I took my little bundle for a pillow, wrapped the quilt about me, not to sleep but rather to dream and wonder what terrible thing had happened to my dear father, as I then thought of him, to bring all this misfortune upon us. I tried to console myself with the thought that there must be some hereafter when we could all meet again sometime. The night wore away at last but I had had no rest. Then I heard the mournful voice of Master calling: "Peter, Peter, are you awake?"

"Yes, sir, Master."

"Make the fire in the kitchen and in here."

"Yes, sir, Master."

"Bring Isaac, the lad, and show him what to do."

"Yes, sir, Master."

"Take him with you to do the chores."

"Yes, sir, Master."

"Peter then told me to bring some water while he split some wood for the Mistress. I asked where I would get the water.

He said: "See dat tree down dare?"

I said "Yes."

He said, "You go to dat tree, when you get dare you see nuther tree uther side dat tree, and when you get dare you'll see little grass uther side dat tree, and uther side dat grass dare is big hole and dat is whare de water is."

I went but failed to find "de big hole," and he upbraided me, saying: "You nice nigger! Can't fin dat well when it's bin dare long while, long fore I comed here and you can't fin it!"

He took the pail and showed me the well. After we returned he asked: "Do you tink you can fin dat well now?"

I said, "I thought I could," and he sent me for another pailful while he carried in the wood after which we were to have something to eat.

We went into the house and Mistress asked: "Peter, have you done all the chores?"

"Yes, mam!" said Peter, and we then sat on the floor, Peter in one corner of the fireplace and I in the other; here we sat until Master and

Mistress had finished their breakfast when she brought us our mush and milk once more.

Master then came and said, "Peter!"

"Yes, sir, Master."

"Have you finished your breakfast?"

"Yes, sir, Master."

"Go and hitch up the mules and bring them ready to put on the grists for the mill." We obeyed and the mules were loaded with three sacks of corn on each except two that carried only two sacks each, these last were to be ridden and the others were to be led.

CHAPTER IV.

AT HOME WITH MISTRESS.

Master and Peter went with the mules and I was left to help Mistress do the washing. I was pleased with this arrangement as I liked her better than the Master. She, wishing to learn my skill as a washer, gave me first the baby's soiled clothes, these I cleaned to her satisfaction; she then gave me Master's clothes which I also washed and then she gave me her own clothes, all of which pleased her. She then asked if I could iron? I told her I would try. The clothes were dried and brought in and I ironed all of them. She was kind to me and complimented my work saying: "You have done very well, my boy, and now you may sit down and rest."

I sat down, but not to rest. The moment I stopped working a great grief came to me so overpowering I could not conceal my feelings and I began to cry. She asked me kindly: "What is the matter, Isaac?" I told her, "I wanted to see my mamma."

She tried to pacify me by saying: "Don't cry and fret about that, Isaac, you will see your mother again, Master will buy her and the rest of them sometime."

I asked: "Why didn't he buy them when he bought me?"

She replied: "My boy, never mind about that, your mother will be sold again soon and you will be together once more."

I asked: "Who bought her?"

Her reply was: "Never mind who bought her, you must not ask questions about such things, not a question, my word is law."

Soon thereafter Master and Peter returned; on entering the house Master asked: "Well, Margaret, how did you get along with the lad?"

She informed him that I had done nicely and that I was a good little worker. His next inquiry was: "Have you taught him how to talk?"

"No," she replied, "but he'll learn without any trouble."

"That's the next thing he must learn," he said and then he called in a loud commanding tone: "Isaac, come here!"

"All right," I answered.

In an angry voice he said: "All right? Is that the way you answer your Master? When I tell you to 'come here' I want you to say, 'Yes, sir, Master,' Now I'll try you once more; Isaac, come here."

I was frightened and again said, "All right."

He was angry. He took up the whip and said: "Isaac, you nigger you, if you don't talk to me as you ought to I shall use this black snake on you. When I call you, you must say, 'yes, sir, Master,' and to your Mistress you must say, 'yes, Madam,' and don't you ever let me hear you say 'all right' to a white man, and when you meet a white man always take off your hat and say 'yes, sir,' or 'no, sir,' and stand to one side till he passes. Remember what I have told you or I shall try the black snake on your back. Now go and help Peter do the chores." . . .

CHAPTER V.

HIRED OUT.

The harvesting was finally all done and the first day of January, 1853, had arrived. The first of January was the time when local sales and hiring took place. Myself, Jim and Peter were among those to be hired out and we were taken to Bardstown for this purpose. Our services for the year were sold at auction. Jim was sold for the year for $150, Peter for $125 and I was sold for $100. The cook, Anna, was taken along and sold outright to the slave dealers, and that was the last we knew of her. Peter and Jim were hired by one Miller, a farmer on the Columbia river, and I was hired to one Yates, a store keeper in Hart county. His store was near the Mammoth cave, around which at that time was a wilderness. His family consisted of himself, his wife, two sons, a woman slave and myself. My work was to do the chores about the house and run on errands to the store, which was about a mile distant. I had a fairly easy time here, my hardest work being to carry water from the cave to the house, the distance being about a mile. I had a yoke which laid across my shoulders, at each end were hooks so I could carry two pails at once. To get the water I had to enter the cave and descend about thirty feet. I was always afraid when I entered the cave because people told all manner of stories about it, saying that there were all kinds of devils and animals living in there who just delighted in catching colored people and killing them.

I managed, so far as I could, to go to the cave when the sun was shining bright so that I could see my way clearly to run if a devil appeared. The two sons of the Master were very mischievous, and when they learned how afraid I was they would go each Sunday and build a fire inside the cave and then send me for water. When I entered the cave and saw the fire I was sure it was the devil, and would run screaming at the top of my voice much to their amusement. They would then go back with me and enter the cave, by which time the fire would be out, and they would then accuse me of lying about seeing the devil. This occurred so often that Master became suspicious. He asked why it was the devils only appeared on Sundays. This I could not explain. He concluded to investigate for himself, and the next Sunday went with me and caught the boys building the fire, and that ended the stories of devils being in the cave and I had no more trouble. I remained at this place till Christmas, when we were given a week's holiday, and on the first of January, 1854, I was sent to my Master's brother, his name was James Madinglay. I remained with him two months. He was the meanest kind of a slave holder. He had two slaves, a girl and a boy. He drank very hard and seldom left his room on account of his being too drunk to do so. He would order the slaves to his room and whip them unmercifully without any cause or provocation. His son was equally as mean as he, he would watch the slaves, and if he saw one idle, only for a moment, he would inform his father and that meant, every time, a severe whipping. We were to husk corn one morning during the husking season, but it rained so very hard that we did not start at once for the crib. For this delay, Master called us all in to be punished. I stood by and saw him whip the other boy severely. I knew my turn would come next, and I started on the run for home as hard as I could run, not stopping till I reached there. Mistress saw me and wished to know my reasons for my appearance. I told her what had taken place and she said it was "all right, stay here till your Master comes home."

I didn't know what Master would say or do, but when he came I told him all about it. He listened quietly till I was through, and then said: "It is all right this time, Isaac, as I have rented my farm for four years and sold you to my brother, John, who lives on the Beech Fork river, about six miles from here; he is not at home now but will be in a few days, so you can 'back' your things and I will take you there in the morning."

I felt very well satisfied with the result and said: "I have nothing to 'back' as all I have is on my back and I can go any time."

The next morning we went to his brother John's farm. There was no one there except the overseer and an old negro woman. The overseer's name was Steward, and he had been engaged to manage what was called "an improved stock farm." In a few days my new Master sent to the farm a fine looking slave girl, an octoroon, she was to take charge as stewardess. Master had won her at a game of poker in St. Louis. This girl he kept for his own use, and she was made Mistress of the stock farm. By stock it will be understood is meant negro slaves.

The stock soon began to arrive, there was a negro with a couple of brood mares, then came Jim and Peter, then two males, then three women, then about the first of April John Madinglay made his appearance with a group of twenty, making thirty slaves all told. There were also brought onto the farm, farming utensils, mules, ten horses, thirty head of cattle, one hundred hogs and fifty sheep. He owned one thousand acres of land, but most of it was covered with brush or bushes. He raised the usual farm products and when these did not require attention we were set to work clearing the land. He had agents out in the country buying slaves and forwarding them to the farm, and soon there were one hundred and twenty slaves on the farm. After harvesting, the surplus negroes were sent to the Southern markets at Grand Gulf, Jackson and Vicksburg, at each of which places he had slave pens.

The time of the removal was kept secret from the slaves, and about ten o'clock the night before, twelve men were sent into the cabins and these hand-cuffed the males. In the morning these were brought out by twos and fastened to a chain about forty or fifty feet long. The women and children not able to walk were packed into wagons and the line of march commenced, the chained men first, the women able to walk next, and the wagons brought up the rear. A beautiful sight for a country that boasts of its freedom! How the boasted Southern chivalry must have delighted in such sights, delighted in them so greatly they were ready to go to war to preserve the "sacred institution" of human slavery! I have tasted its sacredness and felt that its Divinity is devilish. The line of march was to Nashville where they were placed aboard of boats and taken to the different slave pens.

The pens were divided into groups, women in one, men in another, girls and young boys by themselves. Here the buyers came and examined the stock, feeling of them as men do horses, looking into their mouths and eyes and asked questions as to sickness. Then the sales commenced and were held from November till about the first of March, during which time the agents were scouring the country, picking up new stock and forwarding the same to the market. After the first of March, if there were any unsold, they were taken back to the stock farm to work during the summer and shipped with the next lot ready for market. . . .

CHAPTER VI.

BOB, THE CANADIAN.

Among the five slaves brought back to the stock farm unsold, was one named Bob who had come from Canada. He was an engineer and had hired on the steamer Louisville at Cincinnati, Ohio, for the round trip. When they reached New Orleans the cargo was sold, and just as the boat was ready to return, the sheriff came aboard and all negroes found who were not owned by a Whiteman were taken to the city jail, advertised for three months as runaway slaves, and if no owner claimed them they were sold to the highest bidder. This is the way Bob became a slave. At that sale of Bob, my master, John Madinglay, was the purchaser. He took him to Grand Gulf and not being able to sell him there he brought him to the stock farm where he was placed in the hoe gang over which I was boss. My gang consisted of six boys and six girls besides Bob and myself. Bob was a shrewd as well as a powerful man. He was closely watched and not allowed to talk to any of the men, though he could at all times talk to and associate with Rosa and was encouraged to do so. The result was, Bob fell deeply in love with Rosa and talked with her freely. He told her all about his home and life in Canada and proposed that she go there with him. He pictured to her how pleasantly they could live in that land of freedom, where colored people were treated as human beings, and he laid before her all his plans to escape. She apparently consented to his proposals and the time was fixed when they were to start. The stock farm was on the banks of Beech Fork river, and whenever there was a heavy rain this river was swollen to a flood. When this should next occur was the time fixed upon for escape, and I was to go with them, though at first I did not know that Rosa was to go with us.

The flood soon came. I had charge of the skiff and watched eagerly till the water was at its height, when I informed Bob of the situation. I explained to him how we could go over the dams in safety. It was Saturday and I proposed to Bob that we start that night and when evening came I urged Bob to start at once. But Bob said "No!" He was going to take Rosa with him. This was the first I knew of his intentions with reference to Rosa and I told him not to trust her, that she told everything she knew to Master. He refused to start that night, but said he would go next Monday morning as the Master was going away that day and would not return till night. I told him that would never do and tried to impress him with the fact that Rosa could not be trusted; but he insisted that I leave the matter to him and everything would be all right. I was finally persuaded to do as he said. Monday morning came and I got the horse for Master who said he was going to town and told me to go to the field to my work. On reaching the field I informed Bob Master had gone and there was the skiff. At this point of the river there was an elbow around which the distance was ten miles, while across the land it was only three miles. Bob told me to take the boat around the elbow and he and Rosa would meet me by going across the land. I started. The current was strong and I made the distance in good time, reached the other side but no Bob or Rosa was there. I waited and waited for them for about three hours when I concluded to wait no longer. Bob had explained to me the whole route to be taken to reach Canada and so I started alone. I continued down stream till about seven o'clock in the evening. I was halted during the day three different times by men on the shore who had guns and shot at me. The first shot struck the boat but did not injure it. Soon after I was shot at twice, but neither of them came near me. This gave me courage and I thought: "Fire away! You can't hit me!" Still I pulled harder than ever and soon reached the railroad bridge and passed under without being seen. About half of a mile inland I saw a light which I took for a negro cabin. I was fearfully hungry, having had nothing to eat since morning. I pulled my boat ashore and started for the light. After I had gone two or three hundred yards the light disappeared and I started back to the boat. As I drew near I saw two men armed and they had two dogs with them. I turned and ran for a swamp near by, the men and dogs following. I managed to keep out of their way for a couple of hours or more. The number of men had increased to ten and I saw there was no chance for me to escape and the longer I tried to evade them the worse it would be for me. I knew the character of the dogs and what I might expect from them if they should reach me before the men were near and I gave myself up. One of the men said he would take me to his house till morning and then return me to master. I was taken to the depot near by, where there were about fifty men armed, all of whom had been hunting for me. Although I was only a poor negro boy, ignorant and without arms, these men were thoroughly armed with guns, knives and dogs as if they were in pursuit of a wild and ferocious animal. I was taken to the house, given some supper, which I was glad to get as I was as hungry as a bear, was given a place to lie down in a corner, the man and his wife were in another corner in the same room, so also were the dogs. He bolted the door, laid his revolver on a table near his bed in which he and his wife slept.

I took in the situation and made up my mind to have that revolver before morning. I laid down determined not to sleep. My day's work, however, had been a hard one, harder even than it would have been in the field on the old stock farm. I had scarcely laid down before I was fast asleep and knew nothing whatever till the man called me in the morning. My disappointment was great. I feared I had lost my last chance for freedom, still I had a little hope left and did not wholly despair. I was given some breakfast and told to split some wood while he hitched the horses. I watched him, sideways, till he entered the barn and as soon as he was out of sight I took to my heels and ran for the swamp. I must have had a quarter of a mile start before he set the dogs on my track. I heard their loud baying and quickened my speed. If there is anything that will make one almost fly through the air, it is one of those blood hounds on his track, with the knowledge that unless he outstrips them he is liable to be torn in pieces. It is no wonder to me that deer and other animals chased by dogs become so fleet. I have never since heard of such a chase for a deer, but I think of this race of my own, and I must say it has created in me a sympathy for the animal, and I would gladly banish by law, if I could, all such manner of hunting. I reached the swamp pretty well exhausted. Here I hid, and, as luck would have it, the dogs passed on beyond me, baying at every jump. After they had passed I ran for the river and followed it till about four o'clock in the afternoon. If I heard an alarm on one side of the river I swam to the other side and continued my race. I watched for a skiff, not finding one, I concluded to make a raft. I had one about completed and was covering it with brush, in which I hoped to hide from sight of those ashore, when I heard the sound of dogs near by. I did not have time to push off the raft, so I plunged into the water, swam a short distance to a big stump near the shore. The water in this river was almost as black as ink, and an object could not be seen below its surface. I sank in the water, leaving only my nose and mouth above. Here I lay for some time. There were five men on the shore and the dogs were hunting up and down the bank. At last one of the dogs got the scent and started for me with a yelp. The men gathered at once on the bank and, pointing their guns at me, ordered me to swim ashore. I saw there was no further use in my trying to escape and I surrendered.

I was taken to the nearest depot and thence to my Master, who paid fifty dollars for my recovery. I was taken to the garret in his home, handcuffed for the night, and, to make sure I would not escape again, Peter was handcuffed to me. The next morning Peter was released, shackles were placed on my legs, and I remained in this shape till about 10 o'clock, when Master and his brother William, who was his slave agent, came to the garret, took off the shackles, handcuffed my hands behind my back and took me to the punishment room or shanty where I saw Bob lying on a few boards, his throat cut and he was slowly dying in great misery. From him I afterwards learned that about half an hour after I left the field, Master and three slave drivers came to the still house, sent for Bob to come there, which he did, not mistrusting what was before him. As soon as he arrived the four men all pounced upon him like four ravenous wolves upon a lamb. He fought all of them till he was overpowered. They then drove four stakes in the ground and he was tied to these with his back up and the four men took turns lashing him with a raw hide whip, the black snake I have referred to, until his back appeared like a piece of beefsteak pounded. They then took hot coals from the furnace and poured them over his back, after which they took him to the punishment cabin, shackled his feet, chained him to the punishment block and in the night two of them went into the cabin and cut his throat, taking care not to cut the jugular, but cutting just enough so he would die gradually in torture.

Bob's condition was a lesson to the rest of us, and no means were allowed to escape making it an impressive one. He lived in this condition for five days and then his poor soul took its flight to the region where it is hoped no slave holder will ever have the privilege of exercising his power over human beings. . . .

Bob was at last dead and then followed his funeral. A box was made into which he was placed, all the slaves were brought to view his remains, a grave was dug, the improvised coffin was loaded into a cart and we all followed him to his burial. After the remains were lowered into the grave Master preached what was called a funeral sermon. The substance of his words were: "This negro, Bob, was a bad man. I paid my money for him and I was his master. You all know that if he had done right as you have done, he would never have been where he is. He cut his own throat and beat me out of my money. You know that I must be obeyed and if you do not obey me I must whip you; but he was so mean that whipping was of no use to him and it would have been better for you and me if his throat had been cut long ago. There isn't one among you but knows I have done right, as he was a mean, mean negro. You must understand there is no Lord or God who has anything to do with any of you, as I alone am your Master, your maker and your law giver, and when you do what I tell you to do you will get along all right."

After Bob's condition had been impressed upon me sufficiently, as they thought, and before Bob had died, at the time they took me to see him, I was again taken to the garret, from there I was taken to a ladder which stood between the house and the garden. My clothes were taken off and I was strapped to this ladder. Master's wife came forward and said: "Let him tell the whole truth about going away." I don't know, but I think she wished to implicate Rosa. Knowing that Bob was the same as dead and could not be hurt any further, I told them that "I was going to Canada because there I would be a free man." Master then asked: "Who told you that Canada is a country in which you can be free?"

I said: "Bob told me."

He asked how many of the negroes knew about the runaway and I told him, "not one that I know of."

He said: "Don't you know that you are lying to me? Doesn't Rosa know all about it?"

I told him, "No! If I had thought she knew about it I would not have started, because I knew she would tell you."

He asked: "Are you sure none of the other negroes know anything about it?"

I answered, "I am sure, so far as I know."

The Mistress then said: "Isaac, I don't want to see you killed the same as Bob has been; if you will go in the garden and obey my orders I will see that your Master does not hurt you. I want you to never speak to a negro on the place, nor leave the garden without my permission, and when you come to meals come to my dining room and Rosa will serve you and at night you must go to the garret to sleep."

She then spoke to her husband, saying: "Let him go and I will look after him."

I was put in the garden which was surrounded by a high fence, the gate was locked and the key was given to Rosa so that I could not get out without her knowing it.

The above occurred before Bob had died. After I had been in the garden two days, Master and his wife went to visit a neighbor. After they had gone Rosa came to the garden and I asked her to allow me to go and see Bob. She had always been friendly with me and consented, saying, however: "You can go, but do not allow anyone to see you, if you do it will make trouble for me." I went. Bob could talk, but his voice was very weak. It was then he told me the particulars I have related about their treatment of him, and that he had been betrayed by Rosa. He also said: "Isaac, there is just one thing I want to do before I die, and that is to punish Master. I am shackled and chained and can't get three feet from the bed. I want you to bring me a hatchet, ax, or something, and I will be satisfied."

I told him I could not do that as I was watched, but that I would get him the prong of a pitch fork. I went to the garden, got the prong, hid it under my shirt, picked some onions and asked Rosa if I could take the onions to Bob. She consented and I took them to him and left the pitchfork prong which he concealed about his bed and waited for a chance to get even with the Master. But Master was too cautious for him and did not go into the place till Bob had been dead some six hours.

FIVE

From *The Narrative of Bethany Veney: A Slave Woman*

Writing in the book's introduction, Reverend Bishop W. F. Mallalieu points to the inspirational, as opposed to strictly polemical, function of late slave narratives when he wrote, "The biographies of saintly, enduring spirits like that of Betty Veney will be read, and will serve to inspire the discouraged and down-trodden to put their trust in the almighty arm of Jehovah, who alone works deliverance and salvation to all those who put their trust in him."

Although the preface describes the author's life as "uneventful" when compared to the lives of many slaves, the true relativity of that designation comes into focus when Veney writes that her first mistress "was kind to me, as I then counted kindness, never whipping or starving me; but it was not what a free-born white child would have found comforting or needful."

Veney grew up with her mother, grandmother, uncle, and four siblings as the property of James Fletcher in Luray, Virginia. Upon Fletcher's death, when the author was "about nine years old," Veney's family was parceled out to Fletcher's grown children. Her new owner, "Miss Lucy," is remembered as "kind and tender-hearted" and as someone who

---

Originally published: Worcester, MA, 1889; Press of Geo. H. Ellis, 141 Franklin Street, Boston.

"said she hated slavery, and wanted nothing to do with it; but . . . could see no way out of it." When Miss Lucy decided to live with a sister, Veney and her own sister were reunited with their grandmother and uncle, who were the property of "Miss Nasenath." However, any personal rejoicing over this unexpected family reunion was mitigated by the arrival of Miss Nasenath's husband, David Kibbler, "a man of most violent temper, ready to fight anything or anybody who resisted his authority or in any way crossed his path."

In this excerpt, the hardships particular to married slave couples are recalled in heartbreaking detail as Veney and her husband, Jerry, attempt to avoid his sale to the Southern market, where he would be "worked to death in the rice-swamps and cotton-fields."

CHAPTER IV.
COURTSHIP AND MARRIAGE—A SLAVEHOLDER'S IDEA OF ITS REQUIREMENTS—SEPARATION.

Year after year rolled on. Master Jonas Mannyfield lived seven miles from us, on the other side of the Blue Ridge; and he owned a likely young fellow called Jerry. We had always known each other, and now he wanted to marry me. Our masters were both willing; and there was nothing to hinder, except that there was no minister about there to marry us. "No matter for that," Kibbler said to Jerry. "If you want Bett, and she wants you, that's the whole of it." But I didn't think so. I said, "No: never till somebody comes along who can marry us." So it happened, one day, there was a colored man—a peddler, with his cart—on the road, and Jerry brought him in, and said he was ready to be minister for us. He asked us a few questions, which we answered in a satisfactory manner, and then he declared us husband and wife. I did not want him to make us promise that we would always be true to each other, forsaking all others, as the white people do in their marriage service, because I knew that at any time our masters could compel us to break such a promise; and I had never forgotten the lesson learned, so many years before, in the blackberry pasture.

So Jerry and I were happy as, under all the circumstances, we could well be. When he asked his master's consent to our marriage, he told him he had had thoughts of removing to Missouri, in which case he should take him with him, and we would have to be separated; but, if he chose to run the risk, he had nothing to say. Jerry did not think there was any danger, and we were not dissuaded; for hearts that love are much the same in bond or free, in white or black.

Eight or ten months passed on, when one night my brother Stephen, who lived on the Blue Ridge, near Master Mannyfield, came to see me, and, as we talked of many things, he spoke of Jerry in a way that instantly roused my suspicion. I said: "Tell me what is the matter? I know there is something. Is Jerry dead? Is he sold? Tell me what it is." I saw he dreaded to speak, and that frightened me the more.

At last, he said: "'Tis no use, Betty. You have got to know it. Old Look-a-here's people are all in jail for debt." "Old Look-a-here" was the nickname by which Mannyfield was known by the colored people far and near, because he had a way of saying, when he was about to whip one of his slaves, "Now look-a-here, you black rascal," or "you black wench."

The next day was Saturday, and I hurried to complete my task in the corn-field, and then asked my master if I could go to see Jerry. He objected at first, but at last gave me a pass to see my brother, and be gone until Monday morning.

The sun might have been two hours high when I started; but, before I was half over the mountain, night had closed round me its deepest gloom. The vivid flashes of lightning made the carriage path plain at times, and then I could not see a step before me; and the rolling thunder added to my fear and dread. I was dripping wet when, about nine o'clock, I reached the house. It had been my plan to get Stephen to go on with me to Jerry's mother's, and stay the night there; but his mistress, who was sister to my Miss Lucy, declared we must not go on in the storm, and, giving me supper, brought bedding, that I might lie on the kitchen floor and rest me there. In the morning, after a good breakfast, she started us off, with a bag of biscuits to eat by the way. Jerry's mother was glad to go with us; and we hurried along to Jerry, in jail at Little Washington, where he with his fellow-slaves was confined, like sheep or oxen, shut up in stalls, to be sold to pay their owner's debts.

Jerry saw us, as we came along the road, through the prison bars; and the jailer allowed us to talk together there, not, however, without a witness to all we might say. We had committed no offence against God or man. Jerry had not; and yet, like base criminals, we were denied even the consolation of privacy. This was a necessary part of the system of American slavery. Neither wife nor mother could intervene to soften its rigors one jot.

Several months passed, and Mannyfield was still unable to redeem his property; and they were at last put up at auction, and sold to the highest bidder. Frank White, a slave-trader, bought the entire lot, and proceeded at once to make up a gang for the Southern market.

Arrangements were made to start Friday morning; and on Thursday afternoon, chained together, the gang were taken across the stream, and encamped on its banks. White then went to Jerry, and, taking the handcuffs from his wrists, told him to go and stay the night with his wife, and see if he could persuade her to go with him. If he could, he would buy her, and so they need not be separated. He would pass that way in the morning, and see. Of course, Jerry was only too glad to come; and, at first, I thought I would go with him. Then came the consciousness that this inducement was only a sham, and that, once exposed for sale in a Southern market, the bidder with the largest sum of money would be our purchaser singly quite as surely as together; and, if separated, what would I do in a strange land? No: I would not go. It was far better for me to stay where, for miles and miles, I knew every one, and every one knew me. Then came the wish to secrete ourselves together in the mountains, or elsewhere, till White should be gone; but, to do this, detection was sure. Then we remembered that White had trusted us, in letting him come to me, and we felt ashamed, for a moment, as if we had tried to cheat; but what *right* had White to carry him away, or even to own him at all? Our poor, ignorant reasoning found it hard to understand his rights or our own; and we at last decided that, as soon as it was light, Jerry should take to the mountains, and, when White was surely gone, either I would join him there, and we would make for the North together, or he would come back, go to White's mother, who lived a few miles distant, and tell her he would work for her and obey her, but he would never go South to be worked to death in the rice-swamps or cotton-fields.

We talked late into the night; and at last, in the silence and dread, worn out with sorrow and fear, my head on his shoulder, we both dropped asleep.

Daylight was upon us when we waked. The sad consciousness of our condition, and our utter helplessness, overpowered us. I opened the door, and there was my mistress, with pail in hand, going to the spring for water. "Oh, what shall I do? Where shall I go?" cried Jerry, as he saw her. "Have no fear," I said. "Go right along. I know mistress will never betray you." And, with a bound, he was over the fence, into the fields, and off to the mountains.

In a very short time, White and his poor, doomed company came along, and called for Jerry. I had taken my pail to milk the cows; and, seeing me, he sung out, "Woman, where is Jerry, I say?" "I don't know where Jerry is," I answered. Then, turning to Kibbler, who, hearing the outcry, now came out, he said, "You told me that woman wouldn't lie; and you know well enough she is lying now, when she says she don't know where that—rascal is." Kibbler answered very slowly and thoughtfully, "I never knowed her to lie; but may be this time,— may be this time." White then turned to me, and said, "I took off his handcuffs, and let him go to you, and you had no business to serve me so."

It was true I did not know where Jerry was at that time. We had agreed that we would meet that night near the blacksmith's old shop, on the other side of the run; and that was all I knew of his whereabouts, though he had not been gone long enough to be far away. It was true he had trusted us, and I felt very badly; but what else *could* we have done? Kind reader, *what* think you?

I then told him that Jerry had said he was willing to work, and would go to his mother's and serve her, but *never,* if he could help it, would he be carried South.

Then White tried to bargain with Kibbler for my purchase, saying he would give any price he should name for me, because he knew I would then find Jerry. But it was no use. Kibbler had a kind spot in his heart, and would not consent to let me go. So the slave-trader moved on with his human cattle.

Five miles on the road lived David McCoy, another slavetrader. When White reached his house, it was agreed by them that, if McCoy could find Jerry within two days, he should bring him on, and they would meet at Stanton, Va.

CHAPTER V.
MEETING—A LAST INTERVIEW—SEPARATION.

The place where I was to meet Jerry was, as I have said, across the run, in a corn-field, near the blacksmith's shop, the time Friday night.

It had rained hard all day, and the stream was swollen, and pouring and rushing at a fearful rate. I waited till everybody was in bed and asleep, when I lighted my pine knot, and started for the Pass. It was still raining, and the night was very dark. Only by my torch could I see a step before me; and, when I attempted to wade in, as I did in many different places, I found it was no use. I should surely be drowned if I persisted. So, disappointed and grieved, I gave up and went home. The next morning I was able to get over on horseback to milk the cows, but I neither heard nor saw anything of Jerry.

Saturday night came. I knew well that, if not caught by White, Jerry would be round. At last, every one was in bed, and all was still. I waited and listened. I listened and waited. Then I heard his step at the door. I hurriedly opened it, and he came in. His clothes were still damp and stiff from the rain of yesterday. He was frightened and uneasy. He had been hiding around in different places, constantly fearing detection. He had seen me from behind the old blacksmith's shop when I had tried the night before, with my pine knot, to ford the stream; and he was glad, he said, when he saw me go back, for he knew I should be carried down by the current and be drowned, if I had persisted. I went to my mistress's bedroom, and asked her if I might go to the cellar. She knew at once what I meant, and whispered softly, "Betty, has Jerry come?" then, without waiting for reply, added, "Get him some milk and light bread and butter." I was not long in doing so; and the poor fellow ate like one famishing. Then he wanted to know all that had happened, and what White had said when he found he was gone. We talked a long time, and tried to devise some plans for our mutual safety and possible escape from slavery altogether; but, every way we looked, the path was beset with danger and exposure. We were both utterly disheartened. But sleep came at last and, for the time being, relieved us of our fears.

In the morning, which was Sunday, we had our breakfast together, and, as the hours passed, began to feel a little comforted. After dinner, we walked out to the field and strolled about for some time; and, when ready to go back to the house, we each took an armful of fodder along for the horses. As we laid it down and turned to go into the house, David McCoy rode up on horseback. He saw Jerry at once, and called him to come to the fence. The excitement of the last days—the fasting and the fear—had completely cowed and broken whatever of manhood, or even of brute courage, a slave might by any possibility be presumed at any time to be possessed of, and the last remains of these qualities in poor Jerry were gone. He mutely obeyed; and when, with an oath, McCoy commanded him to mount the horse behind him, he mutely seated himself there. McCoy then called to me to go to the house and bring Jerry's clothes. "Never,"—I screamed back to him,— "never, not to save your miserable life." But Jerry said: "O Betty, 'tis no use. We can't help it." I knew this was so. I stifled my anger and my grief, brought his little bundle, into which I tucked a testament and catechism some one had given me, and shook hands "good-by" with him. So we *parted forever,* in this world.

SIX

From *Life and Adventures of Robert, the Hermit of Massachusetts, Who has lived 14 Years in a Cave, secluded from human society. Comprising, An account of his Birth, Parentage, Sufferings, and providential escape from unjust and cruel Bondage in early life— and his reasons for becoming a Recluse.*

Life and Adventures of Robert, the Hermit of Massachusetts *is the tragic account of Robert Voorhis, who had been in the process of buying his freedom from his master when the white acquaintance who had lent him the money tricked Voorhis by selling him to a slave trader. Voorhis was dragged away, without warning, from his wife and children and put aboard a schooner. The anguish that Voorhis suffered some twenty years later when, first as a fugitive and then as a freedman, he returned home to discover his family's fate so overwhelmed him that he retreated from the world and into a life of self-seclusion.*

Henry Trumball, a local resident who gained Voorhis's confidence as someone genuinely interested in his welfare, transcribed the hermit's

---

Originally published: Providence: Printed for H. Trumbull, 1829.

story. Up until the publication of Voorhis's narrative, in 1829, little was known about him, despite the fact that he was known to "every inhabitant of Rhode Island" as the "peaceable and agreeable" hermit who occupied a hill east of the Seekonk River, in neighboring Massachusetts. Some residents speculated that Voorhis had committed a serious crime, while others imagined that he was serving penance for an unjust act. Still, in spite of reportedly hundreds of attempts by curiosity-seekers to discern his origins, Voorhis remained silent on the topic until his encounter with Trumball.

———

FROM *LIFE AND ADVENTURES OF ROBERT THE HERMIT.*

I was born in Princeton (New Jersey) in the year 1769 or '70, and was born, as was my mother (who was of African descent,) in bondage; although my father, as has been represented to me, was not only a pure white blooded Englishman, but a gentleman of considerable eminence—I had no brothers and but one sister, who was three years older than myself; but of her, as of my mother, I have but a faint recollection, as I in my infancy was included in the patrimonial portion of my master's oldest daughter, on her marriage to a Mr. JOHN VOORHIS, by birth a German. When but four years of age I was conveyed by my master to Georgetown (District of Columbia,) to which place he removed with his family, and never have I since been enabled to learn the fate of my poor mother or sister, whom, it is not very improbable, death has long since removed from their unjust servitude.

At the age of 14 or 15, my master apprenticed me to a Shoemaker, to obtain if possible a knowledge of the art; but making but little proficiency, he again took me upon his plantation, where my time was mostly employed in gardening until about the age of nineteen. It was at that age, that I became first acquainted with an agreeable young female (an orphan) by the name of ALLEY PENNINGTON, a native of Cecil county, (Maryland)—she first expressed her attachment to me, and a willingness to become my partner for life, provided I could obtain my freedom, nor can I say that I felt less attachment for one with whom I was confident I could spend my life agreeably—she was indeed the object of my first love, a love which can only be extinguished with my existence; and never at any period previous was the yoke of bondage more goading, or did I feel so sensibly the want of that freedom, the deprivation of which was now the only barrier to my much wished for union with one I so sincerely and tenderly loved.

As my master had uniformly expressed an unwillingness to grant me my freedom, on any other terms than receiving a suitable compensation therefor, my only alternative now to obtain it, was to apply to one with whom I was most intimately acquainted, and to whom I thought I could safely communicate my desires, as he had in more than one instance, expressed much regard for me, and a willingness to serve me—to him I proposed that he should pay to my master the stipulated sum (Fifty Pounds.) demanded for my freedom, and that the bill of sale should remain in his hands, until such time as I should be enabled by the fruits of my industry to repay him, principal and interest, and allow him suitable compensation therefor for his trouble— to this proposal he readily assented, and not only expressed his willingness but his approbation of my much desired union with my beloved ALLEY. My request was immediately complied with, the Fifty Pounds were paid by my good friend (as I then supposed him,) to whom I was by bond transferred as his lawful property, and by whom I was given to understand that I might then seek business for myself, and turn my attention to any that I should conceive the most profitable, and consider myself under no other bondage than as a debtor, to the amount paid for my freedom. The name of one who had manifested so much what I supposed real and disinterested friendship for me, but who finally proved the author of almost all the wretchedness, which I have since endured, ought not to be concealed—it was JAMES BEVINS.

Feeling myself now almost a free man, I did not, as may be supposed suffer many hours to elapse before I hastened to bear the joyful tidings of my good fortune, to one, who, as I had anticipated, received it with unfeigned demonstrations of joy; and who, so far from exhibiting an unwillingness to fulfill her promise, yielded her hand without reluctance or distrust—we were married, lawfully married, and more than three years of domestic felicity passed away, without a misfortune to ruffle our repose—in the course of which the Almighty had not only been pleased to bless us with two children, but myself with so great a share of good health, as to have enabled me by my industry, to earn and refund a very considerable portion of the fifty pounds paid by Bevins for my freedom—of these sums I had neither made any charge, or took any receipts—in this I was brought to see my error, but, alas! Too late.

Bevins, as I have stated, was a man in whom I had placed implicit confidence, and indeed until the period mentioned, supposed him, as regarded myself, incapable of any thing dishonorable, much less of being the author of as great an act of cruelty and injustice, as ever was recorded in the catalogue of human depravity!

It was late one evening, an evening never to be forgotten by me, while sitting in the midst of my innocent and beloved family, amused with the prattle of my eldest child, and enjoying all the felicity which conjugal love and parental affections are productive of, that this monster in human shape (Bevins) accompanied by another, entered, seized and pinioned me! And gave me to understand that I was intended for a Southern market!! It is impossible for me to describe my feelings or those of my poor distracted wife, at that moment! It was in vain that I entreated, in vain that I represented to Bevins that he had already received a very great proportion of the sum paid for my freedom—to which the ruffian made no other reply, than pronouncing me a liar, dragged me like a felon from my peaceable domicile—from my beloved family—whose shrieks would have pierced the heart of any one but a wretch like himself!

In the most secret manner, at eleven at night, I was hurried on board a Schooner, where additional miseries awaited me!—for fear of an escape, I found irons were to be substituted for the ropes with which they had bound me! And while a person was employed in riveting them, I improved the opportunity, which I though probably would be the last, to address the author of my miseries, in words nearly as follows:—"Are these the proofs, master Bevins, of the friendship which you have professed for me! Tell me I pray you, what have I done to merit such barbarous treatment from your hands? Nothing, no nothing! I have nothing wherewith to reproach myself but my own credulity!"—to this he made no reply; shackled and handcuffed, I was precipitated into the hold of the schooner, by the motion of which I perceived was soon under way, and bearing me I knew not whither! So far from feeling any inclination to sleep, it was to me a night of inconceivable wretchedness! I could hear nothing but the shrieks of my poor disconsolate wife, and the moans of her helpless children! Indeed such was my imagination—alas! He alone can have a just conception of my feelings who may have been placed in similar situation, if such a person can be found on earth.

In three days (during which no other food was allowed me but a few pounds of mouldy bread) the Schooner reached the port of her destination—Charleston, S.C.—and from which, without being relieved of my irons, I was conveyed to and lodged in prison, where I was suffered to remain in solitude five days—from thence I was conducted to a place expressly appropriated to the sale of human beings! Where, like the meanest animal of the brute creation, I was disposed of at public auction to the highest bidder.

Resolved on my liberty, and that I would not let pass unimproved the first opportunity that should present, to regain it, I did not remain with my purchaser long enough to learn his name or the price paid for me; who, to win my affections, and the better to reconcile me to my situation, professed much regard for me and made many fair promises (not one of which it is probable he ever intended to perform,) and the better to deceive me, voluntarily granted me the indulgence to walk a few hours unguarded and unattended about the city, without a well authenticated pass—of this I was not ignorant, and therefore sought other and less dangerous means to escape, for I felt that death in its worst forms would be far preferable to slavery.

I carelessly strolled about the wharves among the shipping, where

I at length was so fortunate as to find a Sloop bound direct to Philadelphia—she had completed her lading, her sails were loosed and
every preparation made to haul immediately into the stream—watching a favourable opportunity, while the hands were employed forward,
I unperceived ascended and secreted myself between two casks in the
hold—all beneath was soon well secured by the hatches, and I had the
satisfaction to find myself in less than three hours, from the time that
I was purchased like a bale of goods at auction, stowing snugly away,
and with fair prospects of regaining my liberty! It was at that moment
that a secret joy diffused itself through my soul—I found unexpected
consolation and fortitude, produced by a firm persuasion that by the
assistance of a divine providence I should accomplish my deliverance.

Early in the morning of the fourth day from that of our departure,
we were safely moored along side of one of the Philadelphia wharves.
During the passage of three days and one night, my only nourishment
had been about one fill of spirits, contained in a small viol, with which
I occasionally moistened my lips, for on the third day my thirst had
become intolerable.

I was as fortunate in leaving the sloop unsuspected or discovered,
as I had been in secreting myself aboard her, and as soon as safely on
shore; my first object was to procure lodgings and something to satisfy
the cravings of nature, at a boarding house for seamen. Representing
myself as belonging to a coaster, I was not suspected as any other than
a free man. As I had heard much of the hospitality of the Quakers (or
Friends,) and as a class who were zealous advocated for the emancipation of their fellow beings in bondage, to one of them, on the very day
of my arrival, I made my situation known, concealing nothing; and
begged that he would interest himself so far in my behalf as to advise
me what I had best do, to secure my person from further by unjust
claimants, and to restore to me my bereaved and afflicted family.

The good man listened with much apparent attention to my story,
and seemed somewhat affected thereby, and so far from exhibiting any
disposition to discredit any part of it, presented me with half a crown,
and requested me to call on him in the forenoon of the next day, by

which time (as he said) he would have an opportunity to consult some of his brethren, by whom he thought steps would be taken to redress my wrongs—nor have I any reason to believe that he promised more than he intended to perform, and I believe that by these good people I should have been effectually freed from the shackles of slavery, had not another melancholy instance of adverse fortune, placed me in a situation not to comply with his request. Returning to my lodgings in the evening, I was accused (jocosely, as I at first supposed) by the inmates of the house, of being a run-away slave! Still however persisting in my former story, that I was free and belonged to a coaster, but being unable to reply satisfactorily to their enquiries, as to the name and place of destination of the vessel, I was committed to prison and advertized as a suspected runaway.

By what means my pretended master obtained information of my situation, I could never learn, for after nine days close confinement in prison (during which I was not permitted to communicate with any one but the gaoler) I was once more strongly ironed and delivered over to the charge of the captain of a Charleston packet—to which port as it proved she was bound direct. It will not be necessary to inform you that my treatment was no better than what I had received on my late passage from Maryland—nor do I know that I could have reasonably expected any better, from those who probably considered coloured people as free from feelings as understandings. As soon as we reached Charleston, I was conducted to and delivered over to my reputed master, who had however in my absence, as it appeared, become somewhat sick of his purchase, for the Next day I was with two or three others similarly situated, exposed to sale at public auction.

The person by whom I was next purchased, was a Dr. PETER FERSUE, a man of considerable wealth, and who, had it not been obtained by the toils of his fellow creatures in bondage, might have passed for one not entirely devoid of humanity, for I must say, in justice to him, that it was remarked that those who were held in bondage by him, were treated with less severity than those possessed by some of his neighbors. Perceiving that I was not a little dissatisfied with my situation, and that I possessed a partial knowledge of letters (which I had acquired previous to my marriage) through fear probably that I might instill into the minds of some of my fellow slaves, principles, which might ultimately prove to his disadvantage, I was selected as a house servant, and consequently exempted from many of the privations to which the other slaves were exposed—yet, I became no more reconciled to my situation, nor felt any degree of attachment for him, as I could never harbour a belief but that human beings, whatever might be their complexion were all created equally free; and that it was in direct contradiction to the will of the Supreme Being, that one portion of his creatures should be held in bondage by another, for no other fault than a difference of complexion!—and, I must confess, that my bosom could not but swell with indignation, when placed in a situation to witness the severity with which many of my fellow companions in bondage, at the South, were treated—worn out by constant fatigue, clad in rags, branded with lashes, and otherways treated more like brutes than human beings!

Freedom, the gift of Heaven, was too highly prized by me to permit any thing of less importance to occupy my mind—but, great as were my desires to enjoy it, with him by whom I was wrongfully claimed, I spent eighteen months in servitude, before an opportunity presented to obtain it. The means by which I was finally enabled to effect my escape, were very similar to those which I had practiced in my last attempt—I succeeded in secreting myself in the hold of a brig ready laden, and bound direct to Boston (Massachusetts,) and without an opportunity to provide myself with a drop of water, or a morsel of food of any kind on which to subsist during the passage.

Although the place of my concealment afforded nothing better on which to repose than a water cask, yet I found my berth not so uncomfortable as one would naturally imagine, and I was enabled to endure the calls of hunger and thirst, until the close of the fifth day from that of our departure, when the latter became too oppressive to be longer endured—had I then possessed the wealth of the Indias, it appeared to me, that I should have made a willing exchange for a draught of sweet water; not however until nearly deprived of my senses, did I feel willing to make my situation known to those on board—on the reflection, that should it even cost me my life, that an instantaneous death would be preferable to a lingering one, I seized a fragment of a hoop, with which I crawled to and commenced thumping upon a beam near the hatchway, at the same time hallooing as loud as the strength my lungs would admit of—soon I was heard by the hands on deck, and while some broke out in exclamations of wonder and surprise, others ran affrighted to the cabin, to proclaim to the captain the fact that "the brig was most certainly haunted, and had become the habitation of bodiless spirits, as one or more were at that moment crying out lamentably in the hold!"—bodiless spirits they no doubt concluded they must be, for the hatches being so well secured with a tarpolin, none other, as they supposed, could have obtained access.

The captain less superstitiously inclined, ordered the hatches to be immediately raised, but so great a terror of the sailors, that it was sometime before any could be found of sufficient courage to obey.

The hatches were no sooner removed than I presented myself to their view, trembling through fear, pale as death, and with hardly strength sufficient to support myself!—my appearance was indeed such as almost to confirm the superstitious opinion of the sailors, that the brig must certainly be haunted, for in me they beheld, as they supposed, naught but an apparition! The ghost, probably of some unfortunate shipmate, who on a former voyage for some trifling offence, had been privately and wickedly precipitated from the brig's deck into the ocean!—such indeed is the weakness and superstition peculiar to many of that class of people, who follow the seas for a livelihood.

Those on board became however a little less intimidated, when I assured them that I intended them no harm, and was no other than one of the most unfortunate and miserable of human beings, who had sought that means to escape from unjust and cruel bondage! And then briefly related to them, at what time and in what manner I succeeded in secreting myself unnoticed in the brig's hold; where it was my intention to have remained, if possible, until her arrival at the port of her destination—and concluded with begging them for mercy's sake, to grant me a bucket of fresh water for, indeed, such was my thirst, that a less quantity it appeared to me would have proved insufficient to have allayed it.

The captain (who very fortunately for me, proved to be a Quaker, and with all the tender feeling peculiar to that excellent class of people) gave orders to his men to treat me with kindness, and to assist me on deck, for I had now become so weak and emaciated by long fasting, that I was scarcely able to help myself. "Thy wants shall be supplied (said the good captain, addressing himself to me) but such is thy present weakness, that thee must eat and drink sparingly, or it may be worse for thee!"—this man was truly in practice, as well as by profession, a Christian—for had he been my father, he could not have treated me with more tenderness and compassion—he would not allow me but a single gill of water at a draught, and that quantity but twice in an hour, although five times that quantity would not have satisfied me— and the food allowed me was apportioned accordingly.

In two days after we reached Boston, where I was landed, with permission of the captain to proceed whither I pleased; not however until he had imparted to me some friendly advice, to be cautious with whom I associated on shore, and as I valued my liberty, not to frequent such parts of the town as was inhabited by the most vicious and abandoned of the human race—with which he presented me with some change, and bid me farewell, and never to my knowledge have I since had the happiness to meet with this good man; who, long 'ere this has probably been numbered with the just, and if so, is now I trust reaping the reward of his good deeds in another and better world.

Unacquainted then with the laws of New-England, and fearful that it might not be safe to tarry a long while in a place so populous as Boston, before sunset of the same day I crossed the bridge leading to Charlestown, with an intention of proceeding as far east as Portland— I tarried that night at Lynn, and at about 10 o'clock the next morning reached Salem, where I concluded to remain until the morning ensuing. I applied to a boarding house for seamen for some refreshment, and bespoke lodgings for the night, and in the course of the day met with a gentleman who was in quest of hands for a voyage to India. As my small funds were now nearly exhausted, I thought this not only a favourable opportunity to replenish them, but to place myself beyond the reach of my pretended masters of the south, should they extend their pursuit of me as far east as Massachusetts—to him I therefore offered myself for the voyage, and was accepted.

It cannot be expected that I can recollect, or is it necessary for me to state every minute circumstance that attended me on this voyage, and I will only remark, that although a fresh hand, and totally unacquainted with seamanship, I succeeded in the performance of my duty beyond my expectations, and I believe not only to the satisfaction of my officers, but gained the esteem and good will of my shipmates on board—in proof of this, there is one circumstances that I ought not fail to mention—when about to cross the line, where sailors generally calculate to receive a formal visit from Neptune, the aged Monarch of the deep made his appearance as usual, and with little ceremony introduced himself on board, and while others (who had never before been honored with an interview with his majesty) were compelled to yield to the unpleasant severities of a custom prescribed by him, I was, by the intercession of my shipmates, so fortunate as to escape.

After an absence of about fourteen months, the ship returned in safety to Salem, and with the loss I believe of but one man—when discharge, my wages were punctually paid me, which amounted to a sum not only much greater than what I had ever before been in possession of, but a sum much more considerable than what I once ever expected to possess!—there was indeed as I then thought, but one thing wanting to complete my happiness (to wit.) the presence of my poor unfortunate family!—with this money, thought I, how comfortable could I render the situation of my beloved ALLEY, and my not less beloved children! Who, while I at this moment have enough and to spare, is not improbable, if living, are enduring all the miseries that poverty and oppression are productive of!—reflections like these were sufficient to depress my spirits, and to deprive me of that enjoyment, which sailors so abundantly participate in on their return from a long voyage to their favorite port.

I remained on shore but a short time when I shipped for a second voyage to India—and, would here briefly state, without entering into particulars, that from this period of nine years, I continued to sail as a common hand from the ports of Boston and Salem, to different ports in Europe and India—in which time I never once suffered shipwreck, or met with any very serious disaster!—it is not improbable that there are at the present day, some of my old Commanders and Shipmates still living in or about Boston and Salem, who may have some recollection of "ROBERT."

After my return from my first voyage, I became acquainted with and commenced board in the family of a respectable widow woman, who afforded decent fare, although in a very moderate circumstances—the family was composed of the old lady and three daughters, of the ages of eighteen, twenty-one and twenty-five—it was their house that I continued to "hail" as my home, whenever I returned to port, and so long as I remained on shore; and, almost destitute as I was at this time of other friends, it is not, as I deem it, very extraordinary that I should feel more than a common degree of regard and attachment for the family, and that that attachment should finally lead to greater intimacy—this was indeed the case, and on my return from my second voyage, I entered into the bands of matrimony with one of the daughters—the marriage ceremonies were performed by a Justice Putnam, of Danvers. Here, in justification of myself, for having consented to become the husband of another, when there was a possibility of my first wife being alive, I must state that there were two great inducements—one, that I was strongly urged so to do by those who undoubtedly had the authority to use compulsory means had I declined—and the other, that I had now given up all hopes and expectations of ever meeting again in this world, her, who was the first object of my pledged love.

The day after my marriage I rented a small tenement, which I gave my mother and her daughters liberty to occupy with my wife in my absence, for in three days after I was once more on my favorite element, bound to India—previous to my departure however, I made ample provision for the support of my family, and left a request with the gentleman in whose employ I sailed, to allow them a portion of my wages, in my absence, which was strictly complied with. The voyage proved as usual prosperous, and on my return was received by my friends, not only with the most lively demonstrations of joy, but with the tidings that I had in my absence, for the third time, become a father.

I remained on shore about three months, and such was the harmony that prevailed between us, and such the kind treatment that I received from my companion, that it would have been cruel to have doubted her love and affection for me. At the expiration of the three months, I once more with considerable reluctance bid her adieu, and shipped on board the Herald, Capt. DERBY, bound from Boston to Canton;—on this voyage I was absent but about eighteen months, from the time that we left Boston, which was out port of entry on our return.

As soon as discharged I hastened to Salem with the fruits of my toil, and with fond expectations of being welcomed once more to my peaceful home, by one who had so repeatedly expressed her love and regard for me—but, alas, sadly was I disappointed!—for true it is, that she who I had supposed almost an angel in disposition, had in my absence been transformed to a demon! Cold indeed was the reception that I met with—so far from expressing or manifesting the least degree of joy or satisfaction on the occasion (although I had been between one and two years absent) I was insultingly told by her that "if I had never returned she would have been the last to lament it!"

The cause of this surprising and unexpected alteration in one, whom, from the moment she became my wife, I had treated with so much regard and affection, I was never able to learn—although I did not and could not feel that ardent affection for her, as for one who was the object of my first love, yet my affection for my child was as great as that for my first born—for this I felt willing to make almost any sacrifice, could a reconciliation have been thereby effected; but it could not, and a final separation was the consequence. I continued in Salem eight or ten months longer, supporting myself with the fruits of what

I obtained by labour on board vessels, on the wharves, &c. and then, with light feet but a heavy heart, started in quest of new friends and a new home, bending my course southerly.

I made no longer tarry on the road than to obtain refreshments, until I reached Providence (Rhode Island) where I made application for, and obtained employment for a few days; at the conclusion of which, I obtained a berth on board of one of the Packets plying between Providence and New-York, in which business I continued (with the exception of a part of the time that I was occasionally employed on shore,) eight or nine years—some few of the packet masters with whom I have sailed, some for whom I occasionally wrought on shore, are still living.

Feeling a strong inclination once more to visit the shores of the south, where I had not only been unjustly deprived of my liberty, but where I was inhumanly forced from my beloved wife and two darling children, I took passage (about fifteen years since) on board a sloop for Baltimore, and from thence proceeded direct to Georgetown. As twenty years had elapsed since I there left all that I held most dear in life—and so great a change had time effected in my personal appearance, I felt little or no apprehension that I should be recognized or molested by any, if living, who once professed a claim to me. In this I was not mistaken, for indeed as regarded the town, inhabitants, &c. so great a change had the twenty years produced, that I walked the streets at mid-day unnoticed and unknown. My old master (Voorhis and his wife had been some years dead, and the survivors of the family had removed to parts unknown) Bevins, the wretch by whom I was unjustly deprived of my liberty, and thereby forever separated from my unfortunate family, had a few years previous emigrated to the west—but, the principle object of my visit was not answered—of my wife and children I could obtain no satisfactory information—all that I could learn, was, that soon after my disappearance, their sufferings and deprivations became so great, that my poor wife in a fit of desperation, as was supposed, put an end to her existence, and that her helpless children did not long survive her!—this was enough! yea more than enough, to fill to the brim the bitter cup of my afflictions!—afflictions which had more less attended me through life!—I then felt but little desire to live, as there was nothing then remaining to attach me to this world—it was at that moment that I formed the determination to retire from it—to become a recluse, and mingle thereafter as little as possible with human society.

With this determination I returned direct to Rhode Island, and soon after selected a retired spot well suited to my purpose, being an extreme point of uninhabited land (Fox Point) situated about one mile south of Providence bridge—there I built me a hut and dwelt peaceably therein for several years, and until annoyed and discommoded by the youth of the town, and by labourers employed in levelling the hill in the neighborhood of my dwelling—I then applied to and obtained the consent of the gentleman (Hon. TRISTAM BRUGISS) to whom the land belongs, to build this hut, and permission to improve the spot of ground enclosed during my life—here in solitude I have dwelt more than six years—once or twice a week (and sometimes oftener) I leave my recess, cross over the bridge into Providence, converse a little with those with whom I have become acquainted, obtain a few necessaries, and return again well satisfied to my peaceable dwelling.

PART THREE

Running Inspired by Religion

An engraving of a slave in chains praying. Copyright © Bettmann/Corbis.

SEVEN

From *A Narrative of Some Remarkable Incidents in the Life of Solomon Bayley, Formerly a Slave in the State of Delaware, North America; Written by Himself, and Published for His Benefit; to Which Are Prefixed, a Few Remarks by Robert Hurnard.*

The narrative of Solomon Bayley is significant in documenting how Christian faith was, for some slaves, a foundational touchstone in their lives—driving them forward, sustaining them with hope in the face of the most barbaric circumstances. But, just as importantly, this narrative also challenges popular assumptions that running away necessarily culminated in freedom and underscores relative definitions of the fugitive slave experience

Although the exact date of Solomon Bayley's birth is unknown, it's estimated to have been sometime around 1771. He was born and raised in Delaware but was taken from his wife and family by his master to Virginia. He managed to escape and return to his family in Delaware, living in seclusion there until 1799, when he was recaptured. In time,

---

Originally published: London: Harvey and Darton, 1825.

Bayley was able to purchase his freedom, as well as that of his wife and children.

As this excerpt demonstrates, the author's narrative is steeped in religious fervor. A Methodist, Bayley makes clear, repeatedly, that no less than the hand of God is guiding him. "It is a solemn truth, he is nigh to all them that call on him, with a view to his greatness and their own nothingness. . . . I now believed if every body in the world was engaged against me, that he was able to deliver me out of their hands."

NARRATIVE, &C.

SOLOMON BAYLEY, unto all people, and nations, and languages, grace be unto you, and peace from God our Father, and from the Lord Jesus Christ.

Having lived some months in continual expectation of death, I have felt uneasy in mind about leaving the world, without leaving behind me some account of the kindness and mercy of God towards me. But when I go to tell of his favours, I am struck with wonder at the exceeding riches of his grace. O! that all people would come to admire him for his goodness, and declare his wonders which he doth for the children of men. The Lord tried to leach me his fear when I was a little boy; but I delighted in vanity and foolishness, and went astray. But the Lord found out a way to overcome me, and to cause me to desire his favour, and his great help; and although I thought no one could be more unworthy of his favour, yet he did look on me, and pitied me in my great distress.

I was born a slave in the state of Delaware, and was one of those slaves that were carried out of Delaware into the state of Virginia; and the laws of Delaware did say, that slaves carried out of that state should be free; whereupon I moved to recover my freedom. I employed lawyers, and went to court two days, to have a suit brought to obtain my freedom. After court I went home to stay until the next court, which was about six weeks off. But two days before the court was to sit, I was taken up and put on board of a vessel out of Hunting Creek, bound to Richmond, on the western shore of Virginia, and there put into Richmond jail, and irons were put on me; and I was brought very low. In my distress I was often visited with some symptoms of distraction. At length I was taken out of jail, and put into one of the back country waggons, to go toward the going down of the sun. Now consider, how great my distress must have been, being carried from my wife and children, and from my natural place, and from my chance for freedom.

On the third day my distress was bitter, and I cried out in my heart, "I am past all hope:" and the moment I said I was past all hope, it pleased the father of all mercy to look on me, and he sent a strengthening thought into my heart, which was this: that he that made the heavens and the earth, was able to deliver me. I looked up to the sky, and then to the trees and ground, and I believed in a moment, that if he could make all these, he was able to deliver me. Then did that scripture come into my mind, which I had heard before, and that was, "they that trust in the Lord, shall never be confounded." I believed that was a true word, and I wanted to try that word, and got out of the waggon; but I thought I was not fit to lay hold of the promise: yet another thought came into my mind, and that was, that I did not know to what bounds his mercy would extend. I then made haste and got out of the waggon, and went into the bushes; I squatted down to see what would follow. Now there were three waggons in company, and four white people; they soon missed me, and took out one of the horses and rode back, and were gone about three-quarters of an hour, and then returned, and put the horse in the waggon again, and went on their way; and that was the last I ever saw or heard of them. I sat still where I was till night, and then walked out into the road and looked up to the sky, and I felt very desolate. Oh! the bitterness of distress which I then felt, for having sinned against God; whom if I had been careful to obey in all things, he would have spared me all my troubles. Oh! it is a dangerous thing to cast off fear, and to restrain prayer before God. If we do that which we believe will please him, with a desire to obtain his favour, it is a real prayer; but if we do, or say, that which we believe will displease him, that is to cast off fear, and to restrain prayer before him.

When night came and I walked out of the bushes, I felt very awful. I set off to walk homewards, but soon was chased by dogs, at the same house where the man told the waggoner he had taken up a runaway three days before. But it pleased the highest, to send out a dreadful wind, with thunder and lightning, and rain; which was the means by which I escaped, as I then thought, as I travelled along that night. Next day I was taken with the dysentery, which came on so bad, I thought I must die; but I obtained great favour, and kept on my feet, and so I got down to Richmond; but had liked to have been twice taken, for twice I was pursued by dogs.

But after I got to Richmond, a coloured man pretended to be my friend, and then sent white people to take me up; but a little while before they came, it came expressly into my mind, that he would prove treacherous and betray me. I obeyed the impression immediately, and left the place I was in, and presently there came with clubs to take me, as it did appear, two white men and a coloured man. When I saw them I was in an hollow place on the ground, not far from where the coloured man left me: at sight of them I was struck with horror and fear, and the fear that came into my soul, took such an impression on my animal frame, that I felt very weak: I cried to the Maker of heaven and earth to save me, and he did so. I lay there and prayed to the Lord, and broke persimmon tree bushes, and covered myself: when night came on, I felt as if the great God had heard my cry. Oh! how marvellous is his loving kindness toward men of every description and complexion. Though he is high, yet hath he respect unto the lowly, and will hear the cry of the distressed when they call upon him, and will make known his goodness and his power.

I lay there till night, and then with great fear I went into the town of Richmond, and enquired the way over the river to go to Petersburgh, where I staid near three weeks, in which time, severe and painful were my exercises: I appeared to be shut up in such a straight case, I could not see which way to take. I tried to pray to the Lord for several days together, that he would be pleased to open some way for me to get along. And I do remember, that when I was brought to the very lowest, suddenly a way appeared, and I believe it was in the ordering of a good providence.

It was so; there came a poor distressed coloured man to the same house where I had taken refuge: we both agreed to take a craft, and go down James' River, which was attended with great difficulty, for we met with strict examination twice, and narrowly escaped; we had like to have been drowned twice, once in the river, and once in the bay. But how unable were we to offer unto God that tribute of praise due to his name, for the miracle of grace shewn to us in our deliverance! Surely wisdom and might are his, and all them that walk in pride he is able to abase. Oh!

> *"Let all the world fall down and know*
> *That none but God such power can shew."*

We got safe over to the eastern shore of the Chesapeake Bay, where his wife and mine were. And now, reader, I do not tell thee how glad I was, but will leave thee to judge, by supposing it had been thy own case. We landed near Nandew, and then started for Hunting Creek, and we found both our wives; but we found little or no satisfaction, for we were hunted like partridges on the mountains.

My companion got to work on board of a vessel to get clams, perhaps to get some money to bring suit for his freedom (as he had been sold like me, out of the state of Delaware), if his master should come after him from the back countries, who he said, lived about three hundred and thirty miles from the eastern shore; but poor fellow, they went on board of the vessel where he had been at work, and talked of taking him up and putting him in jail, and of writing to his master in the back countries. He was said to tell them, that he had rather die than to be taken and carried away from his wife again: and it was said, they went down into the cabin and drank, and then came up on deck and seized him, and in the scuffle he slipped out of their hands, and jumped over-board, and tried to swim to an island that was not far off; but they got out the tow boat and went after him, and when they overtook him, he would dive to escape, and still he tried to reach the island: but they watched their opportunity as he rose, when they struck him with the loom of the oar, and knocked his brains out, and he died. And now, reader, consider if you had been carried away from your wife and children, and had got back again, how hard it would seem to be, to be thus chased out of the world; but the great God, whose eyes behold the things that are equal, he continues to make such repent, either in this world, or in the world to come, And now, readers, you have heard of the end of my fellow-sufferer, but I remain as yet, a monument of mercy, thrown up and down on life's tempestuous sea; sometimes feeling an earnest desire to go away and be at rest; but I travel on, in hopes of overcoming at my last combat.

But I will go on to tell of my difficulties. After I came over the bay, I went to see my wife, but was still in trouble; and it was thought best to leave the state of Virginia and go to Dover, and then if my master came after me, to bring suit at Dover, and have a trial for my freedom. The distance from where I then was to Dover, was about one hundred and twenty miles: so I started and travelled at nights, and lay by in the day time. I went on northwards, with great fear and anxiety of mind. It abode on my mind that I should meet with some difficulty before I got to Dover: however I tried to study on the promises of the Almighty, and so travelled on until I came to a place called Anderson's Cross-Roads; and there I met with the greatest trial I ever met with in all my distress. But the greater the trial, the greater the benefit, if the mind be but staid on that everlasting arm of power, whom the winds and the waves obey. It was so, that I called at them cross-roads, to enquire the way to Camden, and I thought I would go to the kitchen where the black people were; but when the door was opened, it was a white man I saw, of a portly appearance, with a sulky down look. Now the day was just a breaking: he raised up out of his bed, and came towards the door and began to examine me, and I did not know what to say to him; so he soon entangled me in my own talk, and said,

I doubt you are a lying: I said I scorn to lie; but I felt very weak and scared, and soon bid him farewell and started. I went some distance along the road, and then went into the woods, and leaned my back against a tree to study, and soon fell to sleep; and when I waked, the sun was up, and I said to myself, if I stand sleeping about here, and that man that examined me in the morning comes to look for me and finds me, he may tie me before I get awake; for the poor fellow that came across the bay with me told me, that he travelled all night, and in the morning he met a coloured man, and passed on, and went into the woods and lay down, and went to sleep; and he said there came white men and tied him, and waked him up to go before the justice; but so it was, he got away from them and found me at Petersburgh. So considering on what he had told me, and that man's examining me in the morning, made me I did not know what to do. I concluded to look for a thick place and lay down, and then another thought came into my mind, and that was, to look for a thin place, and there lie down. So I concluded to do so; withal I thought to take a sally downwards, as I enquired of the man to go upwards, I thought by going a little downwards, would be a dodge, and so I should miss him: I thought this plan would do. I then looked for a thin place, and lay down and slept till about nine o'clock, and then waked; and when I awoke, I felt very strange: I said to myself I never felt so in all my distress: I said something was going to happen to me today.

So I studied about my feelings until I fell to sleep, and when I awoke, there had come two birds near to me; and seeing the little strange looking birds, it roused up all my senses; and a thought came quick into my mind that these birds were sent to caution me to be away out of this naked place; that there was danger at hand. And as I was about to start, it came into my mind with great energy and force, "If you move out of this circle this day, you will be taken;" for I saw the birds went all round me: I asked myself what this meant, and the impression grew stronger, that I must stay in the circle which the birds made. At the same time a sight of my faults came before me, and a scanty sight of the highness and holiness of the great Creator of all things. And now, reader, I will assure thee I was brought very low, and I earnestly asked what I should do: and while I waited to be instructed, my mind was guided back to the back countries, where I left the waggons about sixty or seventy miles from Richmond, towards the sun-setting; and a question arose in my mind, how I got along all that way, and to see if I could believe that the great God had helped me notwithstanding my vileness. I said in my heart, it must be the Lord, or I could not have got along, and the moment I believed in his help, it was confirmed in my mind, if he had begun to help me, and if he did send those birds, he would not let anything come into the circle the birds had made; I therefore tried to confirm myself in the promises of God, and concluded to stay in the circle; and so being weary, travelling all night, I soon fell to sleep; and when I awaked, it was by the noise of the same man that examined me in the morning, and another man, an old conjuror, for so I called him. And the way they waked me was by their walking in the leaves, and coming right towards me. I was then sitting on something about nine inches high from the ground, and when I opened my eyes and saw them right before me, and I in that naked place, and the sun a shining down on me about eleven o'clock, I was struck with dread, but was afraid to move hand or foot: I sat there, and looked right at them; and thought I, here they come right towards me; and the first thought that struck my mind was, am I a going to sit here until they come and lay hands on me? I knew not what to do; but so it was, there stood a large tree about eleven or twelve yards from me, and another big tree had fallen with the top limbs round it: and so it was, through divine goodness, they went the other side of the tree, and the tree that had fallen, was between them and me. Then I fell down flat upon my face, on the ground; as I raised up my head to look, I saw the actions of this old craftsman; he had a stick like a surveyor's rod; he went along following his stick very diligently. The young man that examined me in the morning, had a large club, with the big end downwards, and the small end in his hand; he looked first one side, and then on the other: the old man kept on away past me about sixty yards, and then stopped; and I heard him say, "he h'ant gone this way."

Then he took his stick and threw it over his shoulder, and pointed this way and that way, until he got it right towards me; and then I heard him say, "come let us go this way." Then he turned his course and came right towards me: then I trembled, and cried in my heart to the Lord, and said, what shall I do? What shall I do? And it was impressed on my mind immediately, "Stand still and see the salvation of the Lord;" the word that was spoken to the children of Israel when at the Red Sea. And I said in my heart, bless the Lord, O my soul; I will try the Lord this time. Here they come; and still that word sounded in my heart; "Stand still and see the salvation of the Lord." They came not quite so near me as the circle the birds had made, when the old man sheered off, and went by me; but the young man stopped and looked right down on me, as I thought, and I looked right up into his eyes; and then he stood and looked right into my eyes, and when he turned away, he ran after the old man, and I thought he saw me; but when he overtook the old man, he kept on, and then I knew he had not seen me. Then I said, bless the Lord, he that gave sight to man's eyes, hath kept him from seeing me this day: I looked up among the trees and said, how dreadful is this place. I said, two great powers have met here this day; the power of darkness, and the power of God; and the power of God has overthrown the power of darkness for me a sinner. I thought I must jump and shout, but another thought struck my mind, that it was not a right time to shout; I therefore refrained. But my heart was overwhelmed at the sight of the goodness and power of God, and his gracious readiness to help the stranger in distress: though he is high, yet hath he respect unto the lowly. It is a solemn truth, he is nigh to all them that call on him, with a view to his greatness and their own nothingness: I felt greatly at loss to know how to adore him according to his excellent greatness. I said, has the maker of heaven and earth took my part? I said again, what could all the world do in comparison with him? I now believed if every body in the world was engaged against me, that he was able to deliver me out of their hands.

After a while I moved out of that place, and went away to a small stream of water, and staid there a little while, and then went out of that neighbourhood. But whether I did right or not, I know not; for in moving out of that circle so quickly, I became so bewildered as to be quite lost, and did not know what course to take, or what to do; and I thought it was because my faith failed me so quickly. Oh! what pains God doth take to help his otherwise helpless creatures. O that his kindness and care were more considered and laid to heart, and then there would not be that cause to complain that "the ox knoweth his owner, and the ass his master's crib, but Israel doth not know, my people doth not consider." Oh! how marvellous is his loving-kindness toward people of every description, both high and low, rich and poor. O that all people would study to please him, for his goodness and his power; for his wisdom is great, and he knoweth how to deliver all those that look unto him, and will pass by none, no not the least of all his human creatures; and he will make them see that they are of more value than many sparrows; and that they are not their own, but that they are bought with a price.

Now unto the king immortal, invisible, the only wise God, be glory and honour, dominion and power, now and for ever. Amen.

After this, my understanding was opened to see for what purpose this last trial had happened unto me; and it was impressed on my mind that I had come through difficulties and troubles, in order that my faith and confidence might be tried; and that I might be made strong in the faith to believe that so high and holy an one, who had thus marvellously preserved me, would hereafter help so poor an object as me, out of his great mercy and condescension, and that I might be afraid again to sin against his majesty, who had suffered me to be thus sorely tried, that I might see the greatness of my past transgressions, and his boundless loving-kindness and mercy.

EIGHT

From *The Confessions of Nat Turner, the Leader of the Late Insurrection in Southampton, Va.*

*N*at Turner's confession provides a chilling example of Christian inspiration that sets it apart from any slave narrative recorded. The leader of the largest and most significant slave revolt in American history, Turner was brought up by his mother, a slave who had been kidnapped from Africa, to believe that great things were expected from him. As a child he learned to read, and from the teachings of the Bible grew up associating religion with freedom. Turner grew up to become a charismatic preacher whose religious visions even led some blacks to consider him a prophet. In fact, one such vision—a solar eclipse that Turner took to be a sign from God—inspired his final and most historic act.

On the night of August 22, 1831, Turner, in an ill-fated attempt to free his people, led four accomplices on a three-day rampage through Southampton, Virginia. Going from house to house, the fugitives murdered every white person—regardless of sex or age—whom they encoun-

Originally published: Baltimore: T. R. Gray, 1831.
Editors' note: Subsequent footnotes in this narrative are from the original document.

tered. *Their destination was the arsenal in Jerusalem, Virginia, and along the way Turner's army swelled to as many as seventy slave rebels. However, a militia intercepted the army and killed more than one hundred blacks. Turner escaped but was apprehended weeks later.*

Turner's narrative, dictated to his attorney as a confession made shortly before his execution in November 1831, demonstrates how his fanatical devotion to God led to a "divinely inspired" killing spree that left fifty-seven whites dead. But, just as significantly, Turner's rebellion attests to the extreme lengths slaves were prepared to go to in order to achieve their freedom by any means necessary.

———

CONFESSION.

. . . SIR,—You have asked me to give a history of the motives which induced me to undertake the late insurrection, as you call it—To do so I must go back to the days of my infancy, and even before I was born. I was thirty-one years of age the 2d of October last, and born the property of Benj. Turner, of this county. In my childhood a circumstance occurred which made an indelible impression on my mind, and laid the ground work of that enthusiasm, which has terminated so fatally to many, both white and black, and for which I am about to atone at the gallows. It is here necessary to relate this circumstance—trifling as it may seem, it was the commencement of that belief which has grown with time, and even now, sir, in this dungeon, helpless and forsaken as I am, I cannot divest myself of. Being at play with other children, when three or four years old, I was telling them something, which my mother overhearing, said it had happened before I was I born—I stuck to my story, however, and related somethings which went, in her opinion, to confirm it—others being called on were greatly astonished, knowing that these things had happened, and caused them to say in my hearing, I surely would be a prophet, as the Lord had shewn me things that had happened before my birth. And my father and mother strengthened me in this my first impression, saying in my presence, I was intended for some great purpose, which they had always thought from certain marks on my head and breast—[a parcel of excrescences which I believe are not at all uncommon, particularly among negroes, as I have seen several with the same. In this case he has either cut them off or they have nearly disappeared]—My grand mother, who was very religious, and to whom I was much attached—my master, who belonged to the church, and other religious persons who visited the house, and whom I often saw at prayers, noticing the singularity of my manners, I suppose, and my uncommon intelligence for a child, re-marked I had too much sense to be raised, and if I was, I would never be of any service to any one as a slave—To a mind like mine, restless, inquisitive and observant of every thing that was passing, it is easy to suppose that religion was the subject to which it would be directed, and although this subject principally occupied my thoughts—there was nothing that I saw or heard of to which my attention was not directed—The manner in which I learned to read and write, not only had great influence on my own mind, as I acquired it with the most perfect ease, so much so, that I have no recollection whatever of learning the alphabet—but to the astonishment of the family, one day, when a book was shewn me to keep me from crying, I began spelling the names of different objects—this was a source of wonder to all in the neighborhood, particularly the blacks—and this learning was constantly improved at all opportunities—when I got large enough to go to work, while employed, I was reflecting on many things that would present themselves to my imagination, and whenever an opportunity occurred of looking at a book, when the school children were getting their lessons, I would find many things that the fertility of my own imagination had depicted to me before; all my time, not devoted to my master's service, was spent either in prayer, or in making experiments in casting different things in moulds made of earth, in attempting to make paper, gunpowder, and many other experi-

ments, that although I could not perfect, yet convinced me of its prac-
ticability if I had the means.[1] I was not addicted to stealing in my
youth, nor have ever been—Yet such was the confidence of the negroes
in the neighborhood, even at this early period of my life, in my superior judgment, that they would often carry me with them when they
were going on any roguery, to plan for them. Growing up among
them, with this confidence in my superior judgment, and when this, in
their opinions, was perfected by Divine inspiration, from the circumstances already alluded to in my infancy, and which belief was ever
afterwards zealously inculcated by the austerity of my life and manners, which became the subject of remark by white and black.—
Having soon discovered to be great, I must appear so, and therefore
studiously avoided mixing in society, and wrapped myself in mystery,
devoting my time to fasting and prayer—By this time, having arrived
to man's estate, and hearing the scriptures commented on at meetings,
I was struck with that particular passage which says : "Seek ye the
kingdom of Heaven and all things shall be added unto you." I reflected
much on this passage, and prayed daily for light on this subject—As
I was praying one day at my plough, the spirit spoke to me, saying
"Seek ye the kingdom of Heaven and all things shall be added unto
you." *Question*—what do you mean by the Spirit. *Ans.* The Spirit that
spoke to the prophets in former days—and I was greatly astonished,
and for two years prayed continually, whenever my duty would
permit—and then again I had the same revelation, which fully confirmed me in the impression that I was ordained for some great purpose in the hands of the Almighty. Several years rolled round, in
which many events occurred to strengthen me in this my belief. At this
time I reverted in my mind to the remarks made of me in my childhood, and the things that had been shewn me—and as it had been
said of me in my childhood by those by whom I had been taught to
pray, both white and black, and in whom I had the greatest confidence,

---

1. When questioned as to the manner of manufacturing those different articles, he
was found well informed on the subject.

that I had too much sense to be raised, and if I was, I would never be of any use to any one as a slave. Now finding I had arrived to man's estate, and was a slave, and these revelations being made known to me, I began to direct my attention to this great object, to fulfil the purpose for which, by this time, I felt assured I was intended. Knowing the influence I had obtained over the minds of my fellow servants, (not by the means of conjuring and such like tricks—for to them I always spoke of such things with contempt) but by the communion of the Spirit whose revelations I often communicated to them, and they believed and said my wisdom came from God. I now began to prepare them for my purpose, by telling them something was about to happen that would terminate in fulfilling the great promise that had been made to me—About this time I was placed under an overseer, from whom I ran away—and after remaining in the woods thirty days, I returned, to the astonishment of the negroes on the plantation, who thought I had made my escape to some other part of the country, as my father had done before. But the reason of my return was, that the Spirit appeared to me and said I had my wishes directed to the things of this world, and not to the kingdom of Heaven, and that I should return to the service of my earthly master—"For he who knoweth his Master's will, and doeth it not, shall be beaten with many stripes, and thus, have I chastened you." And the negroes found fault, and murmured against me, saying that if they had my sense they would not serve any master in the world. And about this time I had a vision— and I saw white spirits and black spirits engaged in battle, and the sun was darkened—the thunder rolled in the Heavens, and blood flowed in streams—and I heard a voice saying, "Such is your luck, such you are called to see, and let it come rough or smooth, you must surely bare it." I now withdrew myself as much as my situation would permit, from the intercourse of my fellow servants, for the avowed purpose of serving the Spirit more fully—and it appeared to me, and reminded me of the things it had already shown me, and that it would then reveal to me the knowledge of the elements, the revolution of the planets, the operation of tides, and changes of the seasons. After this revelation in the year 1825, and the knowledge of the elements being made known to me, I sought more than ever to obtain true holiness before the great day of judgment should appear, and then I began to receive the true knowledge of faith. And from the first steps of righteousness until the last, was I made perfect; and the Holy Ghost was with me, and said, "Behold me as I stand in the Heavens"—and I looked and saw the forms of men in different attitudes—and there were lights in the sky to which the children of darkness gave other names than what they really were—for they were the lights of the Saviour's hands, stretched forth from east to west, even as they were extended on the cross on Calvary for the redemption of sinners. And I wondered greatly at these miracles, and prayed to be informed of a certainty of the meaning thereof—and shortly afterwards, while laboring in the field, I discovered drops of blood on the corn as though it were dew from heaven—and I communicated it to many, both white and black, in the neighborhood—and I then found on the leaves in the woods hieroglyphic characters, and numbers, with the forms of men in different attitudes, portrayed in blood, and representing the figures I had seen before in the heavens. And now the Holy Ghost had revealed itself to me, and made plain the miracles it had shown me— For as the blood of Christ had been shed on this earth, and had ascended to heaven for the salvation of sinners, and was now returning to earth again in the form of dew—and as the leaves on the trees bore the impression of the figures I had seen in the heavens, it was plain to me that the Saviour was about to lay down the yoke he had borne for the sins of men, and the great day of judgment was at band. About this time I told these things to a white man (Etheldred T. Brantley) on whom it had a wonderful effect—and he ceased from his wickedness, and was attacked immediately with a cutaneous eruption, and blood oozed from the pores of his skin, and after praying and fasting nine days, he was healed, and the Spirit appeared to me again, and said, as the Saviour had been baptised so should we be also—and when the white people would not let us be baptised by the church, we went down into the water together, in the sight of many who reviled us, and were baptised by the Spirit—After this I rejoiced greatly, and gave thanks to God. And on the 12th of May, 1828, I heard a loud noise in the heavens, and the Spirit instantly appeared to me and said the Serpent was loosened, and Christ had laid down the yoke he had borne for the sins of men, and that I should take it on and fight against the Serpent, for the time was fast approaching when the first should be last and the last should be first. *Ques.* Do you not find yourself mistaken now? *Ans.* Was not Christ crucified. And by signs in the heavens that it would make known to me when I should commence the great work—and until the first sign appeared, I should conceal it from the knowledge of men—And on the appearance of the sign, (the eclipse of the sun last February) I should arise and prepare myself, and slay my enemies with their own weapons. And immediately on the sign appearing in the heavens, the seal was removed from my lips, and I communicated the great work laid out for me to do, to four in whom I had the greatest confidence, (Henry, Hark, Nelson, and Sam)—It was intended by us to have begun the work of death on the 4th July last— Many were the plans formed and rejected by us, and it affected my mind to such a degree, that I fell sick, and the time passed without our coming to any determination how to commence—Still forming new schemes and rejecting them, when the sign appeared again, which determined me not to wait longer.

Since the commencement of 1830, I had been living with Mr. Joseph Travis, who was to me a kind master, and placed the greatest confidence in me; in fact, I had no cause to complain of his treatment to me. On Saturday evening, the 20th of August, it was agreed between Henry, Hark and myself, to prepare a dinner the next day for the men we expected, and then to concert a plan, as we had not yet determined on any. Hark, on the following morning, brought a pig, and Henry brandy, and being joined by Sam, Nelson, Will and Jack, they prepared in the woods a dinner, where, about three o'clock, I joined them.

Q. Why were you so backward in joining them.
A. The same reason that had caused me not to mix with them for years before.

I saluted them on coming up, and asked Will how came he there, he answered, his life was worth no more than others, and his liberty as dear to him. I asked him if he thought to obtain it? He said he would, or lose his life. This was enough to put him in full confidence. Jack, I knew, was only a tool in the hands of Hark, it was quickly agreed we should commence at home (Mr. J. Travis') on that night, and until we had armed and equipped ourselves, and gathered sufficient force, neither age nor sex was to be spared, (which was invariably adhered to.) We remained at the feast until about two hours in the night, when we went to the house and found Austin; they all went to the cider press and drank, except myself. On returning to the house, Hark went to the door with an axe, for the purpose of breaking it open, as we knew we were strong enough to murder the family, if they were awaked by the noise; but reflecting that it might create an alarm in the neighborhood, we determined to enter the house secretly, and murder them whilst sleeping. Hark got a ladder and set it against the chimney, on which I ascended, and hoisting a window, entered and came down stairs, unbarred the door, and removed the guns from their places. It was then observed that I must spill the first blood. On which, armed with a hatchet, and accompanied by Will, I entered my master's chamber, it being dark, I could not give a death blow, the hatchet glanced from his head, he sprang from the bed and called his wife, it was his last word, Will laid him dead, with a blow of his axe, and Mrs. Travis shared the same fate, as she lay in bed. The murder of this family, five in number, was the work of a moment, not one of them awoke; there was a little infant sleeping in a cradle, that was forgotten, until we had left the house and gone some distance, when Henry and Will returned and killed it; we got here, four guns that would shoot, and several old muskets, with a pound or two of powder. We remained some time at the barn, where we paraded; I formed them in a line as soldiers, and after carrying them through all the manoeuvres I was master of, marched them off to Mr. Salathul Francis,' about six hundred yards distant. Sam and Will went to the door and knocked. Mr. Francis asked who was there, Sam replied, it was him, and he had a letter for him, on which he got up and came to the door, they immediately seized him, and dragging him out a little from the door, he was dispatched by repeated blows on the head; there was no other white person in the family. We started from there for Mrs. Reese's, maintaining the most perfect silence on our march, where finding the door unlocked, we entered, and murdered Mrs. Reese in her bed, while sleeping; her son awoke, but it was only to sleep the sleep of death, he had only time to say who is that, and he was no more. From Mrs. Reese's we went to Mrs. Turner's, a mile distant, which we reached about sunrise, on Monday morning. Henry, Austin, and Sam, went to the still, where, finding Mr. Peebles, Austin shot him, and the rest of us went to the house; as we approached, the family discovered us, and shut the door. Vain hope! Will, with one stroke of his axe, opened it, and we entered and found Mrs. Turner and Mrs. Newsome in the middle of a room, almost frightened to death. Will immediately killed Mrs. Turner, with one blow of his axe. I took Mrs. Newsome by the hand, and with the sword I had when I was apprehended, I struck her several blows over the head, but not being able to kill her, as the sword was dull. Will turning around and discovering it, despatched her also. A general destruction of property and search for money and ammunition, always succeeded the murders. By this time my company amounted to fifteen, and nine men mounted, who started for Mrs. Whitehead's, (the other six were to go through a by way to Mr. Bryant's and rejoin us at Mrs. Whitehead's,) as we approached the house we discovered Mr. Richard Whitehead standing in the cotton patch, near the lane fence; we called him over into the lane, and Will, the executioner, was near at hand, with his fatal axe, to send him to an untimely grave. As we pushed on to the house, I discovered some one run round the garden, and thinking it was some of the white family, I pursued them, but finding it was a servant girl belonging to the house, I returned to commence the work of death, but they whom I left, had not been idle; all the family were already murdered, but Mrs. Whitehead and her daughter Margaret. As I came round to the door I saw Will pulling Mrs. Whitehead out of the house, and at the step he nearly severed her head from her body, with his broad axe. Miss Margaret, when I discovered her, had concealed herself in the corner, formed by the projection of the cellar cap from the house; on my approach she fled, but was soon overtaken, and after repeated blows with a sword, I killed her by a blow on the head, with a fence rail. By this time, the six who had gone by Mr. Bryant's, rejoined us, and informed me they had done the work of death assigned them. We again divided, part going to Mr. Richard Porter's, and from thence to Nathaniel Francis,' the others to Mr. Howell Harris,' and Mr. T. Doyles. On my reaching Mr. Porter's, he had escaped with his family. I understood there, that the alarm had already spread, and I immediately returned to bring up those sent to Mr. Doyles, and Mr. Howell Harris'; the party I left going on to Mr. Francis,' having told them I would join them in that neighborhood. I met these sent to Mr. Doyles' and Mr. Harris' returning, having met Mr. Doyle on the road and killed him; and learning from some who joined them, that Mr. Harris was from home, I immediately pursued the course taken by the party gone on before; but knowing they would complete the work of death and pillage, at Mr. Francis' before I could there, I went to Mr. Peter Edwards,' expecting to find them there, but they had been here also. I then went to Mr. John T. Barrow's, they had been here and murdered him. I pursued on their track to Capt. Newit Harris', where I found the greater part mounted, and ready to start; the men now amounting to about forty, shouted and hurrahed as I rode up, some were in the yard, loading their guns, others drinking. They said Captain Harris and his family had escaped, the property in the house they destroyed, robbing him of money and other valuables. I ordered them to mount and march instantly, this was about nine or ten o'clock, Monday morning. I proceeded to Mr. Levi Waller's, two or three miles distant. I took my station in the rear, and as it 'twas my object to carry terror and devastation wherever we went, I placed fifteen or twenty of the best armed and most to be relied on, in front, who generally approached the houses as fast as their horses could run; this was for two purposes, to prevent their escape and strike terror to the inhabitants—on this account I never got to the houses, after leaving Mrs. Whitehead's, until the murders were committed, except in one case. I sometimes got in sight in time to see the work of death completed, viewed the mangled bodies as they lay, in silent satisfaction, and immediately started in quest of other victims—Having murdered Mrs. Waller and ten children, we started for Mr. William Williams'—having killed him and two little boys that were there; while engaged in this, Mrs. Williams fled and got some distance from the house, but she was pursued, overtaken, and compelled to get up behind one of the company, who brought her back, and after showing her the mangled body of her lifeless husband, she was told to get down and lay by his side, where she was shot dead. I then started for Mr. Jacob Williams, where the family were murdered—Here we found a young man named Drury, who had come on business with Mr. Williams—he was pursued, overtaken and shot. Mrs. Vaughan was the next place we visited—and after murdering the family here, I determined on starting for Jerusalem—Our number amounted now to fifty or sixty, all mounted and armed with guns, axes, swords and clubs—On reaching Mr. James W. Parkers' gate, immediately on the road leading to Jerusalem, and about three miles distant, it was proposed to me to call there, but I objected, as I knew he was gone to Jerusalem, and my object was to reach there as soon as possible; but some of the men having relations at Mr. Parker's it was agreed that they might call and get his people. I remained at the gate on the road, with seven or eight; the others going across the field to the house, about half a mile off. After waiting some time for them, I became impatient, and started to the house for them, and on our return we were met by a party of white men, who had pursued our blood-stained track, and who had fired on those at the gate, and dispersed them, which I knew nothing of, not having been at that time rejoined by any of them— Immediately on discovering the whites, I ordered my men to halt and form, as they appeared to be alarmed— The white men, eighteen in number, approached us in about one hundred yards, when one of them fired (this was against the positive orders of Captain Alexander P. Peete, who commanded, and who had directed the men to reserve their fire until within thirty paces). And I discovered about half of them retreating, I then ordered my men to fire and rush on them; the few remaining stood their ground until we approached within fifty yards, when they fired and retreated. We pursued and overtook some of them who we thought we left dead; (they were not killed) after pursuing them about two hundred yards, and rising a little hill, I discovered they were met by another party, and had haulted, and were re-loading their guns, (this was a small party from Jerusalem who knew the negroes were in the field, and had just tied their horses to await their return to the road, knowing that Mr. Parker and family were in Jerusalem, but knew nothing of the party that had gone in with Captain Peete; on hearing the firing they immediately rushed to the spot and arrived just in time to arrest the progress of these barbarous villains, and save the lives of their friends and fellow citizens.) Thinking that those who retreated first, and the party who fired on us at fifty or sixty yards distant, had all only fallen back to meet others with ammunition. As I saw them re-loading their guns, and more coming up than I saw at first, and several of my bravest men being wounded, the others became panick struck and squandered over the field; the white men pursued and fired on us several times. Hark had his horse shot under him, and I caught another for him as it was running by me; five or six of my men were wounded, but none left on the field; finding myself defeated here I instantly determined to go through a private way, and cross the Nottoway river at the Cypress Bridge, three miles below Jerusalem, and attack that place in the rear, as I expected they would look for me on the other road, and I had a great desire to get there to procure arms and ammunition. After going a short distance in this private way, accompanied by about twenty men, I overtook two or three who told me the others were dispersed in every direction. After trying in vain to collect a sufficient force to pro-ceed to Jerusalem, I determined to return, as I was sure they would make back to their old neighborhood, where they would rejoin me, make new recruits, and come down again. On my way back, I called at Mrs. Thomas's, Mrs. Spencer's, and several other places, the white

families having fled, we found no more victims to gratify our thirst for
blood, we stopped at Majr. Ridley's quarter for the night, and being
joined by four of his men, with the recruits made since my defeat, we
mustered now about forty strong. After placing out sentinels, I laid
down to sleep, but was quickly roused by a great racket; starting up, I
found some mounted, and others in great confusion; one of the sentinels having given the alarm that we were about to be attacked, I ordered some to ride round and reconnoitre, and on their return the
others being more alarmed, not knowing who they were, fled in different ways, so that I was reduced to about twenty again; with this I
determined to attempt to recruit, and proceed on to rally in the neighborhood, I had left. Dr. Blunt's was the nearest house, which we
reached just before day; on riding up the yard, Hark fired a gun.
We expected Dr. Blunt and his family were at Maj. Ridley's, as I
knew there was a company of men there; the gun was fired to ascertain
if any of the family were at home; we were immediately fired upon
and retreated, leaving several of my men. I do not know what became
of them, as I never saw them afterwards. Pursuing our course back
and coming in sight of Captain Harris', where we had been the day
before, we discovered a party of white men at the house, on which all
deserted me but two, (Jacob and Nat,) we concealed ourselves in the
woods until near night, when I sent them in search of Henry, Sam,
Nelson, and Hark, and directed them to rally all they could, at the
place we had had our dinner the Sunday before, where they would find
me, and I accordingly returned there as soon as it was dark and remained until Wednesday evening, when discovering white men riding
around the place as though they were looking for some one, and none
of my men joining me, I concluded Jacob and Nat had been taken, and
compelled to betray me. On this I gave up all hope for the present;
and on Thursday night after having supplied myself with provisions
from Mr. Travis's, I scratched a hole under a pile of fence rails in a
field, where I concealed myself for six weeks, never leaving my hiding
place but for a few minutes in the dead of night to get water which
was very near; thinking by this time I could venture out, I began to go

about in the night and eaves drop the houses in the neighborhood; pursuing this course for about a fortnight and gathering little or no intelligence, afraid of speaking to any human being, and returning every morning to my cave before the dawn of day. I know not how long I might have led this life, if accident had not betrayed me, a dog in the neighborhood passing by my hiding place one night while I was out, was attracted by some meat I had in my cave, and crawled in and stole it, and was coming out just as I returned. A few nights after, two negroes having started to go hunting with the same dog, and passed that way, the dog came again to the place, and having just gone out to walk about, discovered me and barked, on which thinking myself discovered, I spoke to them to beg concealment. On making myself known they fled from me. Knowing then they would betray me, I immediately left my hiding place, and was pursued almost incessantly until I was taken a fortnight afterwards by Mr. Benjamin Phipps, in a little hole I had dug out with my sword, for the purpose of concealment, under the top of a fallen tree. On Mr. Phipps' discovering the place of my concealment, he cocked his gun and aimed at me. I requested him not to shoot and I would give up, upon which he demanded my sword. I delivered it to him, and he brought me to prison. During the time I was pursued, I had many hair breadth escapes, which your time will not permit you to relate. I am here loaded with chains, and willing to suffer the fate that awaits me.

I here proceeded to make some inquiries of him after assuring him of the certain death that awaited him, and that concealment would only bring destruction on the innocent as well as guilty, of his own color, if he knew of any extensive or concerted plan. His answer was, I do not. When I questioned him as to the insurrection in North Carolina happening about the same time, he denied any knowledge of it; and when I looked him in the face as though I would search his inmost thoughts, he replied, "I see sir, you doubt my word; but can you not think the same ideas, and strange appearances about this time in the heaven's might prompt others, as well as myself, to this undertaking." I now had much conversation with and asked him many questions, having forborne to do so previously, except in the cases noted in parenthesis; but during his statement, I had, unnoticed by him, taken notes as to some particular circumstances, and having the advantage of his statement before me in writing, on the evening of the third day that I had been with him, I began a cross examination, and found his statement corroborated by every circumstance coming within my own knowledge or the confessions of others whom had been either killed or executed, and whom he had not seen nor had any knowledge since 22d of August last, he expressed himself fully satisfied as to the impracticability of his attempt. It has been said he was ignorant and cowardly, and that his object was to murder and rob for the purpose of obtaining money to make his escape. It is notorious, that he was never known to have a dollar in his life; to swear an oath, or drink a drop of spirits. As to his ignorance, he certainly never had the advantages of education, but he can read and write, (it was taught him by his parents,) and for natural intelligence and quickness of apprehension, is surpassed by few men I have ever seen. As to his being a coward, his reason as given for not resisting Mr. Phipps, shews the decision of his character. When he saw Mr. Phipps present his gun, he said he knew it was impossible for him to escape as the woods were full of men; he therefore thought it was better to surrender, and trust to fortune for his escape. He is a complete fanatic, or plays his part most admirably. On other subjects he possesses an uncommon share of intelligence, with a mind capable of attaining any thing; but warped and perverted by the influence of early impressions. He is below the ordinary stature, though strong and active, having the true negro face, every feature of which is strongly marked. I shall not attempt to describe the effect of his narrative, as told and commented on by himself, in the condemned hole of the prison. The calm, deliberate composure with which he spoke of his late deeds and intentions, the expression of his fiend-like face when excited by enthusiasm, still bearing the stains of the blood of helpless innocence about him; clothed with rags and covered with chains; yet daring to raise his manacled hands to heaven, with a spirit soaring above the attributes of man; I looked on him and my blood curdled in my veins.

I will not shock the feelings of humanity, nor wound afresh the bosoms of the disconsolate sufferers in this unparalleled and inhuman massacre, by detailing the deeds of their fiend-like barbarity. There were two or three who were in the power of these wretches, had they known it, and who escaped in the most providential manner. There were two whom they thought they left dead on the field at Mr. Parker's, but who were only stunned by the blows of their guns, as they did not take time to re-load when they charged on them. The escape of a little girl who went to school at Mr. Waller's, and where the children were collecting for that purpose, excited general sympathy. As their teacher had not arrived, they were at play in the yard, and seeing the negroes approach, ran up on a dirt chimney (such as are common to log houses,) and remained there unnoticed during the massacre of the eleven that were killed at this place. She remained in her hiding place till just before the arrival of a party, who were in pursuit of the murderers, when she came down and fled to a swamp, where, a mere child as she was, with the horrors of the late scene before her, she lay concealed until the next day, when seeing a party go up to the house, she came up, and on being asked how she escaped, replied with the utmost simplicity, "The Lord helped her." She was taken up behind a gentleman of the party, and returned to the arms of her weeping mother Miss Whitehead concealed herself between the bed and the mat that supported it, while they murdered her sister in the same room, without discovering her. She was afterwards carried off, and concealed for protection by a slave of the family, who gave evidence against several of them on their trial. Mrs. Nathaniel Francis, while concealed in a closet heard their blows, and the shrieks of the victims of these ruthless savages; they then entered the closet where she was concealed, and went out without discovering her. While in this hiding place, she heard two of her women in a quarrel about the division of her clothes. Mr. John T. Baron, discovering them approaching his house, told his wife to make her escape, and scorning to fly, fell fighting on his own threshold. After firing his rifle, he discharged his gun at them, and then broke it over the villain who first approached him, but he was overpowered, and slain. His bravery, however, saved from the hands of these monsters, his lovely and amiable wife, who will long lament a husband so deserving of her love. As directed by him, she attempted to escape through the garden, when she was caught and held by one of her servant girls, but another coming to her rescue, she fled to the woods, and concealed herself. Few indeed, were those who escaped their work of death. But fortunate for society, the hand of retributive justice has overtaken them; and not one that was known to be concerned has escaped.

NINE

From *Sunshine and Shadow of Slave Life. Reminiscences as told by Isaac D. Williams to "Tege"*

Sunshine and Shadow of Slave Life *was published toward the end of the nineteenth century, when slave narratives, as a body of work, were no longer documents of social protest intended to overturn slavery but as texts meant to affirm the humanity of African Americans. However, narratives appearing at this time also served a dual purpose specific to the enlightenment of young people. Writing in a preface to the narra-tive, the author, identified only as "Tege," (Isaac D. Williams himself could neither read nor write) tells us that, though slavery has long been abolished, Williams's story was written for a new generation of readers that had "sprung up" since abolition, people for whom "the true stories of the old slave days, with a realistic picture of the condition of the col-ored race at that time, might not only be interesting but also informing."*

The son of a freed father, Williams was born in 1822. He grew up on a Virginia estate that included five large farms—the smallest of which counted 500 acres—and, according to Williams, housed 760 slaves. Williams's status as a free black fell into jeopardy when the estate was

---

Originally published: East Saginaw, MI: Evening News Printing and Binding House, 1885.

forfeited by its mistress over financial troubles. Williams at first had his labor leased out and then, five years later, he was sold outright into slavery for $500. At age thirty-two, Williams set out to escape: "I was born a free man, and by the help of God I was going to be one again."

However, faith in God was not something all slaves possessed from childhood. Turning to God, as the following chapters demonstrate, was a novelty to Williams at the time of his escape. It is only after he was captured and incarcerated for four weeks that his "thoughts were directed to Him whom I never knew before. I felt that without His help I would never be free." Soon, Williams was devout, praying daily for divine guidance, which, in an echo of an incident described by Solomon Bayley in his narrative, even manifests itself in God "blinding" his opponent in order to allow for Williams's escape. For Williams—and for many other fugitives—"God would direct our steps rightly and lead us through the wilderness to the happy land of promise."

CHAPTER I.

. . . The crisis in my life came at last in the summer of the year 1854. I was then a heavy built man, over six feet in height, and weighing over two hundred and sixty pounds, yet there was no superfluous flesh on me—it was clear bone and sinew—and I never knew what it was to have a pain or an ache. I felt vigorous, and with all my weight I stepped as light and elastic as a little child. I felt God had never intended me to be a slave all my life, and this opinion was strengthened when in some of my midnight wanderings I made my way to Allen's woods, not far from Fitzhugh's farm and there held council and long talk with two brothers named James and Joe Westcott, of Boston. They were engaged in getting out ship timber, and painted a vivid picture of the life, enterprise and business of the northern cities. They told me of the growing feeling that slavery was a curse and should be abolished, and also that if ever I attempted to escape, that willing hands and noble hearts would respond to help me, as soon as I got far enough north to be near them. I drank all this magic tale of freedom to be gained, and listened as eagerly as a child does to a marvelous story, and all my thoughts were on the one subject. I was born a free man, and by the help of God I was going to be one again. I was a slave now only through fraud, and I felt I must bend all my energies to get away. I talked with a friend of mine, named Willis, about visiting these Massachusetts men, and all they said to me, but he proved false and told his folks about it, and they in turn told others. At last three farmers united against me, and came to Mr. Fitzhugh with the story, that I was making the negroes on the surrounding farms discontented by talking about freedom and liberty up north, and a great deal to that effect. At this time what is known as the Fillmore law was rigidly enforced, and the penalty for any north-ern man visiting negro quarters and talking to slaves was very severe. The penitentiary and often the bullet was the penalty; and Massa-chusetts men were especially hated for their anti-slavery proclivities. Well, these three farmers offered Fitzhugh five hundred dollars over and above what he could get for me, as they wished me sent out of the county. They claimed that I was in the habit of stealing away at night to visit these Westcott brothers and imbibing dangerous ideas from them, and that these I would disseminate among others' slaves, creat-ing discontent and making them sullen and disobedient. There may have been some truth in this and I should have been more politic in my talk, but out of the fullness of the heart the mouth speaketh, and I could not help it.

Fitzhugh finally agreed to their terms and I was sold to George A. Ayler of Fredericksburg, Virginia, a town situated on the Rappahan-nock river. Thither I was removed and kept by him in a sort of pen, where slaves and cattle were huddled promiscuously together. I was locked up at night in a little room just large enough to stand up in and kept there for nine days; then I was sold to Dr. James, a Tennessee slave dealer, who gave fifteen hundred dollars for me. I kept steadily rising in the slave market, and the doctor intended to ship me with a large gang to Georgia. One day I got leave to go across the road, to get some clothes that we had left in a house just opposite our prison pen. I was accompanied by a friend named Henry Banks, who afterwards accompanied me in my many wanderings when I escaped. As soon as we got over we made our way through the back yard and then struck out for the bridge across the Rappahannock. Being hailed three times as we crossed the bridge, we made no response but only hurried the faster; we soon reached Falmouth, a small place one and one-quarter miles from Fredericksburg. It lay in a sort of hollow at the base of a high hill. We ran and walked up the heights beyond Falmouth and skirted all along the woods until we heard the dread baying of the bloodhounds and then knew the alarm had been given and our pursuers were upon us. We had taken the precaution to bring with us some red onions and spruce pine for the purpose of rubbing our boots so as to divert the scent of the dogs. We could just see the slave hunters with the pack of hounds gliding like a black thread in the distance and then we struck straight into the woods. We went up to a big leafy tree and commenced rubbing our backs vigorously against the bark. This was for the purpose of making the dogs think we had climbed it. The scent of the onions and spruce pine we rubbed on our boots would not be followed by them, while the human scent on the bark would always claim their attention. Escaping slaves frequently have adopted this stratagem and got away successfully when almost captured. Well, on they came, and we could see their fierce eyes and foam-flecked tongues lolling out of their mouths as they rushed savagely after us. They were urged on by the shouts and curses of the slave hunters, and those who have ever been pursued by wolves would have some idea of the situation. Many a poor fugitive slave has been torn limb from limb by those ferocious brutes set on by the human tigers behind them. We started away as soon as possible and heard the crew of demons as they surrounded the tree we had left, and then as we rushed madly off the deep baying sounds gradually died out in the distance. Night came but we tarried not. It was a matter of life or death, and liberty was before us. We traveled in the direction of Fitzhugh's farm where I had left my wife, and by hiding in thickets, swamps and caves in the day time and journeying nights, we at last reached the place. I saw my wife under cover of the darkness and imparted all my plans to her. Banks and I kept together, knowing that union was strength, and we hid in a cave near the farm, that I had discovered in one of my previous wanderings. We staid there for three weeks, and then another change came upon my fortunes.

CHAPTER II.

The cave that Banks and I hid ourselves in, was situated at the head of what was known as Williams' creek, and the sides were very steep, in some places almost perpendicular. The spot chosen by us was where the bank shelved inwards, leaving a space of a few feet between its base and the water's edge. We had picked up an old spade in one of our midnight tramps, and dug quite a hole in the side of the bank so we could nearly stand upright, and had plenty of room to sleep in, as well as a place to roast corn or what other farm truck we could lay our hands on. In order that we would not be smoked out, we dug a hole from the top of the bank clear through to our cave, a distance of some fifteen feet, and then fixed the top of our earthen stovepipe so it wouldn't be noticed, by covering it up with light branches and leaves. The trees grew so thick, and fires in the woods were so common, that we did not apprehend much danger of discovery from that source anyway.

I knew my wife would be watched pretty closely, and it would be impossible for her to bring me food, so we both foraged around at night, picking up what we could and returning to our nest before day-light. We knew also, that just now there would be a great hue and cry after us, and big rewards would be offered for our capture. We were only forty-five miles from Fredericksburg, and it was known where I came from, so we had to be continually on the alert to guard against surprises. Many long hours did Banks and I talk and plan about what we would do, and where our next move should be made. A fugitive slave had everything against him, the laws of the United States, big rewards offered for his capture, and no knowledge of the country he was to pass through. He had no compass to guide him in his long, weary journey for freedom, and was forced to shun every human face. Well might he despair of ever reaching the goal, for, like the Arab, every man's hand was against him, and there were very few good Samaritans to help the unfortunate on his way until he got further north. Where he might have met kindness and encouragement of a practical nature, he would fear and tremble to ask it. So often did hypocrisy clothe itself in the garments of benevolence, and self-interest be the governing motive, that he would find too late that his confidence had been treacherously betrayed. I mention these few facts so my readers will understand the difficulties of our situation and the many unknown perils we would have to face. I was very fortunate in having Banks for a companion, and we mutually cheered each other in those hours of gloom and despair. I would say to him, "Now, Banks, you know I would rather be shot dead than meet the man that bought me, for you know how we both promised we would go freely with him, but when I thought of my birthright, I made up my mind to fool him and try and get away. You know I was born free and was sold by those people, when before God and man they had no right to do so. I've made up my mind to be either a free man or a dead one. I will not go back to my chains again." . . .

All this time the woods that surrounded us were searched through and through, but they never found us. Now and then we would hear the sound of voices or the peculiar bay of the hounds, but they would pass by and our quiet nook was undiscovered. The trees were very thick around where we were, and whatever smoke issued from the small aperture at the top of the bank was lost out of sight before it passed through its leafy way We found out afterwards that there was a reward of three hundred dollars offered for each of us, and often Mullen, White and Bryant, three of the overseers of the Washington estate, were on the watch to capture us.

I had rigged up a sort of a weapon out of an old carving knife blade and tied it on the end of a stout pole. This knife was sharpened so that it would cut most anything, and one morning while I was out alone walking in the woods, near by I suddenly heard the crackling of twigs and bushes, and the next moment two bloodhounds sprang upon me. I slashed at the foremost one and swung the heavy pole around as he sprang at my throat, cutting off his fore legs and laying him writhing and moaning on the ground. The other furious brute, nothing daunted by the fate of his companion, came right at me, and as the stick had fallen out of my hand I had no time to get it, but seizing a large stone that lay handy, I struck him violently on the head, still retaining the stone and following up by a perfect shower of blows until he was dead. I finished the other one the same way and then rushed back to the cave, where I found Banks trembling with fear and apprehension, that I had either been killed or captured. I was covered with blood, fortunately not my own, and I must have looked as though I had come out of a hard conflict. I soon quieted Bank's fears and we both went out at night and buried the dogs, so they would not draw attention to our retreat.

It was only a day or two after this that we were surprised by hearing voices close upon us. We had just returned in the grey of the morning, after being out several hours prospecting for food, when we noticed that we were followed. It seems that we had been observed by that man Mullen, and he was accompanied by Bryant and White. They had seen us on the bank alone and rushed close at our heels. We got into the cave and quickly disappeared from view, trusting they would not discover us. We were soon made painfully aware such was not the case, and the next moment voices were heard close by us, where they all stood with guns ready to shoot us if we resisted. With oaths and all sorts of vile language they commanded us to come out and deliver ourselves up, or else have our brains blown out. I said, "I will come out; but will not give myself up." I walked out, followed by Banks, feeling that my last moments had come. I was resolved to sell my life as dearly as possible. When we stepped out to the edge of the creek,

Mullen presented his gun at my breast and told me to surrender. I said, "Never; I'll die first," and striking the gun to one side, I sprang into the creek and Banks right beside me. We did this so suddenly it threw them off their guard and necessarily destroyed their aim. We both dashed through the creek, and as I climbed up the marsh on the other side, I received a full charge of shot in my right arm and leg, many of which have never been extracted. Banks was shot in the back and we both fell helpless to the ground, bathed in blood. Then they all sprang upon us and rained blows until satisfied we were incapable of further resistance.

CHAPTER III.

We were captured on a quiet Sabbath morning, about ten o'clock, when the sun was smiling brightly, and leaves were rustling with their forest music. While the good people of the land were on their way to God's house to pray for all mankind, here were two poor wayfarers shot down deliberately, by permission of the laws of this very land. Our captors tied our hands so tight with hitching straps, that we were fain to cry out in our great agony, but knowing it would be of no avail, and only gratify the malice of our captors we bore it all in silence. They had a large wagon close by, and in this we were driven to King George county jail. Before reaching there my wrists swelled up so that they covered the hitching strap that I was tied with, and I asked Mullen to loosen it a little so as to relieve my misery. He refused with oaths, saying, "You shall never get away from us; we wont give you a chance," and they struck me repeatedly in the face and kicked each of us. On reaching the jail the sheriff, whose name was Dr. Hunter, came up and looked at us. I then had twenty-nine shot in my right arm and forty in my right leg. The doctor counted the holes in the flesh and said as he gazed at the mangled members, "If they were my niggers I would rather have them shot dead than wounded this way." He abused them roundly for their bad usage of us, not perhaps so much on the grounds of humanity, as because we had depreciated in value, being not so marketable, and the doctor hated to see good property destroyed. Mullen, Bryant and White dared say nothing in reply to him, for he was rich and they were poor, but they cringed and fawned around him like the curs they were. The doctor then had us removed to a comfortable place, and dressed our wounds himself; he was a skillful man, and soon had us on our feet again. We were put in the dungeon or cell where men condemned to be hung were kept, not a very cheerful place to be sure, but I could not help wishing I should meet that fate rather than be a slave again. I thought of the many sad, desperate men this cell had held, and wondered what their inmost secret feelings were with death staring them in the face, and life's moments ebbing swiftly away.

Doctor James, the slave dealer who had bought me from Ayler, was at this time away, further south in Georgia, with a large gang of slaves he had taken there to sell. Knowing this fact the sheriff telegraphed to James' partner in Richmond, and he came on at once, but when he saw how crippled we were he refused to pay the six hundred dollars reward offered for us both, and told Sheriff Hunter to keep us in the jail until James came back. We were well treated while there, which was about twenty-eight days, and during that time my thoughts were directed to Him whom I never knew before. I felt that without His help I would never be free, and I prayed to my Great Father above to be with me in this time of trouble, and in His wisdom I relied. I felt a consciousness of His near presence and it seemed as though some unseen power personally addressed me.

It was impossible to escape from the cell we were confined in. As before stated it was the one in which condemned murderers and those convicted of the most heinous offences were incarcerated. It was very strong and constantly guarded; but Providence seemed to be helping us, for after being in it for about ten days Banks was taken very ill with malarial fever, owing a good deal to the damp walls, and we were removed to a roomier and pleasanter cell up-stairs. It had two windows, one of which faced the jailor's house, and the other was on the opposite side. We had more light than in the dungeon, and altogether it was a vast improvement for us. Nothing could arouse me, however, from the despondent feeling, which weighed me down like a heavy cloud. Promptly as the sun arose I would greet him with a good morning, and as he sank in the west in all his scarlet splendor I would say farewell, hoping I would not live to see him again, for I longed to die and be out of a world that stifled all of my best feelings, and in which on every side I met with only curses and blows.

Shortly after being put in this upper cell I commenced to look around for a means of escape. I pulled off one of the legs of a stove that was stored in a corner of our room, and with this I pried off a board on the side of our cell and found a small strip of iron about a foot long in one corner, which I managed to rip off, and then I put back the board so that everything would look undisturbed. With this iron strip I worked unceasingly on the east window, when I could do so unobserved, but all my efforts seemed in vain; it was too strong for me. The last day we were to be in our prison had come. It was Thursday. How well do I remember it and the sinking feeling that oppressed my heart when the jailor informed us that our master, Dr. James, had returned from Georgia and was now in Fredericksburg, expecting to be at the jail next morning. All hope seemed to leave me and I fully expected to spend my future days in slavery. After a while I grew more composed over the bad news of master's return, and repeated with a calm sort of desperation that I would rather die than see the man that bought me. I then prayed to God that if I was to be captured again not to let me escape out of there, but if I could get away for Him to show me in His wisdom what to do. I had prayed both night and day up to this time and now began to think God had given me up. I got up and walked to the window, saying: "Window, I will never try you again unless in God's name I am told to do so." I turned away and started right across the floor to the opposite side to try and break the other window open. I knew it was the last day I had any chance and I felt desperate. Just at that moment I heard a voice say distinctly to me: "Go back to the window you have left. Since you have declared to do what is ordered in My name I will be with you." I stood still and dared not move either back or forward. The mysterious voice was still ringing in my ears and I felt as one dazed; I feared to go back until my mind became impressed with the idea that it really was the voice of the Great Master I had heard. He had taken pity on me in my extremity and would now help me. Something seemed to say, "Whose name did you invoke?" and I cried aloud, "God's name." I then went right back to the window and an unseen power directed me just what to do. Remember, I had been at work at this window for many weary days and nights and only a few minutes previously had exerted all my strength to burst it open, but in vain. Now, after leaving it and then coming back again in obedience to the mysterious mandate, I was not five minutes in splitting the bottom sill, in which the grates were fastened. While taking out the sash I accidentally broke two of the panes of glass, and this I felt would betray me and lead to discovery of our plans. Now that I knew that all things were ready for us to escape at night this one accident spoiled it all. The guard had to come in twice before nightfall and see if everything was right, and I felt he could not help but notice the broken panes. I put in the sash, broke off the fragment of glass left, put all the pieces in the stove, and listened for the footfall of our jailor. Our fate hung on a very slender thread, for if he saw anything was wrong all was lost, and as the broken glass was so plain before him it seemed almost impossible not to perceive it. At last a heavy tramp was heard and I tried to hold my breath as he came in. How eagerly we both noticed his every movement. The door grated harshly on the rusty hinges and he entered quickly, giving us a searching glance. Then, seeing we were quietly resting, he passed on and deliberately walked up to the broken window and looked out. We thought we were lost, but no; God seemed to blind his mind, and though he saw with his eyes he did not realize that anything was amiss; and finally, after looking for several moments turned unconcernedly on his heel and left us. Then I fell on my knees and said, "Surely, Lord, Thou art with us," and something seemed to murmur in reply, "all will yet be well." But we had still another ordeal to go through, for after supper he would return to see if everything was safe for the night. The minutes were like hours. Our fate seemed to hang on the turn of a die, and we ardently longed for the moments to fly quicker. "Hope deferred truly maketh the heart sick," and I fairly yearned to be out in the fresh air once more. Would the long, long day never go by, dragging along slowly, so slowly? We heard the heavy metallic pendulum with its steady tick, and from time to time the clock would sonorously strike the hour. I prayed that God would blind the jailor's eyes and mind as before, so that he would not see or realize what had been done. Thus silently and prayerfully we awaited his coming. The slanting rays of the sun told us that night was coming on and soon her dark mantle began to fold around our prison home. Under her friendly veil we would make one last desperate effort to free ourselves again. At last the tread of our jailor was heard, and for a moment I wished the earth would open and swallow me, so fearful had I become of discovery. I, who knew not the meaning of nerves, felt completely unstrung, and I quivered and shook with fear. Banks lay close by me, and I said to him: "Remember Daniel was saved even when in the lion's den, and we will yet be saved from these human tigers." As if to verify what I had said, the guard gave but a casual glance around, staid only a few moments, and left. To paint the relief we felt were impossible. I clasped Banks and he me, and looking into each other's eyes we both breathed one mighty prayer of thankfulness to the great overruling power that we felt had saved us.

Now, friends, you may think of this day's experience just as you please, but all I have related is true. I firmly believe, that it was the Good Father in Heaven who took pity on two of the humblest of his creatures, and told me just what to do. You may call me superstitious if you like, but I give the facts as they occurred and shall always cling to the belief that it was God himself who spoke to me, and I feel all the happier in doing so.

Now, that the jailor was gone and we were left to ourselves for the night, we took the bed-clothes and made them into a rope, so that we could lower ourselves from the window to the ground below, a distance of some thirty feet. I went first and found that the rope was ten feet too short, and with a dull heavy thud I dropped to the ground, Banks followed quickly and came down pretty solidly. This was about nine o'clock and we got away undiscovered as it was very dark. That night we made over eighteen miles and reached Fitzhugh's farm once more. We had to make for that first, as we did not know where else to go, and we could there get some plan of operations laid as to our future course.

It was early Friday morning when I quietly knocked on my wife's cabin door and great was her amazement to see me. She said she thought I was gone for good this time and she had never expected to see me again. After getting some food, we went back to the woods, and digging a cave in the side of a gully about two miles from the other one, we lay still during the day, and at night I saw my wife again. She then told me that Fitzhugh at dinner time had said, "Ike has escaped again, and Dr. James after arriving at the jail was fearfully enraged. He now offers a reward of six-hundred dollars for the capture of each, either dead or alive." Fitzhugh said also, he wished I would escape, but thought I had no chance, as there was a patrol of sixteen or twenty men scouring the country after me. This was not very cheering news, to be sure, but it was just what might have been expected.

One night of the following week, I went out after some food to the cabin of a friendly colored man, named John Fleming, and, as I came up the road, I heard some men talking near me. At first I thought that James Arnold, a white man, was bringing home a lot of slaves from the upper farm to their cabins. I knew I had best keep shady till they had passed by, so I went under some cedar bushes, which grew very low on the ground and crawled as near the road as I could without being observed. I was astonished and alarmed at seeing a gang of sixteen white men armed with guns. I heard them distinctly say, that they were going down to my mother's, where they expected to kill or capture me. They were pretty sure I was around there, they said, and would have me dead or alive. One of them remarked, that it was just as cheap to kill me, as the same reward was offered for my head, and he proposed to shoot me on sight. You can imagine the feelings of a poor hunted fugitive, lying within a few yards of the men bent on killing him. The slightest movement and I would be discovered. But how fortunate I was to have overheard them. I had often been at my mother's late at night, and it was by the merest chance I was not there this evening, for to go there had been my intention. I remember that I once saw the head of a colored man rolled out of a sack. He was shot while attempting to escape. There was a heavy reward offered for his head, dead or alive, and the result was a dead head. Now I said to myself, wherever my head goes, my body shall follow it, for I had strong objections to its being removed from my shoulders. I then joined Banks, and told him what had occurred. I said: "Henry, we cannot stay here any longer; we had better risk dying on the road than be killed, as we surely will be, if we keep to the cave." So with this brief talk we made up our minds to go somewhere anyway, we knew not whither, but anywhere from there. Banks had some free folks, cousins of his, who went now and then to Pennsylvania, and he suggested that we go to his mother's home near Fredericksburg and see if she could direct us what route to take. This was on a Saturday in November, 1854, and we had just made all arrangements to start, when we met a colored man named Christopher Nicholas in the woods. He had been severely beaten by his master and had made up his mind to join us if possible, for he had heard of our being somewhere near. Nicholas had been serving in the capacity of miller and had been misused shamefully for very slight causes. He and I were old friends and gladly greeted each other.

We did not get started for our destination till Monday, December 1st, 1854, and the night before I spent with my wife and mother bidding them farewell. We traveled all of Monday night and hid in the thickets in the day time. It took us two nights to reach Fredericksburg, which we did without any interruption, and at last stopped in front of the house where Banks' mother lived. He went in and Nicholas and I stood near the door watching him, for we thought a great deal depended on this interview. No sooner did Banks' mother set eyes on him, than she exclaimed, "Oh my God, child, go out, the white people have just been after you, and are now searching around here; they may be back any moment."

Banks did not wait to hear more. No tender adieus were uttered, for life and liberty were at stake, and casting his eyes on his old mother for the last time in this world, he rushed from her presence. We then fell back in the woods again, going right through Falmouth, taking the Blue Ridge Mountain road and resolving to try our best to reach Pennsylvania, or at any rate to reach the northern states, and from there get to Canada. As we walked along I prayed that God would direct our steps rightly and lead us through the wilderness to the happy land of promise.

We tramped all night along the lonely road and the next day rested as before. At eventide we started again and met with a colored man near Morrisville. We told him we were very hungry and wanted to know which was the way to Warrenton, as we expected food and shelter there. He told us, and, pointing to a hotel ahead, said he was going there and would see that we got something to eat if we went with him. When the hotel was reached he said, "I have to go on a little ways ahead; you go in and I'll be back in a short time and attend to your wants." He pointed to a back door and told us to go in there, and we three started for it while he walked on. I suspected all was not right from his manner and told Banks and Nicholas to hide near by in the woods and I would go in and see if I could get some food for us, for we were about famished. Just as I got to the door I heard voices coming down the road, and, looking up, I saw four men walking rapidly toward the hotel. I sprang from the door and walked straight up to them, going right between the group. I heard the same colored man say to his white companions: "There are three colored fellows in here who enquired of me the way to Warrenton. I believe from their appearance and questions that they are runaway slaves, and probably there is a good reward for their capture." I recognized the Judas that would betray us as our quondam friend of a few minutes before, and knew that he expected to find three men, not one, which explains why he did not notice me as I was alone. I hastily cut around in the woods and got my companions and we started, resolving to be more guarded in the future. However, we had to eat; the engine must have fuel to keep it going; so, coming to a little cabin by the wayside, which we knew was likely to be occupied by a colored family, we knocked timidly at the door and asked for food. We were kindly welcomed by its inmates, and after a hearty meal and a short rest we started for Warrenton, having been directed the proper way by our friend. He also told us the name of the colored man whom he thought had met and tried to deceive us. He said the fellow made many a five or ten dollars in the mean business of informing on runaway slaves. He would get their confidence and then betray it for a trifling sum. I mentally put him down in my memory and resolved that if we ever met he would feel badly about it. Doing good to those that spitefully use you is one of the most difficult of the Christian roads to grace, and few there are who travel therein. We reached Warrenton late at night and passed through its silent streets unmolested.

CHAPTER IV.

We did not tarry in Warrenton, but kept right on, taking the Alexandria railroad, and when the day began to dawn and the sun to peep forth we hid in the woods, and by nightfall were up and off on our long journey again. We had not covered much ground before we were stopped by an old man with a gun and a large dog. We asked him for something to eat and he replied by enquiring where we were going. We said we were carpenters, and were hired in Alexandria to go to work in Warrenton. He said: "Where are your passes?"

"We have none," I replied.

Then he looked daggers at us and said: "You cannot go any further; you must come with me," and he made a menacing motion with his gun, which he hastily unslung off his back.

"But we have to go," I said, "for we were hired to go there, and go we will, and neither you nor your dog will stop us."

"We'll see about that," he remarked, and as we quickly moved away from him he brought the gun to his shoulder and fired at us, but in his excitement he aimed too high and the charge went harmlessly through the air. Then he set his dog on us. With a fierce growl he bounded like a tiger at my throat, but by a well-directed kick I laid him out, and he returned to his aged master howling piteously. His owner gave up following us, and the last I saw of him he was shaking his fist in impotent rage. I could not help but admire the courage of the old man, who all alone halted three stout, desperate fellows like ourselves. As his frail body stood out in bold relief beneath the lengthening shadows of the evening I could but think of the power he represented. In that menacing hand stretched out to grasp us lay oppression and a grinding tyranny that had covered the land with rivers of tears and wails of agony. It was backed up by all the laws which the ingenuity of man could devise to prevent our escape and to tighten our bonds.

On leaving the old man we retraced our steps toward Warrenton so as to mislead him, for we knew he would be likely to get a posse of slave-hunters and pursue us. Then when out of his sight we doubled in the woods and once more resumed our journey toward what we supposed was the north. For over two days and nights we had gone without food and now the exercise of walking increased our hunger, and having big frames to keep supplied with flesh and blood we endured great suffering. They say one suffers most in the first stages of hunger; that later on the senses not being so bright a sort of insensibility steals over the mind and an indifference to all one's surroundings. I know that I could have eaten almost anything, and I longed for the sight of a friendly cabin where we could rest and supply the inner man. We had no idea where the city of Alexandria was and would have avoided it as if it were the plague, after Banks' experience there. So you may imagine our surprise and fright when on walking into a town from the railroad on a dark night, when but few lights could be seen, as it was after twelve o'clock, to find in the morning that we were in the center of Alexandria.

Banks said: "Why, this is the place where I was captured. I remember seeing that building," pointing to a peculiarly shaped edifice. "We must get out of here, and that right quick."

As only the first gray streaks of dawn had begun to appear we managed to steal away without being molested and reached the woods with quick-beating hearts and anxious faces. Then when night came on we crept out and got on the railroad track and walked toward Washington, which was only eight miles distant. Coming very near Washington we reached a tollgate and bought a cigar apiece from the man who kept it, who took us for Washington darkies. He also gave us some food, and we started out again greatly refreshed. We had a little money, which came very handy in emergencies like the present, for these cigars were the same as passports to us. The moment we got them we struck boldly for Washington and got in that same night without being stopped. You see going to the city we were not so likely to be suspected of being runaways as we would be if fleeing from it, and now as we had got there the plan we adopted was this: All of us lit our cigars and put our hats on one side of our heads as though we were out on a lark together. Then I directed Nicholas to go across the street while Banks and I strolled along together in a free and easy sort of style. This would be about the last thing the authorities would expect in runaways. We passed along the elegant streets, looking everybody in the face and acting as though we feared nothing. We were not suspected in the least, and I heard some one say "Just see those fellows; they seem to be having a good time." I had told Nicholas to watch Banks and me and to turn as we turned. We met several policemen and passed them without their saying a word to us. Not knowing how to get through Washington it was our intention to turn down toward the river and follow its course until we got in the suburbs of the city. It was a cold, rainy night; a sort of drizzling sleet fell that wet us to the very marrow. We had heard of the Baltimore railroad and wanted to reach it if possible and take the track leading to Philadelphia. So we wandered around through the rain nearly all night. At last we saw lights appear in the different homes near where we lay concealed. People were just starting their fires for the day, and we looked for morning to throw some light on the subject and help us find our way, for we were completely lost and knew not where to turn, and I had about given up all hope of finding the railroad. We were benumbed with the cold and wet, and concluded to go up to some house and risk being captured—food and warmth to keep the human engine going being requisites that must be had at any risk. Just as we started we heard the distant rumbling of a train coming into Washington from Baltimore, as we afterward found. We had been wandering around, as the Jews did in the wilderness, and were only about forty rods from the railroad we had been searching for all night. This inspired us with fresh life, and instead of visiting any house we made a breakfast of hope and warmed ourselves with a good brisk trot. It was barely daylight when we started, and we walked until sunrise told us we had better be careful and hide from view, for the track stood up pretty high and we could easily be seen from a great distance. We then fell back into the woods again, and as the rainfall had ceased we made a rousing fire and dried our clothes by it the best way we could. The numerous hunters, with good pointer dogs, that were in the woods kept us dodging a good deal throughout the day, and we feared they might mistake us for three black crows and shoot us as legitimate game.

We spent two nights walking on the railroad, turning off into the woods in the daytime and resuming our tramp at nightfall, and had nothing to eat during that time. We came upon some colored wood-choppers hard at work felling the numerous pine trees that grew in that section of the country. These men treated us kindly and gave us something to eat. They did not ask us any questions, but the looks of some of them were eloquent with sympathy, and we knew they understood how we were situated when with a warm pressure of the hand they wished us God-speed on our journey. We did not stay long with them, for the white overseer was expected soon, and there would be great danger of being captured by him. In the early part of the second night while marching along we were suddenly confronted by three white men who had charge of a gang of white laborers on the railroad. They asked us where we were going in such a hurry and I replied "We are on our way to Baltimore."

"Where have you been working?" said the tallest, who seemed to be a man in authority and better dressed than the others.

"We have been chopping wood down here," I said.

"Who for?"

"For John Brown," I replied at random, speaking the first name that came into my mind.

Then they turned and walked along behind us, muttering among themselves in a manner that made my blood run cold, for I knew they had suspicions that all was not right, and I distinctly heard something said about runaway slaves. They kept close to us until we reached some shanties in which a lot of railroad laborers were staying. Then they ran quickly up to them, while we hurried on just as fast as we could run. It was well we did, for almost the next moment we heard the gang after us shouting, swearing and running. Then we knew it was to be a race for life and liberty, and we ran with all the swiftness we were capable of, the whole pack close at our heels. We had one advantage; it was very dark and our enemies had no fire-arms with them, while they evidently thought we had, for no one of them advanced much ahead of the rest. No doubt there were some very fleet runners among such a crowd, that might have easily overtaken us, but we three had good staying power, especially old man Nicholas, who, though over sixty years of age, left both Banks and me far in the rear. He was lithe, active, and didn't have as much flesh to carry along as we had. At last they stopped chasing us and with a parting shout of "We'll get you yet," they turned back. The next morning before daylight we knew we were nearing the city of Baltimore, for the place was beginning to bestir itself. Winter was upon us and the sun arose late. Long before his rays reached the earth the great city was awake and all was life and bustle. We heard the distant city cries, the whistles of the factories and the whirr of many wheels. How we were to get through Baltimore we did not know. We finally climbed up a high hill, and watched every train as it passed into Baltimore from Washington and carefully noted where it went through. Then early that night we entered on the railway track and started through, going right by the station. After walking about half way, we came to where a lot of tracks ran together and made the mistake of taking a false turn on a side track that led in an entirely different direction, causing us to miss the main trunk line. We discovered this at last and as an excuse for turning back, in case we were observed, we went into a little general store where most everything, from candy up to a suit of clothes was sold. We pretended we wished to buy a suit and selected one for each of us and told the proprietor we would call and get them the next evening. I had him write down my name, which I gave as James Walker. After retracing our steps quite a way we met a train right at the turn going to Philadelphia and just leaving Baltimore. We walked by the side of it until the suburbs of the city were reached, through the long gates that led across the river. After getting outside we traveled all night until daylight, when we came upon a man chopping wood a little distance from the track. I said, "Boys, let us go and see who this man is. He looks like a colored man."

By this time we were quite hungry and I, seeing the others hesitate a little, said, "Let us go, anyway, and see what we can do with him and if he will do anything for us." Generally in speaking to the colored people we met in this manner, I would first study the expression of their faces and try to judge whether they would be false or not. If, on inspection I was favorably impressed, I would be perfectly frank with them and say that we were trying to reach the free states and if they wanted to betray us they could do so. This appealing to their better nature and placing confidence in them, often won them over to our cause. At heart they were all on our side, and it was only self-interest that made them our enemies. We then approached the man who was chopping and he, looking up, nodded a cheery good morning. I rather liked his looks and so resolved to trust him. We briefly stated our case and asked for a little food to help us on our way. We told him where we were intending to go, and he greatly disappointed us by saying that we were on the wrong road. He told us we were now on the road to Havre de Grace, and if we ever struck that place were gone sure, for all through that region, there were lots of poor white people who just laid for such fellows as us and many of them made a regular living out of capturing runaway slaves. It was well we met him, else we might have ran our heads into a trap. You may be sure this news took us right aback and we asked him where we could go with more safety. He volunteered to show us and after going part of the way, said, "You take the road through the woods here straight to the eight mile turnpike, which is just eight miles from Baltimore." We were greatly disappointed at having to retrace our steps and to know that all our last night's tramp was in vain.

We now started on a narrow road that wound its way through the woods and was thickly shaded by trees forming an arch overhead. This was the first time we had traveled by daylight since our escape, and would not have done so now had not the thick woods hidden us from view so that we could quickly get into the thickets if we met anyone. A portion of our way lay through an old corduroy road that finally brought up at a sort of inlet or arm of the river, where there were a couple of vessels loading with wood. We avoided them and walked along until at a break in the woods we suddenly came upon a gang of white men digging iron ore out of the side of a high hill. They saw us and we concluded to put on a bold face and go up to them. What to say came into my mind and I told the boys to keep quiet and let me talk to the fellows. "Keep a stiff upper lip Banks and you, Nicholas, don't look so scared," I said. I was used to ship-carpenters' talk from meeting the down-easters near Fitzhugh's farm and could talk something like them, so I stepped up to a group of stout fellows and said: "Good morning, gentlemen. Would you please tell me the direction to the eight-mile stone, as I want to go to Baltimore and wish to get back before night."

One of them said, "Where did you come from?"

I replied, "From our vessel down here, which came in last night to get some wood."

Two of them remarked to the others that they had seen some vessels there this morning and then, their suspicions being allayed, they gave us full directions and we went on our way rejoicing. Shortly after we met another group and walked up to them in the same manner and with the same result, for several had noticed the vessels and believed that we were part of the crew. We reached the eight-mile stone about four o'clock in the afternoon and then went into the woods and had a good rest and sleep to make up for our long tramp.

Snow and sleet began to fall as night set in, and to keep ourselves warm we had to trot pretty lively. We took the turnpike again and as the trees gradually closed in around us the darkness was intense. We could almost feel it, so to speak, and we groped blindly on our way. Suddenly we heard a most unearthly howl close behind us, and, looking around, beheld two fiery balls that twinkled like stars and then disappeared. Next we heard the heavy breathing of some animal near us. Another melancholy wail followed and was echoed back by several more from the adjacent thickets.

"Wolves!" said Nicholas. "Those fellows we met warned us of them and said they were quite numerous in some parts of the woods."

We knew that these American wolves were neither very large nor dangerous, and were terrible cowards, but they seemed to gather recruits at every step and came crowding and howling close at our heels, indulging in furious snaps frequently, as if to whet their appetites for a meal. I had made up my mind not to form the adipose tissue and general make-up of any wolf if I could help it, but matters began to look a little bit dubious. Anyone can realize how he would feel if on a dark, stormy night a dozen or more fierce brutes were so near that he could feel their hot breath. I think now, with feelings of horror, of how their vicious jaws came together snappingly as they anticipated how much they would enjoy devouring us. Then we did the worst thing we could have done under the circumstances, by starting to run. One of them immediately sprang at Banks and bit one of his hands. Then we all faced them and kicked hard with our big cowhide boots until they retreated a respectful distance. Afterward when we started again on they came, and spying an old cowshed near by we rushed in and closed the entrance.

Here we staid for several hours, until a faint glimmer of light through the broken rafters told us daylight was upon us, and shortly after the wolves went away. After an hour or two of brisk walking to restore circulation of the blood, we arrived at a little house, and on knocking found no one home but an old woman. On asking her for something to eat she said she had nothing cooked in the house and her husband was not home. She gave us some oatmeal bread but had

no meat for us. We were hungry enough to consider the bread a deli-
cacy and it tasted good enough for us to smack our lips over. We then
went into the woods again.

About ten o'clock a man came near by to cut his Christmas fuel.
He had a team of oxen and a wagon. It was customary to get especially
fine wood and to cut greens and decorations for Christmas festivities.
The humblest cabins toward the holidays would be beautifully fes-
tooned with twigs and rosy tinted leaves. This man was of so light a
complexion that I thought he was a white man at first, but on looking
closer I saw that he was colored and then I felt safer. I asked him if he
could help us to get something to eat and assist us on our way by telling us where to go. He said he could not assist us personally but would
put us in the way of being very materially helped. He would send a
man who could put us in the right direction at night and in the meantime he would supply our immediate wants by bringing us some food.

He did not himself assist runaways, but in heart and soul was full
of sympathy for them and helped them indirectly by putting them on
the track of the great underground railway by which many were res-
cued from slavery, and whose direct dealings with us will be related in
the next chapter.

CHAPTER V.

Our new found friend gave us many cheering accounts of successful
escapes that had been made around there. He said that slaves had run
out of the fields in broad daylight, and as they were so near Pennsylvania they escaped. As he was about to return home with his load,
to get some food, we were left to ourselves an hour or so. He had advised us not to run or show any alarm if white men should come suddenly upon us, as it would have a bad look and make them think we
were runaways. We should take right to the road where there were lots
of colored people going and coming and thus would not be especially
selected as objects of suspicion, although we ran our chances and
might be questioned. He said we should always be ready with a prompt
and reasonable reply.

Our friend was not gone long and brought us all we wanted to eat of corn and flour bread and we made a very hearty meal. He then told us he would send a man by the name of Stephen Whipper, who was paid by northern people to help escaping slaves on their way north, in their grand strike for freedom. He was one of the advanced guard of the underground railroad, and had to conduct all his operations with great secrecy, in order not to be a marked man himself and his noble efforts be made unavailable.

The term underground was used as symbolical of the secret manner in which our friends had to work in order to help us. The objective terminus was at St. Catharines, Ontario, twelve miles from Niagara Falls, where a depot of supplies was established and an outfit given to each escaped fugitive, such as an axe, a spade and a decent suit of clothes.

The underground railroad company was originally organized by a band of Quakers in the border states, particularly in Pennsylvania, near the Maryland line. They found out those families on the routes between the slave states and the great north, that were favorably disposed toward the slaves and would help them on their journey. There would be stations on the way from which the poor fleeing ones would be passed from one to the other and after the border was crossed, they would be given into the hands of parties who would have charge of one or more freight cars into which this human freight was carefully locked and covered from view with empty boxes and other material. Then all stations on the road were carefully watched by their friends, and if danger was apprehended, this car would be laid off on the way and taken on later, till finally our destination was reached. You will see by my own experiences the real workings of this noble system, whose aim was to help those who would help themselves, by words of encouragement and, what was more practical, by money and personal effort. In a later chapter I will allude again to this humane outspring of the anti-slavery movement of those days and merely say that such men as William Lloyd Garrison, Wendell Phillips and many others were enrolled among its most active members.

This man Whipper was described to us as having a yellow complexion and being of a stern taciturn disposition. He had an indomitable will and was very earnest in the good work he was embarked in. We were to stand by the side of the woods and when he came along the road, which would be about dark, we were to silently follow him. There were certain peculiarities of gait and dress that he would be known by, and we were told to be careful to ask no questions but do as he said, for his judgment was good and he was an able worker in this peculiar field of labor. Our friend then said good-bye and wished us good speed on our journey.

Just as the sun disappeared we beheld a stranger, a tall, lithe, active man, striding along with a very determined air. There was a look of stern resolution about the closely compressed lips, that bespoke the man of iron will and resolute purpose. The very nature of the humane enterprise he was embarked in called for all those qualities, and in addition there was a certain amount of self-sacrifice about the way he lived, for he took heavy risks and you may say could never call his life his own. If the authorities ever could prove anything against him they would be only too glad to do so, and even to be seen talking to any who were afterwards found out to be refugees would be cause for grave suspicion. As he came by we could see him give us a keen, furtive glance, and a very significant look which we interpreted to mean, "follow me," and silently he led the way with three anxious ones in Indian file closely after him.

There was something very significant in this silent procession, and we began to realize this was the commencement of our feeling the protecting and guiding arm of our warm sympathizers in the free north. We were merely touching the finger tips as yet, but knew the warm grasp would soon be around us and the mysterious agency of the underground railway, so hated by southerners, was beginning to gather us in. Their many outstretched strong arms and helping hands were extended all over the south, and were as an anchor of hope to be grasped by poor, helpless ones who longed to breathe the fresh air of liberty.

After five miles of ground had been covered, Whipper made a gesture for us to halt, and then without a word left us a few minutes and went into a house by the wayside. He soon returned with a man, whom he said briefly would take us away in his wagon and in whose hands he would leave us. Then, without even giving us time to thank him, he turned on his heel and left as mysteriously as he came and that was all we ever saw of him. He was one of the spokes in the wheel, that had commenced to roll us onward to happiness and the land of hope. Now we came to the second spoke that was attached to this axle of humanity, and it soon commenced to revolve.

I said to Banks: "This is all God's doing. He is working for us and he guides us so we go to the right ones, who will assist and help such as we. It was He directed me to speak to that man cutting his Christmas wood, and now the train is started, the chariot will roll on until British soil is reached and we can snap our fingers at our pursuers and their whole system of human tyranny."

The man in whose hands we found ourselves, had a kindly, benevolent face, and cheered us greatly by saying he had just returned, from taking several fugitive slaves to Columbia. He had them concealed under a load of hay and drove by many who would quickly have stopped him if they had suspected the character of his freight. He told us as it was night we might start for Columbia ourselves, for if he went with us, so shortly after being seen on the way there the day before, he might be stopped and asked some awkward questions and it was very important for his future usefulness, that no one should think he was in active sympathy with fleeing slaves. He gave us full directions of the route we should take, and the way to find out the house of a man living there who would help us along, telling us the street and locality so we could easily find him on our arrival.

PART FOUR

Running by Any Means Necessary

The "resurrection" of Henry Box Brown in Philadelphia.
From Narrative of the Life of Henry Box Brown.
Image courtesy of Documenting the American South,
the University of North Carolina at Chapel Hill Libraries.

TEN

From *Incidents in the Life of a Slave Girl. Written by Herself.*

*T*he most famous of all slave narratives written by a woman, Harriet Jacobs's Incidents in the Life of a Slave Girl, Written by Herself *is a stunning accomplishment on a number of levels but none more so than for its detailed account of sexual dynamics and violence under slavery. Originally self-published in 1861 under the pen name Linda Brent in order to protect her family, Jacobs's autobiography was for generations taken to be a work of fiction until its authenticity was verified in the 1980s.*

Born to slave parents in 1813, Jacobs was raised in Edenton, North Carolina. She resided with her parents, a brother, and grandmother until age six, when her mother died. Jacobs was then taken from her family and sent to live with her mother's mistress, Margaret Horniblow, who taught the slave child to read and write. Upon her mistress's death in 1825, Jacobs was bequeathed to her mistress's three-year-old niece, Mary Matilda. In light of Matilda's young age, her father, Dr. James Norcom ("Dr. Flint" in the narrative) became Jacobs's master.

Unwanted sexual advances and abuse followed for a decade until, desperate and no longer able to withstand Norcom's behavior, Jacobs secluded herself in a crawlspace above her grandmother's home. There, against all hardships, she hid from her master for seven years, awaiting the opportunity to escape to the North with her children. With almost no ventilation or light, Jacobs confined herself to an area that was slightly larger than a coffin. Her miraculous tale of survival is a rare, early account of one African American woman's resistance to the most drastic measures, and one of the earliest works by an African American woman writer.

———

XXI.
THE LOOPHOLE OF RETREAT.

A small shed had been added to my grandmother's house years ago. Some boards were laid across the joists at the top, and between these boards and the roof was a very small garret, never occupied by any thing but rats and mice. It was a pent roof, covered with nothing but shingles, according to the southern custom for such buildings. The garret was only nine feet long, and seven wide. The highest part was three feet high, and sloped down abruptly to the loose board floor. There was no admission for either light or air. My uncle Philip, who was a carpenter, had very skillfully made a concealed trap door, which communicated with the storeroom. He had been doing this while I was waiting in the swamp. The storeroom opened upon a piazza. To this hole I was conveyed as soon as I entered the house. The air was stifling; the darkness total. A bed had been spread on the floor. I could sleep quite comfortably on one side; but the slope was so sudden that I could not turn on the other without hitting the roof. The rats and mice ran over my bed; but I was weary, and I slept such sleep as the wretched may, when a tempest has passed over them. Morning came. I knew it only by the noises I heard; for in my small den day and night were all the same. I suffered for air even more than for light. But I was not comfortless. I heard the voices of my children. There was joy and there was sadness in the sound. It made my tears flow. How I longed to speak to them! I was eager to look on their faces; but there was no hole, no crack, through which I could peep. This continued darkness was oppressive. It seemed horrible to sit or lie in a cramped position day after day, without one gleam of light. Yet I would have chosen this, rather than my lot as a slave, though white people considered it an easy one; and it was so compared with the fate of others. I was never cruelly over-worked; I was never lacerated with the whip from head to foot; I was never so beaten and bruised that I could not turn from one side to the other; I never had my heel-strings cut to prevent my running away; I was never chained to a log and forced to drag it about, while I toiled in the fields from morning till night; I was never branded with hot iron, or torn by bloodhounds. On the contrary, I had always been kindly treated, and tenderly cared for, until I came into the hands of Dr. Flint. I had never wished for freedom till then. But though my life in slavery was comparatively devoid of hardships, God pity the woman who is compelled to lead such a life!

My food was passed up to me through the trap-door my uncle had contrived; and my grandmother, my uncle Phillip, and aunt Nancy would seize such opportunities as they could, to mount up there and chat with me at the opening. But of course this was not safe in the daytime. It must all be done in darkness. It was impossible for me to move in an erect position, but I crawled about my den for exercise. One day I hit my head against something, and found it was a gimlet. My uncle had left it sticking there when he made the trap-door. I was as rejoiced as Robinson Crusoe could have been in finding such a treasure. It put a lucky thought into my head. I said to myself, "Now I will have some light. Now I will see my children." I did not dare to begin my work during the daytime, for fear of attracting attention. But I groped round; and having found the side next the street, where I could frequently see my children, I stuck the gimlet in and waited for evening. I bored three rows of holes, one above another; then I bored out the interstices between. I thus succeeded in making one hole about an inch long and an inch broad. I sat by it till late into the night, to enjoy the little whiff of air that floated in. In the morning I watched for my children. The first person I saw in the street was Dr. Flint. I had a shuddering, superstitious feeling that it was a bad omen. Several familiar faces passed by. At last I heard the merry laughing of children, and presently two sweet little faces were looking up at me, as though they knew I was there, and were conscious of the joy they imparted. How I longed to *tell* them I was there!

My condition was now a little improved. But for weeks I was tormented by hundreds of little red insects, fine as a needle's point, that pierced through my skin, and produced an intolerable burning. The good grandmother gave me herb teas and cooling medicines, and finally I got rid of them. The heat of my den was intense, for nothing but thin shingles protected me from the scorching summer's sun. But I had my consolations. Through my peeping-hole I could watch the children, and when they were near enough, I could hear their talk. Aunt Nancy brought me all the news she could hear at Dr. Flint's. From her I learned that the doctor had written to New York to a colored woman, who had been born and raised in our neighborhood, and had breathed his contaminating atmosphere. He offered her a reward if she could find out any thing about me. I know not what was the nature of her reply; but he soon after started for New York in haste, saying to his family that he had business of importance to transact. I peeped at him as he passed on his way to the steamboat. It was a satisfaction to have miles of land and water between us, even for a little while; and it was a still greater satisfaction to know that he believed me to be in the Free States. My little den seemed less dreary than it had done. He returned, as he did from his former journey to New York, without obtaining any satisfactory information. When he passed our house next morning, Benny was standing at the gate. He had heard them say that he had gone to find me, and he called out, "Dr. Flint, did you bring my mother home? I want to see her." The doctor stamped his foot at him in a rage, and exclaimed, "Get out of the way, you little damned rascal! If you don't, I'll cut off your head."

Benny ran terrified into the house, saying, "You can't put me in jail again. I don't belong to you now." It was well that the wind carried the words away from the doctor's ear. I told my grandmother of it, when we had our next conference at the trap-door; and begged of her not to allow the children to be impertinent to the irascible old man.

Autumn came, with a pleasant abatement of heat. My eyes had become accustomed to the dim light, and by holding my book or work in a certain position near the aperture I contrived to read and sew. That was a great relief to the tedious monotony of my life. But when winter came, the cold penetrated through the thin shingle roof, and I was dreadfully chilled. The winters there are not so long, or so severe, as in northern latitudes; but the houses are not built to shelter from cold, and my little den was peculiarly comfortless. The kind grandmother brought me bed-clothes and warm drinks. Often I was obliged to lie in bed all day to keep comfortable; but with all my precautions, my shoulders and feet were frostbitten. O, those long, gloomy days, with no object for my eye to rest upon, and no thoughts to occupy my mind, except the dreary past and the uncertain future! I was thankful when there came a day sufficiently mild for me to wrap myself up and sit at the loophole to watch the passers by. Southerners have the habit of stopping and talking in the streets, and I heard many conversations not intended to meet my ears. I heard slave-hunters planning how to catch some poor fugitive. Several times I heard allusions to Dr. Flint, myself, and the history of my children, who, perhaps, were playing near the gate. One would say, "I wouldn't move my little finger to catch her, as old Flint's property." Another would say, "I'll catch *any* nigger for the reward. A man ought to have what belongs to him, if he *is* a damned brute." The opinion was often expressed that I was in the Free States. Very rarely did any one suggest that I might be in the vicinity. Had the least suspicion rested on my grandmother's house, it would have been burned to the ground. But it was the last place they thought of. Yet there was no place, where slavery existed, that could have afforded me so good a place of concealment.

Dr. Flint and his family repeatedly tried to coax and bribe my children to tell something they had heard said about me. One day the doctor took them into a shop, and offered them some bright little silver pieces and gay handkerchiefs if they would tell where their mother was. Ellen shrank away from him, and would not speak; but Benny spoke up, and said, "Dr. Flint, I don't know where my mother is. I guess she's in New York; and when you go there again, I wish you'd ask her to come home, for I want to see her; but if you put her in jail, or tell her you'll cut her head off, I'll tell her to go right back."

XXII.
CHRISTMAS FESTIVITIES.

Christmas was approaching. Grandmother brought me materials, and I busied myself making some new garments and little playthings for my children. Were it not that hiring day is near at hand, and many families are fearfully looking forward to the probability of separation in a few days, Christmas might be a happy season for the poor slaves. Even slave mothers try to gladden the hearts of their little ones on that occasion. Benny and Ellen had their Christmas stockings filled. Their imprisoned mother could not have the privilege of witnessing their surprise and joy. But I had the pleasure of peeping at them as they went into the street with their new suits on. I heard Benny ask a little playmate whether Santa Claus brought him any thing. "Yes," replied the boy; "but Santa Claus ain't a real man. It's the children's mothers that put things into the stockings." "No, that can't be," replied Benny, "for Santa Claus brought Ellen and me these new clothes, and my mother has been gone this long time."

How I longed to tell him that his mother made those garments, and that many a tear fell on them while she worked!

Every child rises early on Christmas morning to see the John-kannaus. Without them, Christmas would be shorn of its greatest at-traction. They consist of companies of slaves from the plantations, generally of the lower class. Two athletic men, in calico wrappers, have a net thrown over them, covered with all manner of bright-colored stripes. Cows' tails are fastened to their backs, and their heads are decorated with horns. A box, covered with sheepskin, is called the gumbo box. A dozen beat on this, while others strike triangles and jawbones, to which bands of dancers keep time. For a month pre-vious they are composing songs, which are sung on this occasion.

These companies, of a hundred each, turn out early in the morning, and are allowed to go round till twelve o'clock, begging for contributions. Not a door is left unvisited where there is the least chance of obtaining a penny or a glass of rum. They do not drink while they are out, but carry the rum home in jugs, to have a carousal. These Christmas donations frequently amount to twenty or thirty dollars. It is seldom that any white man or child refuses to give them a trifle. If he does, they regale his ears with the following song:—

> *"Poor massa, so dey say;*
> *Down in de heel, so dey say;*
> *Got no money, so dey say;*
> *Not one shillin, so dey say;*
> *God A'mighty bress you, so dey say."*

Christmas is a day of feasting, both with white and colored people. Slaves, who are lucky enough to have a few shillings, are sure to spend them for good eating; and many a turkey and pig is captured, without saying "By your leave, sir." Those who cannot obtain these, cook a 'possum, or a raccoon, from which savory dishes can be made. My grandmother raised poultry and pigs for sale; and it was her established custom to have both a turkey and a pig roasted for Christmas dinner.

On this occasion, I was warned to keep extremely quiet, because two guests had been invited. One was the town constable, and the other was a free colored man, who tried to pass himself off for white, and who was always ready to do any mean work for the sake of currying favor with white people. My grandmother had a motive for inviting them. She managed to take them all over the house. All the rooms on the lower floor were thrown open for them to pass in and out; and after dinner, they were invited up stairs to look at a fine mocking bird my uncle had just brought home. There, too, the rooms were all thrown open, that they might look in. When I heard them talking on the piazza, my heart almost stood still. I knew this colored man had spent many nights hunting for me. Every body knew he had the blood of a slave father in his veins; but for the sake of passing himself off for white, he was ready to kiss the slaveholders' feet. How I despised him! As for the constable, he wore no false colors. The duties of his office were despicable, but he was superior to his companion, inasmuch as he did not pretend to be what he was not. Any white man, who could raise money enough to buy a slave, would have considered himself degraded by being a constable; but the office enabled its possessor to exercise authority. If he found any slave out after nine o'clock, he could whip him as much as he liked; and that was a privilege to be coveted. When the guests were ready to depart, my grandmother gave each of them some of her nice pudding, as a present for their wives. Through my peep-hole I saw them go out of the gate, and I was glad when it closed after them. So passed the first Christmas in my den.

XXIII.
STILL IN PRISON.

When spring returned, and I took in the little patch of green the aperture commanded, I asked myself how many more summers and winters I must be condemned to spend thus. I longed to draw in a plentiful draught of fresh air, to stretch my cramped limbs, to have room to stand erect, to feel the earth under my feet again. My relatives were constantly on the lookout for a chance of escape; but none offered that seemed practicable, and even tolerably safe. The hot summer came again, and made the turpentine drop from the thin roof over my head.

During the long nights, I was restless for want of air, and I had no room to toss and turn. There was but one compensation; the atmosphere was so stifled that even mosquitos would not condescend to buzz in it. With all my detestation of Dr. Flint, I could hardly wish him a worse punishment, either in this world or that which is to come, than to suffer what I suffered in one single summer. Yet the laws allowed *him* to be out in the free air, while I, guiltless of crime, was pent up in here, as the only means of avoiding the cruelties the laws allowed him to inflict upon me! I don't know what kept life within me. Again and again, I thought I should die before long; but I saw the leaves of another autumn whirl through the air, and felt the touch of another winter. In summer the most terrible thunder storms were acceptable, for the rain came through the roof, and I rolled up my bed that it might cool the hot boards under it. Later in the season, storms sometimes wet my clothes through and through, and that was not comfortable when the air grew chilly. Moderate storms I could keep out by filling the chinks with oakum.

But uncomfortable as my situation was, I had glimpses of things out of doors, which made me thankful for my wretched hiding-place. One day I saw a slave pass our gate, muttering, "It's his own, and he can kill it if he will." My grandmother told me that woman's history. Her mistress had that day seen her baby for the first time, and in the lineaments of its fair face she saw a likeness to her husband. She turned the bondwoman and her child out of doors, and forbade her ever to return. The slave went to her master, and told him what had happened. He promised to talk with her mistress, and make it all right. The next day she and her baby were sold to a Georgia trader.

Another time I saw a woman rush wildly by, pursued by two men. She was a slave, the wet nurse of her mistress's children. For some trifling offence her mistress ordered her to be stripped and whipped. To escape the degradation and the torture, she rushed to the river, jumped in, and ended her wrongs in death.

Senator Brown, of Mississippi, could not be ignorant of many such facts as these, for they are of frequent occurrence in every Southern State. Yet he stood up in the Congress of the United States, and declared that slavery was "a great moral, social, and political blessing; a blessing to the master, and a blessing to the slave!"

I suffered much more during the second winter than I did during the first. My limbs were benumbed by inaction, and the cold filled them with cramp. I had a very painful sensation of coldness in my head; even my face and tongue stiffened, and I lost the power of

speech. Of course it was impossible, under the circumstances, to sum-
mon any physician. My brother William came and did all he could
for me. Uncle Phillip also watched tenderly over me; and poor grandmother crept up and down to inquire whether there were any signs of
returning life. I was restored to consciousness by the dashing of cold
water in my face, and found myself leaning against my brother's arm,
while he bent over me with streaming eyes. He afterwards told me he
thought I was dying, for I had been in an unconscious state sixteen
hours. I next became delirious, and was in great danger of betraying
myself and my friends. To prevent this, they stupefied me with drugs.
I remained in bed six weeks, weary in body and sick at heart. How
to get medical advice was the question. William finally went to a
Thompsonian doctor, and described himself as having all my pains
and aches. He returned with herbs, roots, and ointment. He was especially charged to rub on the ointment by a fire; but how could a fire
be made in my little den? Charcoal in a furnace was tried, but there
was no outlet for the gas, and it nearly cost me my life. Afterwards
coals, already kindled, were brought up in an iron pan, and placed
on bricks. I was so weak, and it was so long since I had enjoyed the
warmth of a fire, that those few coals actually made me weep. I think
the medicines did me some good; but my recovery was very slow. Dark
thoughts passed through my mind as I lay there day after day. I tried
to be thankful for my little cell, dismal as it was, and even to love it, as
part of the price I had paid for the redemption of my children. Sometimes I thought God was a compassionate Father, who would forgive
my sins for the sake of my sufferings. At other times, it seemed to me
there was no justice or mercy in the divine government. I asked why
the curse of slavery was permitted to exist, and why I had been so
persecuted and wronged from youth upward. These things took the
shape of mystery, which is to this day not so clear to my soul as I trust
it will be hereafter.

    In the midst of my illness, grandmother broke down under the
weight of anxiety and toil. The idea of losing her, who had always
been my best friend and a mother to my children, was the sorest trial I

had yet had. O, how earnestly I prayed that she might recover! How hard it seemed, that I could not tend upon her, who had so long and so tenderly watched over me!

One day the screams of a child nerved me with strength to crawl to my peeping-hole, and I saw my son covered with blood. A fierce dog, usually kept chained, had seized and bitten him. A doctor was sent for, and I heard the groans and screams of my child while the wounds were being sewed up. O, what torture to a mother's heart, to listen to this and be unable to go to him!

But childhood is like a day in spring, alternately shower and sunshine. Before night Benny was bright and lively, threatening the destruction of the dog; and great was his delight when the doctor told him the next day that the dog had bitten another boy and been shot. Benny recovered from his wounds; but it was long before he could walk.

When my grandmother's illness became known, many ladies, who were her customers, called to bring her some little comforts, and to inquire whether she had every thing she wanted. Aunt Nancy one night asked permission to watch with her sick mother, and Mrs. Flint replied, "I don't see any need of your going. I can't spare you." But when she found other ladies in the neighborhood were so attentive, not wishing to be outdone in Christian charity, she also sallied forth, in magnificent condescension, and stood by the bedside of her who had loved her in her infancy, and who had been repaid by such grievous wrongs. She seemed surprised to find her so ill, and scolded uncle Phillip for not sending for Dr. Flint. She herself sent for him immediately, and he came. Secure as I was in my retreat, I should have been terrified if I had known he was so near me. He pronounced my grandmother in a very critical situation, and said if her attending physician wished it, he would visit her. Nobody wished to have him coming to the house at all hours, and we were not disposed to give him a chance to make out a long bill.

As Mrs. Flint went out, Sally told her the reason Benny was lame was, that a dog had bitten him. "I'm glad of it," she replied. "I wish he had killed him. It would be good news to send to his mother. *Her* day will come. The dogs will grab *her* yet." With these Christian words she and her husband departed, and, to my great satisfaction, returned no more.

I heard from uncle Phillip, with feelings of unspeakable joy and gratitude, that the crisis was passed and grandmother would live. I could now say from my heart, "God is merciful. He has spared me the anguish of feeling that I caused her death."

XXIV.

THE CANDIDATE FOR CONGRESS.

The summer had nearly ended, when Dr. Flint made a third visit to New York, in search of me. Two candidates were running for Congress, and he returned in season to vote. The father of my children was the Whig candidate. The doctor had hitherto been a stanch Whig; but now he exerted all his energies for the defeat of Mr. Sands. He invited large parties of men to dine in the shade of his trees, and supplied them with plenty of rum and brandy. If any poor fellow drowned his wits in the bowl, and, in the openness of his convivial heart, proclaimed that he did not mean to vote the Democratic ticket, he was shoved into the street without ceremony.

The doctor expended his liquor in vain. Mr. Sands was elected; an event which occasioned me some anxious thoughts. He had not emancipated my children and if he should die, they would be at the mercy of his heirs. Two little voices, that frequently met my ear, pleaded with me not to let their father depart without striving to make their freedom secure. Years had passed since I had spoken to him. I had not even seen him since the night I passed him, unrecognized in my disguise of a sailor. I supposed he would call before he left, to say something to my grandmother concerning the children, and I resolved what course to take.

The day before his departure for Washington I made arrangements, towards evening, to get from my hiding-place into the storeroom below. I found myself so stiff and clumsy that it was with great difficulty I could hitch from one resting place to another. When I reached the storeroom my ankles gave way under me, and I sank exhausted on the floor. It seemed as if I could never use my limbs again. But the purpose I had in view roused all the strength I had. I crawled on my hands and knees to the window, and, screened behind a barrel, I waited for his coming. The clock struck nine, and I knew the steamboat would leave between ten and eleven. My hopes were failing. But presently I heard his voice, saying to some one, "Wait for me a moment. I wish to see aunt Martha." When he came out, as he passed the window, I said, "Stop one moment, and let me speak for my children." He started, hesitated, and then passed on, and went out of the gate. I closed the shutter I had partially opened, and sank down behind the barrel. I had suffered much; but seldom had I experienced a leaner pang than I then felt. Had my children, then, become of so little consequence to him? And had he so little feeling for their wretched mother that he would not listen a moment while she pleaded for them? Painful memories were so busy within me, that I forgot I had not hooked the shutter, till I heard some one opening it. I looked up. He had come back. "Who called me?" said he, in a low tone. "I did," I replied. "Oh, Linda," said he, "I knew your voice; but I was afraid to answer, lest my friend should hear me. Why do you come here? Is it possible you risk yourself in this house? They are mad to allow it. I shall expect to hear that you are all ruined." I did not wish to implicate him, by letting him know my place of concealment; so I merely said, "I thought you would come to bid grandmother good by, and so I came here to speak a few words to you about emancipating my children. Many changes may take place during the six months you are gone to Washington and it does not seem right for you to expose them to the risk of such changes. I want nothing for myself; all I ask is, that you will free my children, or authorize some friend to do it, before you go."

He promised he would do it, and also expressed a readiness to make any arrangements whereby I could be purchased.

I heard footsteps approaching, and closed the shutter hastily. I wanted to crawl back to my den, without letting the family know what I had done; for I knew they would deem it very imprudent. But he stepped back into the house to tell my grandmother that he had spoken with me at the storeroom window, and to beg of her not to allow me to remain in the house over night. He said it was the height of madness for me to be there; that we should certainly all be ruined. Luckily, he was in too much of a hurry to wait for a reply, or the dear old woman would surely have told him all.

I tried to go back to my den, but found it more difficult to go up than I had to come down. Now that my mission was fulfilled, the little strength that had supported me through it was gone, and I sank helpless on the floor. My grandmother, alarmed at the risk I had run, came into the storeroom in the dark, and locked the door behind her. "Linda," she whispered, "where are you?"

"I am here by the window," I replied. "I *couldn't* have him go away without emancipating the children. Who knows what may happen?"

"Come, come, child," said she, "it won't do for you to stay here another minute. You've done wrong; but I can't blame you, poor thing!"

I told her I could not return without assistance, and she must call my uncle. Uncle Phillip came, and pity prevented him from scolding me. He carried me back to my dungeon, laid me tenderly on the bed, gave me some medicine, and asked me if there was any thing more he could do. Then he went away, and I was left with my own thoughts— starless as the midnight darkness around me.

My friends feared I should become a cripple for life; and I was so weary of my long imprisonment that, had it not been for the hope of serving my children, I should have been thankful to die; but, for their sakes, I was willing to bear on.

XXV.
COMPETITION IN CUNNING.

Dr. Flint had not given me up. Every now and then he would say to my grandmother that I would yet come back, and voluntarily surrender myself; and that when I did, I could be purchased by my relatives, or any one who wished to buy me. I knew his cunning nature too well not to believe that this was a trap laid for me; and so all my friends understood it. I resolved to match my cunning against his cunning. In order to make him believe that I was in New York, I resolved to write him a letter dated from that place. I sent for my friend Peter, and asked him if he knew any trustworthy seafaring person, who would carry such a letter to New York, and put it in the post office there. He said he knew one that he would trust with his own life to the ends of the world. I reminded him that it was a hazardous thing for him to undertake. He said he knew it, but he was willing to do any thing to help me. I expressed a wish for a New York paper, to ascertain the names of some of the streets. He run his hand into his pocket, and said, "Here is half a one, that was round a cap I bought of a pedler yesterday." I told him the letter would be ready the next evening. He bade me good by, adding, "Keep up your spirits, Linda; brighter days will come by and by."

My uncle Phillip kept watch over the gate until our brief interview was over. Early the next morning, I seated myself near the little aperture to examine the newspaper. It was a piece of the New York Herald; and, for once, the paper that systematically abuses the colored people, was made to render them a service. Having obtained what information I wanted concerning streets and numbers, I wrote two letters, one to my grandmother, the other to Dr. Flint. I reminded him how he, a gray-headed man, had treated a helpless child, who had been placed in his power, and what years of misery he had brought upon her. To my grandmother, I expressed a wish to have my children sent to me at the north, where I could teach them to respect themselves, and set them a virtuous example; which a slave mother was not allowed to do at the south. I asked her to direct her answer to a certain street in Boston, as I did not live in New York, though I went there sometimes. I dated these letters ahead, to allow for the time it would take to carry them, and sent a memorandum of the date to the messenger. When my friend came for the letters, I said, "God bless and reward you, Peter, for this disinterested kindness. Pray be careful. If you are detected, both you and I will have to suffer dreadfully. I have not a relative who would dare to do it for me." He replied, "You may trust to me, Linda. I don't forget that your father was my best friend, and I will be a friend to his children so long as God lets me live."

It was necessary to tell my grandmother what I had done, in order that she might be ready for the letter, and prepared to hear what Dr. Flint might say about my being at the north. She was sadly troubled. She felt sure mischief would come of it. I also told my plan to aunt Nancy, in order that she might report to us what was said at Dr. Flint's house. I whispered it to her through a crack, and she whispered back, "I hope it will succeed. I shan't mind being a slave all *my* life, if I can only see you and the children free."

I had directed that my letters should be put into the New York post office on the 20th of the month. On that evening of the 24th my aunt came to say that Dr. Flint and his wife had been talking in a low voice about a letter he had received, and that when he went to his office he promised to bring it when he came to tea. So I concluded I should hear my letter read the next morning. I told my grandmother Dr. Flint would be sure to come, and asked her to have him sit near a certain door, and leave it open, that I might hear what he said. The next morning I took my station within sound of that door, and re-mained motionless as a statue. It was not long before I heard the gate slam, and the well-known footsteps enter the house. He seated him-self in the chair that was placed for him, and said, "Well, Martha, I've brought you a letter from Linda. She has sent me a letter also. I know exactly where to find her; but I don't choose to go to Boston for her. I had rather she would come back of her own accord, in a respectable manner. Her uncle Phillip is the best person to go for her. With *him,* she would feel perfectly free to act. I am willing to pay his expenses going and returning. She shall be sold to her friends. Her children are free; at least I suppose they are; and when you obtain her freedom, you'll make a happy family. I suppose, Martha, you have no objection to my reading to you the letter Linda has written to you."

He broke the seal, and I heard him read it. The old villain! He had suppressed the letter I wrote to grandmother, and prepared a substitute of his own, the purport of which was as follows:—

"Dear Grandmother: I have long wanted to write to you; but the disgraceful manner in which I left you and my children made me ashamed to do it. If you knew how much I have suffered since I ran away, you would pity and forgive me. I have purchased freedom at a dear rate. If any arrangement could be made for me to return to the south without being a slave, I would gladly come. If not, I beg of you to send my children to the north. I cannot live any longer without them. Let me know in time, and I will meet them in New York or Philadelphia, whichever place best suits my uncle's convenience. Write as soon as possible to your unhappy daughter, LINDA."

"It is very much as I expected it would be," said the old hypocrite, rising to go. "You see the foolish girl has repented of her rashness, and wants to return. We must help her to do it, Martha. Talk with Phillip about it. If he will go for her, she will trust to him, and come back. I should like an answer tomorrow. Good morning, Martha."

As he stepped out on the piazza, he stumbled over my little girl. "Ah, Ellen, is that you?" he said, in his most gracious manner. "I didn't see you. How do you do?"

"Pretty well, sir," she replied. "I heard you tell grandmother that my mother is coming home. I want to see her."

"Yes, Ellen, I am going to bring her home very soon," rejoiced he; "and you shall see her as much as you like, you little curly-headed nigger."

This was as good as a comedy to me, who had heard it all; but grandmother was frightened and distressed, because the doctor wanted my uncle to go for me.

The next evening Dr. Flint called to talk the matter over. My uncle told him that from what he had heard of Massachusetts, he judged he should be mobbed if he went there after a runaway slave. "All stuff and nonsense, Phillip!" replied the doctor. "Do you suppose I want you to kick up a row in Boston? The business can all be done quietly. Linda writes that she wants to come back. You are her relative, and she would trust *you*. The case would be different if I went. She might object to coming with *me;* and the damned abolitionists, if they knew I was her master, would not believe me, if I told them she had begged to go back. They would get up a row; and I should not like to see Linda dragged through the streets like a common negro. She has been very ungrateful to me for all my kindness; but I forgive her, and want to act the part of a friend towards her. I have no wish to hold her as my slave. Her friends can buy her as soon as she arrives here."

Finding that his arguments failed to convince my uncle, the doctor "let the cat out of the bag," by saying that he had written to the mayor of Boston, to ascertain whether there was a person of my description at the street and number from which my letter was dated. He had omitted this date in the letter he had made up to read to my grandmother. If I had dated from New York, the old man would probably have made another journey to that city. But even in that dark region, where knowledge is so carefully excluded from the slave, I had heard enough about Massachusetts to come to the conclusion that slaveholders did not consider it a comfortable place to go to in search of a runaway. That was before the Fugitive Slave Law was passed; before Massachusetts had consented to become a "nigger hunter" for the south.

My grandmother, who had become skittish by seeing her family always in danger, came to me with a very distressed countenance, and said, "What will you do if the mayor of Boston sends him word that you haven't been there? Then he will suspect the letter was a trick; and maybe he'll find out something about it, and we shall all get into trouble. O Linda, I wish you had never sent the letters."

"Don't worry yourself, grandmother," said I. "The mayor of Boston won't trouble himself to hunt niggers for Dr. Flint. The letters will do good in the end. I shall get out of this dark hole some time or other."

"I hope you will, child," replied the good, patient old friend. "You have been here a long time; almost five years; but whenever you do go, it will break your old grandmother's heart. I should be expecting every day to hear that you were brought back in irons and put in jail. God help you, poor child! Let us be thankful that some time or other we shall go 'where the wicked cease from troubling, and the weary are at rest.' " My heart responded, Amen.

The fact that Dr. Flint had written to the mayor of Boston convinced me that he believed my letter to be genuine, and of course that he had no suspicion of my being any where in the vicinity. It was a great object to keep up this delusion, for it made me and my friends feel less anxious, and it would be very convenient whenever there was a chance to escape. I resolved, therefore, to continue to write letters from the north from time to time.

Two or three weeks passed, and as no news came from the mayor of Boston, grandmother began to listen to my entreaty to be allowed to leave my cell, sometimes, and exercise my limbs to prevent my becoming a cripple. I was allowed to slip down into the small storeroom, early in the morning, and remain there a little while. The room was all filled up with barrels, except a small open space under my trap-door. This faced the door, the upper part of which was of glass, and purposely left uncurtained that the curious might look in. The air of this place was close; but it was so much better than the atmosphere of my cell, that I dreaded to return. I came down as soon as it was light, and remained till eight o'clock, when people began to be about, and there was danger that some one might come on the piazza. I had tried various applications to bring warmth and feeling into my limbs, but without avail. They were so numb and stiff that it was a painful effort to move; and had my enemies come upon me during the first mornings I tried to exercise them a little in the small unoccupied space of the storeroom, it would have been impossible for me to have escaped.

ELEVEN

From *Narrative of the Life of Henry Box Brown, Written by Himself.*

As the title of this 1851 narrative indicates, Henry "Box" Brown fled slavery through truly ingenious means. Brown was born in Louisa County, Virginia, in 1815. At age fifteen, he was sent to work in Richmond, where he met his wife, Nancy, a fellow slave with whom he had three children. Their sudden sale by his master to a North Carolina slave trader in 1848 left Brown heartbroken, devastated, and determined to escape.

At Brown's request and in exchange for payment, Samuel Smith, a white shopkeeper with ties to the abolitionist movement, helped orchestrate Brown's extraordinary escape. Packaging the fugitive in a wooden box and shipped as "dry goods" via Adams Express Co., Smith arranged for Brown to be delivered to the offices of the Pennsylvania Anti-Slavery Society in Philadelphia. After traveling for twenty-seven hours, Brown arrived, having spent portions of the trip on his head. He became a popular speaker on the abolitionist circuit, often traveling with the box that was his namesake on display.

———

Originally published: Manchester: Printed by Lee and Glynn, 1851.

CHAPTER VII.

I had for a long while been a member of the choir in the Affeviar church in Richmond, but after the severe family affliction to which I have just alluded in the last chapter and the knowledge that these cruelties were perpetrated by ministers and church members, I began strongly to suspect the christianity of the slave-holding church members and hesitated much about maintaining, my connection with them. The suspicion of these slave-dealing christians was the means of keeping me absent from all their churches from the time that my wife and children were torn from me, until Christmas day in the year 1848; and I would not have gone then but being a leading member of the choir, I yielded to the entreaties of my associates to assist at a concert of sacred music which was to be got up for the benefit of the church. My friend Dr. Smith, who was the conductor of the under-ground railway, was also a member of the choir, and when I had consented to attend he assisted me in selecting twenty four pieces to be sung on the occasion.

On the day appointed for our concert I went along with Dr. Smith, and the singing commenced at half-past three o'clock, P.M. When we had sung about ten pieces and were engaged in singing the following verse—

> *Again the day returns of holy rest,*
> *Which, when he made the world, Jehovah blest;*
> *When, like his own, he bade our labours cease,*
> *And all be piety, and all be peace,*

the members were rather astonished at Dr. Smith, who stood on my right hand, suddenly closing his book, and sinking down upon his seat his eyes being at the same time filled with tears. Several of them began to inquire what was the matter with him, but he did not tell them. I guessed what it was and afterwards found out that I had judged of the circumstances correctly. Dr. Smith's feelings were overcome with a sense of doing wrongly in singing for the purpose of obtaining money to assist those who were buying and selling their fellow-men. He thought at that moment he felt reproved by Almighty God for lending his aid to the cause of slave-holding religion; and it was under this impression he closed his book and formed the resolution which he still acts upon, of never singing again or taking part in the services of a pro-slavery church. He is now in New England publicly advocating the cause of emancipation.

After we had sung several other pieces we commenced the anthem, which run thus—

> *Vital spark of heavenly flame,*
> *Quit, O! quit the mortal frame,—*

these words awakened in me feelings in which the sting of former sufferings was still sticking fast, and stimulated by the example of Dr. Smith, whose feelings I read so correctly, I too made up my mind that I would be no longer guilty of assisting those bloody dealers in the bodies and souls of men; and ever since that time I have steadfastly kept my resolution.

I now began to get weary of my bonds; and earnestly panted after liberty. I felt convinced that I should be acting in accordance with the will of God, if I could snap in sunder those bonds by which I was held body and soul as the property of a fellow man. I looked forward to the good time which every day I more and more firmly believed would yet come, when I should walk the face of the earth in full possession of all that freedom which the finger of God had so clearly written on the constitutions of man, and which was common to the human race; but of which, by the cruel hand of tyranny, I, and millions of my fellow-men, had been robbed.

I was well acquainted with a store-keeper in the city of Richmond, from whom I used to purchase my provisions; and having formed a favourable opinion of his integrity, one day in the course of a little conversation with him, I said to him if I were free I would be able to do business such as he was doing; he then told me that my occupation (a tobacconist) was a money-making one, and if I were free I had no need to change for another. I then told him my circumstances in regard to my master, having to pay him 25 dollars per month, and yet that he refused to assist me in saving my wife from being sold and taken away to the South, where I should never see her again; and even refused to allow me to go and see her until my hours of labour were over. I told him this took place about five months ago, and I had been meditating my escape from slavery since, and asked him, as no person was near us, if he could give me any information about how I should proceed. I told him I had a little money and if he would assist me I would pay him for so doing. The man asked me if I was not afraid to speak that way to him; I said no, for I imagined he believed that every man had a right to liberty. He said I was quite right, and asked me how much money I would give him if he would assist me to get away. I told him that I had 166 dollars and that I would give him the half; so we ultimately agreed that I should have his service in the attempt for 86. Now I only wanted to fix upon a plan. He told me of several plans by which others had managed to effect their escape, but none of them exactly suited my taste. I then left him to think over what would be best to be done, and, in the mean time, went to consult my friend Dr. Smith, on the subject. I mentioned the plans which the store-keeper had suggested, and as he did not approve either of them very much, I still looked for some plan which would be more certain and more safe, but I was determined that come what may, I should have my freedom or die in the attempt.

One day, while I was at work, and my thoughts were eagerly feasting upon the idea of freedom, I felt my soul called out to heaven to breathe a prayer to Almighty God. I prayed fervently that he who seeth in secret and knew the inmost desires of my heart, would lend me his aid in bursting my fetters asunder, and in restoring me to the possession of those rights, of which men had robbed me; when the idea suddenly flashed across my mind of shutting myself up in a box, and getting myself conveyed as dry goods to a free state.

Being now satisfied that this was the plan for me, I went to my friend Dr. Smith and, having acquainted him with it, we agreed to have it put

at once into execution not however without calculating the chances
of danger with which it was attended; but buoyed up by the pros-
pect of freedom and increased hatred to slavery I was willing to dare
even death itself rather than endure any longer the clanking of those
galling chains. It being still necessary to have the assistance of the
store-keeper, to see that the box was kept in its right position on its
passage, I then went to let him know my intention, but he said although he was willing to serve me in any way he could, he did not
think I could live in a box for so long a time as would be necessary to
convey me to Philadelphia, but as I had already made up my mind, he
consented to accompany me and keep the box right all the way.

My next object was to procure a box, and with the assistance of
a carpenter that was very soon accomplished, and taken to the place
where the packing was to be performed. In the mean time the store-
keeper had written to a friend in Philadelphia, but as no answer had
arrived, we resolved to carry out our purpose as best we could. It
was deemed necessary that I should get permission to be absent from
my work for a few days, in order to keep down suspicion until I had
once fairly started on the road to liberty; and as I had then a gathered
finger I thought that would form a very good excuse for obtaining
leave of absence; but when I showed it to one overseer, Mr. Allen, he
told me it was not so bad as to prevent me from working, so with a
view of making it bad enough, I got Dr. Smith to procure for me some
oil of vitriol in order to drop a little of this on it, but in my hurry I
dropped rather much and made it worse than there was any occasion
for, in fact it was very soon eaten in to the bone, and on presenting it
again to Mr. Allen I obtained the permission required, with the advice
that I should go home and get a poultice of flax-meal to it, and keep it
well poulticed until it got better. I took him instantly at his word and
went off directly to the store-keeper who had by this time received an
answer from his friend in Philadelphia, and had obtained permission
to address the box to him, this friend in that city, arranging to call
for it as soon as it should arrive. There being no time to be lost, the
store-keeper, Dr. Smith, and myself, agreed to meet next morning at

four o'clock, in order to get the box ready for the express train. The box which I had procured was three feet one inch wide, two feet six inches high, and two feet wide: and on the morning of the 29th day of March, 1849, I went into the box—having previously bored three gimlet holes opposite my face, for air, and provided myself with a bladder of water, both for the purpose of quenching my thirst and for wetting my face, should I feel getting faint. I took the gimlet also with me, in order that I might bore more holes if I found I had not sufficient air. Being thus equipped for the battle of liberty, my friends nailed down the lid and had me conveyed to the Express Office, which was about a mile distant from the place where I was packed. I had no sooner arrived at the office than I was turned heels up, while some person nailed something on the end of the box. I was then put upon a waggon and driven off to the depôt with my head down, and I had no sooner arrived at the depôt, than the man who drove the waggon tumbled me roughly into the baggage car, where, however, I happened to fall on my right side.

The next place we arrived at was Potomac Creek, where the baggage had to be removed from the cars, to be put on board the steamer; where I was again placed with my head down, and in this dreadful position had to remain nearly an hour and a half, which, from the sufferings I had thus to endure, seemed like an age to me, but I was forgetting the battle of liberty, and I was resolved to conquer or die. I felt my eyes swelling as if they would burst from their sockets; and the veins on my temples were dreadfully distended with pressure of blood upon my head. In this position I attempted to lift my hand to my face but I had no power to move it; I felt a cold sweat coming over me which seemed to be a warning that death was about to terminate my earthly miseries, but as I feared even that, less than slavery, I resolved to submit to the will of God, and under the influence of that impression, I lifted up my soul in prayer to God, who alone, was able to deliver me. My cry was soon heard, for I could hear a man saying to another, that he had travelled a long way and had been standing there two hours, and he would like to get somewhat to sit down; so perceiving my box, standing on end, he threw it down and then two sat upon it. I was thus relieved from a state of agony which may be more easily imagined than described. I could now listen to the men talking, and heard one of them asking the other what he supposed the box contained; his companion replied he guessed it was "THE MAIL." I too thought it was a mail but not such a mail as he supposed it to be.

The next place at which we arrived was the city of Washington, where I was taken from the steam-boat, and again placed upon a waggon and carried to the depôt right side up with care; but when the driver arrived at the depôt I heard him call for some person to help to take the box off the waggon, and some one answered him to the effect that he might throw it off; but, says the driver, it is marked "this side up with care;" so if I throw it off I might break something, the other answered him that it did not matter if he broke all that was in it, the railway company were able enough to pay for it. No sooner were these words spoken than I began to tumble from the waggon, and falling on the end where my head was, I could hear my neck give a crack, as if it had been snapped asunder and I was knocked completely insensible. The first thing I heard after that, was some person saying, "There is no room for the box, it will have to remain and be sent through to-morrow with the luggage train"; but the Lord had not quite forsaken me, for in answer to my earnest prayer He so ordered affairs that I should not be left behind; and I now heard a man say that the box had come with the express, and it must be sent on. I was then tumbled into the car with my head downwards again, but the car had not proceeded far before, more luggage having to be taken in, my box got shifted about and so happened to turn upon its right side; and in this position I remained till I got to Philadelphia, of our arrival in which place I was informed by hearing some person say, "We are in port and at Philadelphia." My heart then leaped for joy, and I wondered if any person knew that such a box was there.

Here it may be proper to observe that the man who had promised to accompany my box failed to do what he promised; but, to prevent it remaining long at the station after its arrival, he sent a telegraphic message to his friend, and I was only twenty seven hours in the box, though travelling a distance of three hundred and fifty miles.

I was now placed in the depot amongst the other luggage, where I lay till seven o'clock p.m., at which time a waggon drove up, and I heard a person inquire for such a box as that in which I was. I was then placed on a waggon and conveyed to the house where my friend in Richmond had arranged I should be received. A number of persons soon collected round the box after it was taken in to the house, but as I did not know what was going on I kept myself quiet. I heard a man say, "Let us rap upon the box and see if he is alive"; and immediately a rap ensued and a voice said, tremblingly, "Is all right within?" to which I replied—"All right." The joy of the friends was very great; when they heard that I was alive they soon managed to break open the box, and then came my resurrection from the grave of slavery. I rose a freeman, but I was too weak, by reason of long confinement in that box, to be able to stand, so I immediately swooned away. After my recovery from the swoon the first thing, which arrested my attention, was the presence of a number of friends, every one seeming more anxious than another, to have an opportunity of rendering me their assistance, and of bidding me a hearty welcome to the possession of my natural rights, I had risen as it were from the dead; I felt much more than I could readily express; but as the kindness of Almighty God had been so conspicuously shown in my deliverance, I burst forth into the following him of thanksgiving,

> *I waited patiently, I waited patiently for the Lord, for the Lord;*
> *And he inclined unto me, and heard my calling:*
> *I waited patiently, I waited patiently for the Lord,*
> *And he inclined unto me, and heard my calling:*
> *And he hath put a new song in my mouth,*
> *Even a thanksgiving, even a thanksgiving, even a thanks-*
>   *giving unto our God.*
> *Blessed, Blessed, Blessed, Blessed is the man, Blessed is the*
>   *man,*

Blessed is the man that hath set his hope, his hope in the Lord;
[torn page] my God, Great, Great, Great,
Great are the wondrous works which thou hast done.
Great are the wondrous works which thou hast done, which
    thou hast done: If I should declare them and speak of
    them, they would be more, more, more than I am able
    to express.
I have not kept back thy loving kindness and truth from the
    great congregation. I have not kept back thy loving
    kindness and truth from the great congregation.
Withdraw not thou thy mercy from me,
Withdraw not thou thy mercy from me, O Lord;
Let thy loving kindness and thy truth always preserve me,
Let all those that seek thee be joyful and glad,
Let all those that seek thee be joyful and glad, be joyful, and
    glad, be joyful and glad, be joyful, be joyful, be joyful,
    be joyful, be joyful and glad—be glad in thee.
And let such as love thy salvation,
And let such as love thy salvation, say, always,
The Lord be praised,
The Lord be praised.
Let all those that seek thee be joyful and glad,
And let such as love thy salvation, say always,
The Lord be praised,
The Lord be praised,
The Lord be praised.

I was then taken by the hand and welcomed to the houses of the following friends:—Mr. J. Miller, Mr. M'Kim, Mr. and Mrs. Motte, Mr. and Mrs. Davis, and many others, by all of whom I was treated in the kindest manner possible. But it was thought proper that I should not remain long in Philadelphia, so arrangements were made for me to proceed to Massachusetts, where, by the assistance of a few Anti-slavery friends, I was enabled shortly after to arrive. I went to New

York, where I became acquainted with Mr. H. Long, and Mr. Eli Smith, who were very kind to me the whole time I remained there. My next journey was to New Bedford, where I remained some weeks under the care of Mr. H. Ricketson, my finger being still bad from the effects of the oil of vitriol with which I dressed it before I left Richmond. While I was here I heard of a great Anti-slavery meeting which was to take place in Boston, and being anxious to identify myself with that public movement, I proceeded there and had the pleasure of meeting the hearty sympathy of thousands to whom I related the story of my escape. I have since attended large meetings in different towns in the states of Maine, New Hampshire, Vermont, Connecticut, Rhode Island, Pennsylvania, and New York, in all of which places I have found many friends and have endeavoured, according to the best of my abilities, to advocate the cause of the emancipation of the slave; with what success I will not pretend to say—but with a daily increasing confidence in the humanity and justice of my cause, and in the assurance of the approbation of Almighty God.

I have composed the following song in commemoration of my fete in the box:—

Air:—"UNCLE NED."

I.

Here you see a man by the name of Henry Brown,
Ran away from the South to the North;
Which he would not have done but they stole all his rights,
But they'll never do the like again.
Chorus—Brown laid down the shovel and the hoe,
Down in the box he did go;
No more Slave work for Henry Box Brown,
In the box by Express he did go.

II.

Then the orders they were given, and the cars did start away;
Roll along—roll along—roll along,

Down to the landing, where the steamboat lay,
To bear the baggage off to the north.
CHORUS.

III.

When they packed the baggage on, they turned him on his head,
There poor Brown liked to have died;
There were passengers on board who wished to sit down,
And they turned the box down on its side.
CHORUS

IV.

When they got to the cars they threw the box off,
And down upon his head he did fall,
Then he heard his neck crack, and he thought it was broke,
But they never threw him off any more.
CHORUS.

V.

When they got to Philadelphia they said he was in port,
And Brown then began to feel glad,
He was taken on the waggon to his final destination,
And left, "this side up with care."
CHORUS.

VI.

The friends gathered round and asked if all was right,
As down on the box they did rap,
Brown answered them, saying; "yes all is right!"
He was then set free from his pain.
CHORUS.

TWELVE

From *Running a Thousand Miles for Freedom; or, the Escape of William and Ellen Craft from Slavery.*

Published in 1860, William Craft's memoir of escape from slavery with his wife, Ellen, is one of the most extraordinary fugitive accounts ever written. Born to a biracial slave mother and her mother's master, Ellen was so light in appearance that she was mistaken as one of her master's white family members. In order to alleviate the problem, Ellen's mistress gave the eleven-year-old as a gift to a daughter in Macon, Georgia, where Ellen met William. The couple was married in 1846, when Ellen was twenty. Before starting a family, however, the Crafts were determined to have their freedom and to raise their children as freed people.

Escape from slavery, an enormous challenge for any black, was further complicated for the Crafts by the great distance that the nearest free state, Pennsylvania, was from their home in Georgia. Running away required traveling through a series of slave states and involved the considerable risk at every step of being apprehended and returned as fugitives to their master. There was also the obstacle of neither William nor Ellen being able to read or write.

Originally published: London: William Tweedie, 337, Strand. 1860.

During the Christmas holiday season of 1848, the Crafts devised an incredible and dangerous plan to secure their freedom: Ellen would disguise herself as a white male slave-owner—complete with suit and spectacles befitting a gentleman of the time—who was traveling with her slave companion (William) to Philadelphia. The risk of exposure was heightened by the fact that the couple had to employ public transportation and accommodations the entire way. Their ultimate triumph makes their story a classic in fugitive slave literature.

PART 1.

. . . My wife was torn from her mother's embrace in childhood, and taken to a distant part of the country. She had seen so many other children separated from their parents in this cruel manner, that the mere thought of her ever becoming the mother of a child, to linger out a miserable existence under the wretched system of American slavery, appeared to fill her very soul with horror; and as she had taken what I felt to be an important view of her condition, I did not, at first, press the marriage, but agreed to assist her in trying to devise some plan by which we might escape from our unhappy condition, and then be married.

We thought of plan after plan, but they all seemed crowded with insurmountable difficulties. We knew it was unlawful for any public conveyance to take us as passengers, without our master's consent. We were also perfectly aware of the startling fact, that had we left without this consent the professional slave-hunters would have soon had their ferocious bloodhounds baying on our track, and in a short time we should have been dragged back to slavery, not to fill the more favourable situations which we had just left, but to be separated for life, and put to the very meanest and most laborious drudgery; or else have been tortured to death as examples, in order to strike terror into the hearts of others, and thereby prevent them from even attempting to escape from their cruel taskmasters. It is a fact worthy of remark, that nothing seems to give the slaveholders so much pleasure as the catching and torturing of fugitives. They had much rather take the keen and poisonous lash, and with it cut their poor trembling victims to atoms, than allow one of them to escape to a free country, and expose the infamous system from which he fled.

The greatest excitement prevails at a slave-hunt. The slaveholders and their hired ruffians appear to take more pleasure in this inhuman pursuit than English sportsmen do in chasing a fox or a stag. Therefore, knowing what we should have been compelled to suffer, if caught and taken back, we were more than anxious to hit upon a plan that would lead us safely to a land of liberty.

But, after puzzling our brains for years, we were reluctantly driven to the sad conclusion, that it was almost impossible to escape from slavery in Georgia, and travel 1,000 miles across the slave States. We therefore resolved to get the consent of our owners, be married, settle down in slavery, and endeavour to make ourselves as comfortable as possible under that system; but at the same time ever to keep our dim eyes steadily fixed upon the glimmering hope of liberty, and earnestly pray God mercifully to assist us to escape from our unjust thraldom.

We were married, and prayed and toiled on till December, 1848, at which time (as I have stated) a plan suggested itself that proved quite successful, and in eight days after it was first thought of we were free from the horrible trammels of slavery, and glorifying God who had brought us safely out of a land of bondage.

Knowing that slaveholders have the privilege of taking their slaves to any part of the country they think proper, it occurred to me that, as my wife was nearly white, I might get her to disguise herself as an invalid gentleman, and assume to be my master, while I could attend as his slave, and that in this manner we might effect our escape. After I thought of the plan, I suggested it to my wife, but at first she shrank from the idea. She thought it was almost impossible for her to assume that disguise, and travel a distance of 1,000 miles across the slave

States. However, on the other hand, she also thought of her condition. She saw that the laws under which we lived did not recognize her to be a woman, but a mere chattel, to be bought and sold, or otherwise dealt with as her owner might see fit. Therefore the more she contemplated her helpless condition, the more anxious she was to escape from it. So she said, "I think it is almost too much for us to undertake; however, I feel that God is on our side, and with his assistance, notwithstanding all the difficulties, we shall be able to succeed. Therefore, if you will purchase the disguise, I will try to carry out the plan."

But after I concluded to purchase the disguise, I was afraid to go to any one to ask him to sell me the articles. It is unlawful in Georgia for a white man to trade with slaves without the master's consent. But, notwithstanding this, many persons will sell a slave any article that he can get the money to buy. Not that they sympathize with the slave, but merely because his testimony is not admitted in court against a free white person.

Therefore, with little difficulty I went to different parts of the town, at odd times, and purchased things piece by piece, (except the trowsers which she found necessary to make,) and took them home to the house where my wife resided. She being a ladies' maid, and a favourite slave in the family, was allowed a little room to herself; and amongst other pieces of furniture which I had made in my overtime, was a chest of drawers; so when I took the articles home, she locked them up carefully in these drawers. No one about the premises knew that she had anything of the kind. So when we fancied we had everything ready the time was fixed for the flight. But we knew it would not do to start off without first getting our master's consent to be away for a few days. Had we left without this, they would soon have had us back into slavery, and probably we should never have got another fair opportunity of even attempting to escape.

Some of the best slaveholders will sometimes give their favourite slaves a few days' holiday at Christmas time; so, after no little amount of perseverance on my wife's part, she obtained a pass from her mistress, allowing her to be away for a few days. The cabinet-maker with whom I worked gave me a similar paper, but said that he needed my services very much, and wished me to return as soon as the time granted was up. I thanked him kindly; but somehow I have not been able to make it convenient to return yet; and, as the free air of good old England agrees so well with my wife and our dear little ones, as well as with myself, it is not at all likely we shall return at present to the "peculiar institution" of chains and stripes.

On reaching my wife's cottage she handed me her pass, and I showed mine, but at that time neither of us were able to read them. It is not only unlawful for slaves to be taught to read, but in some of the States there are heavy penalties attached, such as fines and imprisonment, which will be vigorously enforced upon any one who is humane enough to violate the so-called law. . . .

However, at first, we were highly delighted at the idea of having gained permission to be absent for a few days; but when the thought flashed across my wife's mind, that it was customary for travellers to register their names in the visitors' book at hotels, as well as in the clearance or Custom-house book at Charleston, South Carolina—it made our spirits droop within us.

So, while sitting in our little room upon the verge of despair, all at once my wife raised her head, and with a smile upon her face, which was a moment before bathed in tears, said, "I think I have it!" I asked what it was. She said, "I think I can make a poultice and bind up my right hand in a sling, and with propriety ask the officers to register my name for me." I thought that would do.

It then occurred to her that the smoothness of her face might betray her; so she decided to make another poultice, and put it in a white handkerchief to be worn under the chin, up the cheeks, and to tie over the head. This nearly hid the expression of the countenance, as well as the beardless chin.

The poultice is left off in the engraving, because the likeness could not have been taken well with it on.

My wife, knowing that she would be thrown a good deal into the company of gentlemen, fancied that she could get on better if she had something to go over the eyes; so I went to a shop and bought a pair of green spectacles. This was in the evening.

We sat up all night discussing the plan, and making preparations. Just before the time arrived, in the morning, for us to leave, I cut off my wife's hair square at the back of the head, and got her to dress in the disguise and stand out on the floor. I found that she made a most respectable looking gentleman.

My wife had no ambition whatever to assume this disguise, and would not have done so had it been possible to have obtained our liberty by more simple means; but we knew it was not customary in the South for ladies to travel with male servants; and therefore, notwithstanding my wife's fair complexion, it would have been a very difficult task for her to have come off as a free white lady, with me as her slave; in fact, her not being able to write would have made this quite impossible. We knew that no public conveyance would take us, or any other slave, as a passenger, without our master's consent. This consent could never be obtained to pass into a free State. My wife's being muffled in the poultices, &c., furnished a plausible excuse for avoiding general conversation, of which most Yankee travellers are passionately fond.

There are a large number of free negroes residing in the southern States; but in Georgia (and I believe in all the slave States,) every coloured person's complexion is prima facie evidence of his being a slave; and the lowest villain in the country, should he be a white man, has the legal power to arrest, and question, in the most inquisitorial and insulting manner, any coloured person, male or female, that he may find at large, particularly at night and on Sundays, without a written pass, signed by the master or some one in authority; or stamped free papers, certifying that the person is the rightful owner of himself.

If the coloured person refuses to answer questions put to him, he may be beaten, and his defending himself against this attack makes him an outlaw, and if he be killed on the spot, the murderer will be exempted from all blame; but after the coloured person has answered the questions put to him, in a most humble and pointed manner, he may then be taken to prison; and should it turn out, after further examination, that he was caught where he had no permission or legal right to be, and that he has not given what they term a satisfactory account of himself, the master will have to pay a fine. On his refusing to do this, the poor slave may be legally and severely flogged by public officers. Should the prisoner prove to be a free man, he is most likely to be both whipped and fined.

The great majority of slaveholders hate this class of persons with a hatred that can only be equalled by the condemned spirits of the infernal regions. They have no mercy upon, nor sympathy for, any negro whom they cannot enslave. They say that God made the black man to be a slave for the white, and act as though they really believed that all free persons of colour are in open rebellion to a direct command from heaven, and that they (the whites) are God's chosen agents to pour out upon them unlimited vengeance. For instance, a Bill has been introduced in the Tennessee Legislature to prevent free negroes from travelling on the railroads in that State. It has passed the first reading. The bill provides that the President who shall permit a free negro to travel on any road within the jurisdiction of the State under his supervision shall pay a fine of 500 dollars; any conductor permitting a violation of the Act shall pay 250 dollars; provided such free negro is not under the control of a free white citizen of Tennessee, who will vouch for the character of said free negro in a penal bond of one thousand dollars. The State of Arkansas has passed a law to banish all free negroes from its bounds, and it came into effect on the 1st day of January, 1860. Every free negro found there after that date will be liable to be sold into slavery, the crime of freedom being unpardonable. The Missouri Senate has before it a bill providing that all free negroes above the age of eighteen years who shall be found in the State after September, 1860, shall be sold into slavery; and that all such negroes as shall enter the State after September, 1861, and remain there twenty-four hours, shall also be sold into slavery for ever. Mississippi, Kentucky, and Georgia, and in fact, I believe, all the slave

States, are legislating in the same manner. Thus the slaveholders make it almost impossible for free persons of colour to get out of the slave States, in order that they may sell them into slavery if they don't go. If no white persons travelled upon railroads except those who could get some one to vouch for their character in a penal bond of one thousand dollars, the railroad companies would soon go to the "wall." Such mean legislation is too low for comment; therefore I leave the villainous acts to speak for themselves.

But the Dred Scott decision is the crowning act of infamous Yankee legislation. The Supreme Court, the highest tribunal of the Republic, composed of nine Judge Jeffries's, chosen both from the free and slave States, has decided that no coloured person, or persons of African extraction, can ever become a citizen of the United States, or have any rights which white men are bound to respect. That is to say, in the opinion of this Court, robbery, rape, and murder are not crimes when committed by a white upon a coloured person.

Judges who will sneak from their high and honourable position down into the lowest depths of human depravity, and scrape up a decision like this, are wholly unworthy the confidence of any people. I believe such men would, if they had the power, and were it to their temporal interest, sell their country's independence, and barter away every man's birthright for a mess of pottage. Well may Thomas Campbell say—

> *United States, your banner wears,*
> *Two emblems,—one of fame;*
> *Alas, the other that it bears*
> *Reminds us of your shame!*
> *The white man's liberty in types*
> *Stands blazoned by your stars;*
> *But what's the meaning of your stripes?*
> *They mean your Negro-scars.*

When the time had arrived for us to start, we blew out the lights, knelt down, and prayed to our Heavenly Father mercifully to assist us, as he did his people of old, to escape from cruel bondage; and we shall ever feel that God heard and answered our prayer. Had we not been sustained by a kind, and I sometimes think special, providence, we could never have overcome the mountainous difficulties which I am now about to describe.

After this we rose and stood for a few moments in breathless silence,—we were afraid that some one might have been about the cottage listening and watching our movements. So I took my wife by the hand, stepped softly to the door, raised the latch, drew it open, and peeped out. Though there were trees all around the house, yet the foliage scarcely moved; in fact, everything appeared to be as still as death. I then whispered to my wife, "Come my dear, let us make a desperate leap for liberty!" But poor thing, she shrank back, in a state of trepidation. I turned and asked what was the matter; she made no reply, but burst into violent sobs, and threw her head upon my breast. This appeared to touch my very heart, it caused me to enter into her feelings more fully than ever. We both saw the many mountainous difficulties that rose one after the other before our view, and knew far too well what our sad fate would have been, were we caught and forced back into our slavish den. Therefore on my wife's fully realizing the solemn fact that we had to take our lives, as it were, in our hands, and contest every inch of the thousand miles of slave territory over which we had to pass, it made her heart almost sink within her, and, had I known them at that time, I would have repeated the following encouraging lines, which may not be out of place here—

> *The hill, though high, I covet to ascend,*
> *The difficulty will not me offend;*
> *For I perceive the way to life lies here:*
> *Come, pluck up heart, let's neither faint nor fear;*
> *Better, though difficult, the right way to go,—*
> *Than wrong, though easy, where the end is woe.*

However, the sobbing was soon over, and after a few moments of silent prayer she recovered her self-possession, and said, "Come,

William, it is getting late, so now let us venture upon our perilous journey."

We then opened the door, and stepped as softly out as "moonlight upon the water." I locked the door with my own key, which I now have before me, and tiptoed across the yard into the street. I say tiptoed, because we were like persons near a tottering avalanche, afraid to move, or even breathe freely, for fear the sleeping tyrants should be aroused, and come down upon us with double vengeance, for daring to attempt to escape in the manner which we contemplated.

We shook hands, said farewell, and started in different directions for the railway station. I took the nearest possible way to the train, for fear I should be recognized by some one, and got into the negro car in which I knew I should have to ride; but my master (as I will now call my wife) took a longer way round, and only arrived there with the bulk of the passengers. He obtained a ticket for himself and one for his slave to Savannah, the first port, which was about two hundred miles off. My master then had the luggage stowed away, and stepped into one of the best carriages.

But just before the train moved off I peeped through the window, and, to my great astonishment, I saw the cabinet-maker with whom I had worked so long, on the platform. He stepped up to the ticket-seller, and asked some question, and then commenced looking rapidly through the passengers, and into the carriages. Fully believing that we were caught, I shrank into a corner, turned my face from the door, and expected in a moment to be dragged out. The cabinet-maker looked into my master's carriage, but did not know him in his new attire, and, as God would have it, before he reached mine the bell rang, and the train moved off.

I have heard since that the cabinet-maker had a presentiment that we were about to "make tracks for parts unknown;" but, not seeing me, his suspicions vanished, until he received the startling intelligence that we had arrived safely in a free State.

As soon as the train had left the platform, my master looked round in the carriage, and was terror-stricken to find a Mr. Cray—an old friend of my wife's master, who dined with the family the day before, and knew my wife from childhood—sitting on the same seat.

The doors of the American railway carriages are at the ends. The passengers walk up the aisle, and take seats on either side: and as my master was engaged in looking out of the window, he did not see who came in.

My master's first impression, after seeing Mr. Cray, was, that he was there for the purpose of securing him. However, my master thought it was not wise to give any information respecting himself, and for fear that Mr. Cray might draw him into conversation and recognise his voice, my master resolved to feign deafness as the only means of self-defence.

After a little while, Mr. Cray said to my master, "It is a very fine morning, sir." The latter took no notice, but kept looking out of the window. Mr. Cray soon repeated this remark, in a little louder tone, but my master remained as before. This indifference attracted the attention of the passengers near, one of whom laughed out. This, I suppose, annoyed the old gentleman; so he said, "I will make him hear;" and in a loud tone of voice repeated, "It is a very fine morning, sir."

My master turned his head, and with a polite bow said, "Yes," and commenced looking out of the window again.

One of the gentlemen remarked that it was a very great deprivation to be deaf. "Yes," replied Mr. Cray, "and I shall not trouble that fellow any more." This enabled my master to breathe a little easier, and to feel that Mr. Cray was not his pursuer after all.

The gentlemen then turned the conversation upon the three great topics of discussion in first-class circles in Georgia, namely, Niggers, Cotton, and the Abolitionists.

My master had often heard of abolitionists, but in such a connection as to cause him to think that they were a fearful kind of wild animal. But he was highly delighted to learn, from the gentlemen's conversation, that the abolitionists were persons who were opposed to oppression; and therefore, in his opinion, not the lowest, but the very highest, of God's creatures.

Without the slightest objection on my master's part, the gentlemen left the carriage at Gordon, for Milledgeville (the capital of the State).

We arrived at Savannah early in the evening, and got into an omnibus, which stopped at the hotel for the passengers to take tea. I stepped into the house and brought my master something on a tray to the omnibus, which took us in due time to the steamer, which was bound for Charleston, South Carolina.

Soon after going on board, my master turned in; and as the captain and some of the passengers seemed to think this strange, and also questioned me respecting him, my master thought I had better get out the flannels and opodeldoc which we had prepared for the rheumatism, warm them quickly by the stove in the gentleman's saloon, and bring them to his berth. We did this as an excuse for my master's retiring to bed so early.

While at the stove one of the passengers said to me, "Buck, what have you got there?" "Opodeldoc, sir," I replied. "I should think it's opo-devil," said a lanky swell, who was leaning back in a chair with his heels upon the back of another, and chewing tobacco as if for a wager; "it stinks enough to kill or cure twenty men. Away with it, or I reckon I will throw it overboard!"

It was by this time warm enough, so I took it to my master's berth, remained there a little while, and then went on deck and asked the steward where I was to sleep. He said there was no place provided for coloured passengers, whether slave or free. So I paced the deck till a late hour, then mounted some cotton bags, in a warm place near the funnel, sat there till morning, and then went and assisted my master to get ready for breakfast.

He was seated at the right hand of the captain, who, together with all the passengers, inquired very kindly after his health. As my master had one hand in a sling, it was my duty to carve his food. But when I went out the captain said, "You have a very attentive boy, sir; but you had better watch him like a hawk when you get on to the North. He seems all very well here, but he may act quite differently there. I know several gentlemen who have lost their valuable niggers among them d—d cut-throat abolitionists."

Before my master could speak, a rough slave-dealer, who was sitting opposite, with both elbows on the table, and with a large piece of broiled fowl in his fingers, shook his head with emphasis, and in a deep Yankee tone, forced through his crowded mouth the words, "Sound doctrine, captain, very sound." He then dropped the chicken into the plate, leant back, placed his thumbs in the armholes of his fancy waistcoat, and continued, "I would not take a nigger to the North under no consideration. I have had a deal to do with niggers in my time, but I never saw one who ever had his heel upon free soil that was worth a d—n." "Now stranger," addressing my master, "if you have made up your mind to sell that ere nigger, I am your man; just mention your price, and if it isn't out of the way, I will pay for him on this board with hard silver dollars." This hard-featured, bristly-bearded, wire-headed, red-eyed monster, staring at my master as the serpent did at Eve, said, "What do you say, stranger?" He replied, "I don't wish to sell, sir; I cannot get on well without him."

"You will have to get on without him if you take him to the North," continued this man; "for I can tell ye, stranger, as a friend, I am an older cove than you, I have seen lots of this ere world, and I reckon I have had more dealings with niggers than any man living or dead. I was once employed by General Wade Hampton, for ten years, in doing nothing but breaking 'em in; and everybody knows that the General would not have a man that didn't understand his business. So I tell ye, stranger, again, you had better sell, and let me take him down to Orleans. He will do you no good if you take him across Mason's and Dixon's line; he is a keen nigger, and I can see from the cut of his eye that he is certain to run away." My master said, "I think not, sir; I have great confidence in his fidelity." "Fi-devil," indignantly said the dealer, as his fist came down upon the edge of the saucer and upset a cup of hot coffee in a gentleman's lap. (As the scalded man jumped up the trader quietly said, "Don't disturb yourself, neighbour; accidents will happen in the best of families.") "It always makes me mad to hear a man talking about fidelity in niggers. There isn't a d—d one on 'em who wouldn't cut sticks, if he had half a chance."

By this time we were near Charleston; my master thanked the captain for his advice, and they all withdrew and went on deck, where the trader fancied he became quite eloquent. He drew a crowd around him, and with emphasis said, "Cap'en, if I was the President of this mighty United States of America, the greatest and freest country under the whole universe, I would never let no man, I don't care who he is, take a nigger into the North and bring him back here, filled to the brim, as he is sure to be, with d—d abolition vices, to taint all quiet niggers with the hellish spirit of running away. These air, cap'en, my flat-footed, every day, right up and down sentiments, and as this is a free country, cap'en, I don't care who hears 'em; for I am a Southern man, every inch on me to the backbone." "Good!" said an insignificant-looking individual of the slave-dealer stamp. "Three cheers for John C. Calhoun and the whole fair sunny South!" added the trader. So off went their hats, and out burst a terrific roar of irregular but continued cheering. My master took no more notice of the dealer. He merely said to the captain that the air on deck was too keen for him, and he would therefore return to the cabin.

While the trader was in the zenith of his eloquence, he might as well have said, as one of his kit did, at a great Filibustering meeting, that "When the great American Eagle gets one of his mighty claws upon Canada and the other into South America, and his glorious and starry wings of liberty extending from the Atlantic to the Pacific, oh! then, where will England be, ye gentlemen? I tell ye, she will only serve as a pocket-handkerchief for Jonathan to wipe his nose with."

On my master entering the cabin he found at the breakfast-table a young southern military officer, with whom he had travelled some distance the previous day.

After passing the usual compliments the conversation turned upon the old subject,—niggers.

The officer, who was also travelling with a man-servant, said to my master, "You will excuse me, Sir, for saying I think you are very likely to spoil your boy by saying 'thank you' to him. I assure you, sir, nothing spoils a slave so soon as saying, 'thank you' and 'if you please' to him. The only way to make a nigger toe the mark, and to keep him in his place, is to storm at him like thunder, and keep him trembling like a leaf. Don't you see, when I speak to my Nod, he darts like lightning; and if he didn't I'd skin him."

Just then the poor dejected slave came in, and the officer swore at him fearfully, merely to teach my master what he called the proper way to treat me.

After he had gone out to get his master's luggage ready, the officer said, "That is the way to speak to them. If every nigger was drilled in this manner, they would be as humble as dogs, and never dare to run away."

The gentleman urged my master not to go to the North for the restoration of his health, but to visit the Warm Springs in Arkansas.

My master said, he thought the air of Philadelphia would suit his complaint best; and, not only so, he thought he could get better advice there.

The boat had now reached the wharf. The officer wished my master a safe and pleasant journey, and left the saloon.

There were a large number of persons on the quay waiting the arrival of the steamer but we were afraid to venture out for fear that some one might recognize me; or that they had heard that we were gone, and had telegraphed to have us stopped. However, after remaining in the cabin till all the other passengers were gone, we had our luggage placed on a fly, and I took my master by the arm, and with a little difficulty he hobbled on shore, got in and drove off to the best hotel, which John C. Calhoun, and all the other great southern fire-eating statesmen, made their head-quarters while in Charleston.

On arriving at the house the landlord ran out and opened the door: but judging, from the poultices and green glasses, that my master was an invalid, he took him very tenderly by one arm and ordered his man to take the other.

My master then eased himself out, and with their assistance found no trouble in getting up the steps into the hotel. The proprietor made me stand on one side, while he paid my master the attention and homage he thought a gentleman of his high position merited.

My master asked for a bed-room. The servant was ordered to show a good one, into which we helped him. The servant returned. My master then handed me the bandages, I took them downstairs in great haste, and told the landlord my master wanted two hot poultices as quickly as possible. He rang the bell, the servant came in, to whom he said, "Run to the kitchen and tell the cook to make two hot poultices right off, for there is a gentleman upstairs very badly off indeed!"

In a few minutes the smoking poultices were brought in. I placed them in white handkerchiefs, and hurried upstairs, went into my master's apartment, shut the door, and laid them on the mantel-piece. As he was alone for a little while, he thought he could rest a great deal better with the poultices off. However, it was necessary to have them to complete the remainder of the journey. I then ordered dinner, and took my master's boots out to polish them. While doing so I entered into conversation with one of the slaves. I may state here, that on the sea-coast of South Carolina and Georgia the slaves speak worse English than in any other part of the country. This is owing to the frequent importation, or smuggling in, of Africans, who mingle with the natives. Consequently the language cannot properly be called English or African, but a corruption of the two.

The shrewd son of African parents to whom I referred said to me, "Say, brudder, way you come from, and which side you goin day wid dat ar little don up buckra" (white man)?

I replied, "To Philadelphia."

"What!" he exclaimed, with astonishment, "to Philumadelphy?"

"Yes," I said.

"By squash! I wish I was going wid you! I hears um say dat dare's no slaves way over in dem parts; is um so?"

I quietly said, "I have heard the same thing."

"Well," continued he, as he threw down the boot and brush, and, placing his hands in his pockets, strutted across the floor with an air of independence—"Gorra Mighty, dem is de parts for Pompey; and I hope when you get dare you will stay, and nebber follow dat buckra back to dis hot quarter no more, let him be eber so good."

I thanked him; and just as I took the boots up and started off, he caught my hand between his two, and gave it a hearty shake, and, with tears streaming down his cheeks, said: —

"God bless you, broder, and may de Lord be wid you. When you gets de freedom, and sitin under your own wine and fig-tree, don't forget to pray for poor Pompey."

I was afraid to say much to him, but I shall never forget his earnest request, nor fail to do what little I can to release the millions of unhappy bondmen, of whom he was one.

At the proper time my master had the poultices placed on, came down, and seated himself at a table in a very brilliant dining-room, to have his dinner. I had to have something at the same time, in order to be ready for the boat; so they gave me my dinner in an old broken plate, with a rusty knife and fork, and said, "Here, boy, you go in the kitchen." I took it and went out, but did not stay more than a few minutes, because I was in a great hurry to get back to see how the invalid was getting on. On arriving I found two or three servants waiting on him; but as he did not feel able to make a very hearty dinner, he soon finished, paid the bill, and gave the servants each a trifle, which caused one of them to say to me, "Your massa is a big bug"— meaning a gentleman of distinction—"he is the greatest gentleman dat has been dis way for dis six months." I said, "Yes, he is some pumpkins," meaning the same as "big bug."

When we left Maçon, it was our intention to take a steamer at Charleston through to Philadelphia; but on arriving there we found that the vessels did not run during the winter, and I have no doubt it was well for us they did not; for on the very last voyage the steamer made that we intended to go by, a fugitive was discovered secreted on board, and sent back to slavery. However, as we had also heard of the Overland Mail Route, we were all right. So I ordered a fly to the door, had the luggage placed on; we got in, and drove down to the Custom-house Office, which was near the wharf where we had to obtain tickets, to take a steamer for Wilmington, North Carolina. When we reached the building, I helped my master into the office, which was crowded with passengers. He asked for a ticket for himself and one for his slave to Philadelphia. This caused the principal officer—a very mean-looking, cheese-coloured fellow, who was sitting there—to look up at us very suspiciously, and in a fierce tone of voice he said to me, "Boy, do you belong to that gentleman?" I quickly replied, "Yes, sir" (which was quite correct). The tickets were handed out, and as my master was paying for them the chief man said to him, "I wish you to register your name here, sir, and also the name of your nigger, and pay a dollar duty on him."

My master paid the dollar, and pointing to the hand that was in the poultice, requested the officer to register his name for him. This seemed to offend the "high-bred" South Carolinian. He jumped up, shaking his head; and, cramming his hands almost through the bottom of his trousers pockets, with a slave-bullying air, said, "I shan't do it."

This attracted the attention of all the passengers. Just then the young military officer with whom my master travelled and conversed on the steamer from Savannah stepped in, somewhat the worse for brandy; he shook hands with my master, and pretended to know all about him. He said, "I know his kin (friends) like a book;" and as the officer was known in Charleston, and was going to stop there with friends, the recognition was very much in my master's favour.

The captain of the steamer, a good-looking jovial fellow, seeing that the gentleman appeared to know my master, and perhaps not wishing to lose us as passengers, said in an off-hand sailor-like manner, "I will register the gentleman's name, and take the responsibility upon myself." He asked my master's name. He said, "William Johnson." The names were put down, I think, "Mr. Johnson and slave." The captain said, "It's all right now, Mr. Johnson." He thanked him kindly, and the young officer begged my master to go with him, and have something to drink and a cigar; but as he had not acquired these accomplishments, he excused himself, and we went on board and came off to Wilmington, North Carolina. When the gentleman finds out his mistake, he will, I have no doubt, be careful in future not to pretend to have an intimate acquaintance with an entire stranger. During the voyage the captain said, "It was rather sharp shooting this morning, Mr. Johnson. It was not out of any disrespect to you, sir; but they make it a rule to be very strict at Charleston. I have known families to be detained there with their slaves till reliable information could be received respecting them. If they were not very careful, and d—d abolitionist might take off a lot of valuable niggers."

My master said, "I suppose so," and thanked him again for helping him over the difficulty.

We reached Wilmington the next morning, and took the train for Richmond, Virginia. I have stated that the American railway carriages (or cars, as they are called), are constructed differently to those in England. At one end of some of them, in the South, there is a little apartment with a couch on both sides for the convenience of families and invalids; and as they thought my master was very poorly, he was allowed to enter one of these apartments at Petersburg, Virginia, where an old gentleman and two handsome young ladies, his daughters, also got in, and took seats in the same carriage. But before the train started, the gentleman stepped into my car, and questioned me respecting my master. He wished to know what was the matter with him, where he was from, and where he was going. I told him where he came from, and said that he was suffering from a complication of complaints, and was going to Philadelphia, where he thought he could get more suitable advice than in Georgia.

The gentleman said my master could obtain the very best advice in Philadelphia. Which turned out to be quite correct, though he did not receive it from physicians, but from kind abolitionists who understood his case much better. The gentleman also said, "I reckon your master's father hasn't any more such faithful and smart boys as you." "O, yes, sir, he has," I replied, "lots of 'em." Which was literally true. This seemed all he wished to know. He thanked me, gave me a ten-cent piece, and requested me to be attentive to my good master.

I promised that I would do so, and have ever since endeavoured to keep my pledge. During the gentleman's absence, the ladies and my master had a little cosy chat. But on his return, he said, "You seem to be very much afflicted, sir." "Yes, sir," replied the gentleman in the poultices. "What seems to be the matter with you, sir; may I be allowed to ask?" "Inflammatory rheumatism, sir." "Oh! that is very bad, sir," said the kind gentleman: "I can sympathise with you; for I know from bitter experience what the rheumatism is." If he did, he knew a good deal more than Mr. Johnson.

The gentleman thought my master would feel better if he would lie down and rest himself; and as he was anxious to avoid conversation, he at once acted upon this suggestion. The ladies politely rose, took their extra shawls, and made a nice pillow for the invalid's head. My master wore a fashionable cloth cloak, which they took and covered him comfortably on the couch. After he had been lying a little while the ladies, I suppose, thought he was asleep; so one of them gave a long sigh, and said, in a quiet fascinating tone, "Papa, he seems to be a very nice young gentleman." But before papa could speak, the other lady quickly said, "Oh! dear me, I never felt so much for a gentleman in my life!" To use an American expression, "They fell in love with the wrong chap."

After my master had been lying a little while he got up, the gentleman assisted him in getting on his cloak, the ladies took their shawls, and soon all were seated. They then insisted upon Mr. Johnson taking some of their refreshments, which of course he did, out of courtesy to the ladies. All went on enjoying themselves until they reached Richmond, where the ladies and their father left the train. But, before doing so, the good old Virginian gentleman, who appeared to be much pleased with my master, presented him with a recipe, which he said was a perfect cure for the inflammatory rheumatism. But the invalid not being able to read it, and fearing he should hold it upside down in pretending to do so, thanked the donor kindly, and placed it in his waistcoat pocket. My master's new friend also gave him his card, and requested him the next time he travelled that way to do him the kindness to call; adding, "I shall be pleased to see you, and so will my daughters." Mr. Johnson expressed his gratitude for the proffered hospitality, and said he should feel glad to call on his return. I have not the slightest doubt that he will fulfil the promise whenever that return takes place. After changing trains we went on a little beyond Fredericksburg, and took a steamer to Washington. . . .

For the purpose of somewhat disguising myself, I bought and wore a very good second-hand white beaver, an article which I had never indulged in before. So just before we arrived at Washington, an uncouth planter, who had been watching me very closely, said to my master, "I reckon, stranger, you are 'spiling' that ere nigger of yourn, by letting him wear such a devilish fine hat. Just look at the quality on it; the President couldn't wear a better. I should just like to go and kick it overboard." His friend touched him, and said, "Don't speak so to a gentleman." "Why not?" exclaimed the fellow. He grated his short teeth, which appeared to be nearly worn away by the incessant chewing of tobacco, and said, "It always makes me itch all over, from head to toe, to get hold of every d—d nigger I see dressed like a white man. Washington is run away with spiled and free niggers. If I had my way I would sell every d—d rascal of 'em way down South, where the devil would be whipped out on 'em."

This man's fierce manner made my master feel rather nervous, and therefore he thought the less he said the better; so he walked off without making any reply. In a few minutes we were landed at Washington, where we took a conveyance and hurried off to the train for Baltimore.

We left our cottage on Wednesday morning, the 21st of December, 1848, and arrived at Baltimore, Saturday evening, the 24th (Christmas Eve). Baltimore was the last slave port of any note at which we stopped.

On arriving there we felt more anxious than ever, because we knew not what that last dark night would bring forth. It is true we were near the goal, but our poor hearts were still as if tossed at sea; and, as there was another great and dangerous bar to pass, we were afraid our liberties would be wrecked, and, like the ill-fated Royal Charter, go down for ever just off the place we longed to reach.

They are particularly watchful at Baltimore to prevent slaves from escaping into Pennsylvania, which is a free State. After I had seen my master into one of the best carriages, and was just about to step into mine, an officer, a full-blooded Yankee of the lower order, saw me. He came quickly up, and, tapping me on the shoulder, said in his unmistakable native twang, together with no little display of his authority, "Where are you going, boy?" "To Philadelphia, sir," I humbly replied. "Well, what are you going there for?" "I am travelling with my master, who is in the next carriage, sir." "Well, I calculate you had better get him out; and be mighty quick about it, because the train will soon be starting. It is against my rules to let any man take a slave past here, unless he can satisfy them in the office that he has a right to take him along."

The officer then passed on and left me standing upon the platform, with my anxious heart apparently palpitating in the throat. At first I scarcely knew which way to turn. But it soon occurred to me that the good God, who had been with us thus far, would not forsake us at the eleventh hour. So with renewed hope I stepped into my master's carriage, to inform him of the difficulty. I found him sitting at the farther end, quite alone. As soon as he looked up and saw me, he smiled. I also tried to wear a cheerful countenance, in order to break the shock of the sad news. I knew what made him smile. He was aware that if we were fortunate we should reach our destination at five o'clock the next morning, and this made it the more painful to communicate what the officer had said; but, as there was no time to lose, I went up to him and asked him how he felt. He said "Much better," and that he thanked God we were getting on so nicely. I then said we were not getting on quite so well as we had anticipated. He anxiously and quickly asked what was the matter. I told him. He started as if struck by lightning, and exclaimed, "Good Heavens! William, is it possible that we are, after all, doomed to hopeless bondage?" I could say nothing, my heart was too full to speak, for at first I did not know what to do. However we knew it would never do to turn back to the "City of Destruction," like Bunyan's Mistrust and Timorous, because they saw lions in the narrow way after ascending the hill Difficulty; but press on, like noble Christian and Hopeful, to the great city in which dwelt a few "shining ones." So, after a few moments, I did all I could to encourage my companion, and we stepped out and made for the office: but how or where my master obtained sufficient courage to face the tyrants who had power to blast all we held dear, heaven only knows! Queen Elizabeth could not have been more terror-stricken, on being forced to land at the traitors' gate leading to the Tower, than we were on entering that office. We felt that our very existence was at stake, and that we must either sink or swim. But, as God was our present and mighty helper in this as well as in all former trials, we were able to keep our heads up and press forwards.

On entering the room we found the principal man, to whom my master said, "Do you wish to see me, sir?" "Yes," said this eagle-eyed officer; and he added, "It is against our rules, sir, to allow any person to take a slave out of Baltimore into Philadelphia, unless he can satisfy us that he has a right to take him along." "Why is that?" asked my master, with more firmness than could be expected. "Because, sir," continued he, in a voice and manner that almost chilled our blood, "if we should suffer any gentleman to take a slave past here into Philadelphia; and should the gentleman with whom the slave might be travelling turn out not to be his rightful owner; and should the proper master come and prove that his slave escaped on our road, we shall have him to pay for; and, therefore, we cannot let any slave pass here without receiving security to show, and to satisfy us, that it is all right."

This conversation attracted the attention of the large number of bustling passengers. After the officer had finished, a few of them said, "Chit, chit, chit"; not because they thought we were slaves endeavouring to escape, but merely because they thought my master was a slaveholder and invalid gentleman, and therefore it was wrong to detain him. The officer, observing that the passengers sympathised with my master, asked him if he was not acquainted with some gentleman in Baltimore that he could get to endorse for him, to show that I was his property, and that he had a right to take me off. He said, "No;" and added, "I bought tickets in Charleston to pass us through to Philadelphia, and therefore you have no right to detain us here." "Well, sir," said the man, indignantly, "right or no right, we shan't let you go." These sharp words fell upon our anxious hearts like the crack of doom, and made us feel that hope only smiles to deceive.

For a few moments perfect silence prevailed. My master looked at me, and I at him, but neither of us dared to speak a word, for fear of making some blunder that would tend to our detection. We knew that the officers had power to throw us into prison, and if they had done so we must have been detected and driven back, like the vilest felons, to a life of slavery, which we dreaded far more than sudden death.

We felt as though we had come into deep waters and were about being overwhelmed, and that the slightest mistake would clip asunder the last brittle thread of hope by which we were suspended, and let us down for ever into the dark and horrible pit of misery and degradation from which we were straining every nerve to escape. While our hearts were crying lustily unto Him who is ever ready and able to save, the conductor of the train that we had just left stepped in. The officer asked if we came by the train with him from Washington; he said we did, and left the room. Just then the bell rang for the train to leave; and had it been the sudden shock of an earthquake it could not have given us a greater thrill. The sound of the bell caused every eye to flash with apparent interest, and to be more steadily fixed upon us than before. But, as God would have it, the officer all at once thrust his fingers through his hair, and in a state of great agitation said, "I really don't know what to do; I calculate it is all right." He then told the clerk to run and tell the conductor to "let this gentleman and slave pass;" adding, "As he is not well, it is a pity to stop him here. We will let him go." My master thanked him, and stepped out and hobbled across the platform as quickly as possible. I tumbled him unceremoniously into one of the best carriages, and leaped into mine just as the train was gliding off towards our happy destination.

Contextualizing the Runaway Experience:
A Brief History of Slavery in America

Brenda E. Stevenson

Slavery, the institution and the people who were part of it, has had tremendous and long-lasting influence on American history and the American people. Common perceptions of the slaves and slaveholders, shrouded in mythology almost from the beginning, have changed dramatically over time. But lingering notions of Southern difference and black inferiority—both intimately linked to slavery—still remain along with a host of related questions about race and democracy. To study the history of slavery in the United States, therefore, is also to explore some of the fundamental questions that confront Americans of every generation.

Africans came with the first Europeans to the Americas in exploratory and exploitative missions as seamen, pirates, workers, and slaves. Scholars have documented the presence of Africans on the expeditions of Columbus to the Caribbean, Cortez to Mexico, Narváez in Florida, Cabeza de Vaca in the American Southwest, Hawkins in Brazil, Balboa in the Pacific, Pizarro in Peru, DeSoto in the North American Southeast, and Jesuit missionaries in Canada.

The first Africans designated as slave laborers arrived in the Caribbean in 1518. A century later, the first blacks were brought to Jamestown, Virginia, where, for the next few decades, they were given a status similar to that of indentured servants.

Initially Europeans brought only small numbers of Africans to the New World. However, as the need for labor grew with expansions in agriculture, mining, and other businesses, so, too, did the number of black slaves. Brazil and the Caribbean had the largest numbers of imports and for the longest span of time, with Brazil and Cuba maintaining importation until the 1880s. Figures are imprecise, but over the period Brazil received at least 4 million slaves; the French Caribbean, 1.6 million; the Dutch Caribbean, 0.5 million; the English Caribbean, 1.8 million; the Spanish Caribbean and mainland colonies, 1.6 million; and those British mainland colonies, subsequently the United States, 450,000.

Slavery in the New World began simply as one part of a long history of international trade in goods and people both in Europe and in Africa. Slavery developed differently in different colonies, but the institution was recognizable. Many civilizations of the past had embraced forced labor and every continent, including the Americas and Africa, had witnessed it prior to the initiation of the transatlantic slave trade in the 16th century. Many blacks who arrived in the New World, therefore, were familiar with a system of labor known as slavery. In Africa, slavery had been practiced in Algiers, the Sudan, the Hausa city states, Zanzibar, and among the Fulani and other ethnic groups, including the Wolof, Sherbro and Mende, the Temme, Ashanti, Yoruba, Kongo, Lozi, and Duala.

Their familiarity with the institution in their ancestral homelands, however, did not diminish the horrors the blacks were to encounter in the Americas. Slavery in Africa usually was quite different from New World forms. In Africa slaves usually were persons who had been captured in war, although some were born or sold into bondage. Treatment often depended on the origin of their status. Prisoners of war generally had a harsher life. They could be sold and frequently were. Women often were forced into concubinage. Some were even sacrificed by victorious kings or rulers in religious ceremonies. Others were held for many years, sometimes through generations, and became part of the clan, or extended family, and were treated as valued workers. Native-born slaves, on the other hand, customarily were not sold and had some important privileges such as the right to inherit property and to marry free people.

Indigenous African slavery seemed to be more conducive to family stability and cohesiveness than the American institutions. Some West African societies, for example, forbade interference in a slave's marriage and allowed slaves to buy their freedom and the freedom of family members. Others forbade masters from having sexual relations with their slaves' wives. Some freed women when they gave birth. They also had greater class mobility with some passing from slave status to become soldiers and artisans.

Slavery in any society usually can be explained better, however, through a discussion of the slave's restrictions rather than his or her privileges. Most precolonial West African slaves could not become priests, hold important religious posts, or visit sacred places or the residence of the local chief. Some were not allowed to dress as free persons, or marry or be buried near them.

Slavery in Africa, as elsewhere, was not a static institution. It changed drastically over time usually as a response to cultural, economic, and military factors. The invasions of North African Arabs in the eleventh and twelfth centuries and the Europeans from the sixteenth through the nineteenth centuries caused great escalations in the numbers enslaved and tremendous changes in the status and function of the enslaved. The desire and, eventually, the need of West Africans to trade with Europeans for weapons and other prized goods prompted some Africans to get involved in the slave trade to such an extent that they could no longer draw on their traditional reserves of slaves.

The Atlantic slave trade was dangerous, controversial, and lucrative work. For Europeans in particular the trade was extremely profitable. It was indeed the foundation on which colonial agriculture and shipbuilding and European mercantilism and industry were built in the seventeenth and eighteenth centuries. The slave trade also brought profits to African middlemen, or caboceers, and the chiefs and rulers who traded their gold, ivory, dyewoods, slaves, and foodstuffs for European weaponry, textiles, liquor, glass beads, and brass rings. As greater demands from the New World made the trade more lucrative, more and more slaves were abducted through armed raids.

African villages, however, did not passively comply with slave trading raids; they fought back. Famed Ibo autobiographer Olaudah Equiano noted that the phenomenon of enemies coming into his village to take slaves was so prevalent during his childhood that often the men and the women took weapons to the fields in case of a surprise attack. "Even our women are warriors," Equiano recalled, "and march boldly out to fight along with the men. Our whole district is a kind of militia."[1] Other West Africans who had been harassed by slave procurers went to the source of the problem, European traders, and attacked the company forts. Would-be slaves tried all kinds of ways to escape, sometimes sneaking away, getting help from people passing by, overpowering the guard watching them, and committing suicide. Most of them did not escape, but they did establish a tradition of resistance that followed the slaves to the Americas.

Once they reached the forts on the coast, slavers placed them in temporary holding pens known as baracoons. The capture and transport to baracoons was a brutal experience physically and emotionally for the Africans. Their greatest anxiety derived from their fears—of their slavers, the slave ships, and their fate. Olaudah Equiano's response probably was a typical one. "The first object which saluted my eyes when I arrived on the coast was the sea, and a slave ship, which was as then riding at anchor and waiting for its cargo," Equiano recalled. "These filled me with astonishment, which was soon converted into terror."[2] He had entered a completely different world. None of what he had experienced, however, from the time of his capture to his arrival on the coast in a slave coffle, had prepared Equiano for the horrors of the Middle Passage, the trip across the Atlantic Ocean.

Equiano did not know what to make of these strange people who looked, spoke, and behaved so differently from himself. "I was now persuaded that I had got into a world of bad spirits," he recalled, "and that they were going to kill me. Their complexions too differing so much from ours, their long hair, and the language they spoke, which was very different from any I had ever heard, united to confirm me in this belief. . . . [Q]uite overpowered with horror and anguish, I . . . fainted."[3]

Conditions aboard the slave ships during their voyages from Africa to America, which could take three weeks to three months, often were torture. Segregated by gender, the blacks were chained together and packed so tightly that they often were forced to lie on their sides in spoon fashion. Clearances in ships' holds often were only two to four feet high. During periods of good weather, the slavers allowed the Africans on deck for sun and washing. In bad weather or because of some perceived threat, they had to remain below, chained to one another, lying in their own feces, urine, blood, and vomit. "The floor of the rooms," one eighteenth-century ship observer wrote, "was so covered with blood and mucus which had proceeded from them in consequence of . . . [dysentery], that it resembled a slaughter-house."[4] Both shipboard personnel and American coastline observers reported that sometimes an approaching slave ship could be smelled before it could be seen.

More than two hundred attempts at on-board slave mutinies are documented. Slaves also resisted through hunger strikes, violent outbursts, refusal to cooperate, and suicide. Mortality rates varied greatly: sometimes as low as 10 percent, rarely as high as 100 percent. Still, it is estimated that several million Africans died before they ever reached the Americas.

The first blacks to arrive in the British colony of Virginia reportedly came in 1619. The previous summer the English ship *Treasurer* left Virginia to acquire salt, goats, and other provisions. Shortly thereafter, it came into contact with a Dutch man-of-war, and the two vessels sailed on together. They "happened upon" a Spanish frigate carrying slaves and other cargo. They seized the Spanish vessel and divided the cargo between them. Exactly how many Africans the Spanish ship was carrying we do not know, but the Dutch ship took on a hundred and sailed back to Jamestown after becoming separated from the *Treasurer*. By the time it arrived in Jamestown in August 1619, there were twenty Africans aboard; the other eighty had died at sea. The *Treasurer* eventually reached Jamestown, too, with one African. The others—perhaps as many as twenty-nine—had been sold in Bermuda. From that point, Virginia's black population grew slowly but steadily; there were three hundred blacks in 1649 and two thousand, or 5 percent of the population, by 1671.

The first Africans in Virginia, however, had an uncertain status. Slavery was not a formal, legalized institution in the colony until the 1660s, and subsequent laws made slavery more inescapable for more Africans as larger numbers of them began to arrive. The system's increasing presence can be attributed to numerous conditions. Most important, indentures did not keep pace with the growing needs for labor. Colonial administrators also actively encouraged black slavery, extending in 1635 the headright system, which rewarded those who imported persons to the colonies with 50 acres of Virginia land for each person so imported, to also include those who sponsored the arrival of blacks. At about the same time, there was a belief that blacks, unlike Europeans or the indigenous peoples, could work in the hot Southern sun and that they had a natural immunity to diseases like malaria and yellow fever. Moreover, the rise of the Company of Royal Adventurers Trading to Africa and its later merger with the Royal African Company guaranteed mainland planters greater access to slave imports. By the end of the seventeenth century, therefore, increasing numbers of slaves were entering Virginia and other colonies. Soon they were even the majority in many of Virginia's tidewater and Southside counties (those south of the James River). By 1750, they numbered more than 101,000 in Virginia while whites numbered 130,000.

By the 1670s, Africans lived in all of the British mainland colonies. Slaves were mentioned in Maryland's official documents by 1638, and the colony legally formalized the institution in 1663. The Lords Proprietors of Carolina, four of whom were members of the Royal African Company, expected slavery to play an important role in that colony's economic development and guaranteed its practice even before settlement. They, too, offered economic inducements for slave importation through the headright system. By 1710, the black population of 4,100 in what would become South Carolina almost equaled that of the whites. When the colony separated in 1729, South Carolina had 10,000 whites and 20,000 slaves while North Carolina had 30,000 whites and 6,000 slaves.

Georgia was late to embrace the institution. It legally banned slavery at the colony's founding, but, at the behest of settlers who saw slavery flourishing in neighboring South Carolina, Georgia repealed the prohibition in 1750. Advertisements in the colony's *Gazette* soon read like so many others of the era: "To be Sold on Thursday next, at publick vendue. Ten Likely Gold Coast New Negroes. Just imported from the West Indies, consisting of eight stout men and two women."[5]

Blacks were slaves in the Dutch colony of New Netherlands long before the British took over the colony in 1664 and renamed it New York. Slaves from Angola and Brazil routinely worked the farms of the Hudson River Valley even though the British did not legalize the institution until 1684. By the end of the seventeenth century, only slightly more than 2,000 were in the colony, but by 1771 the 20,000 slaves made up nearly 12 percent of New York residents.

New Jersey under the Swedish and Dutch had few slaves, but that changed once the British gained control of the colony in 1664 and, as in South Carolina and Virginia, offered land incentives for the importation of Africans. By 1745, New Jersey had 4,600 slaves in a total population of about 61,000.

Bondage fell on less fertile ground in Pennsylvania, where Quakers, for moral reasons, and artisans, on economic principle, opposed any increases in slavery. Before William Penn received his land grant, however, the Dutch had imported African slaves. And there always were those who wanted slave labor as eagerly as the Royal African Company wanted to sell slaves. The conflict was symbolized by the tax placed on slave imports by Pennsylvania: a duty of 20 shillings for every African imported in 1700 was doubled in 1705. When the colony's Assembly passed another law in 1712 that completely outlawed the importation of blacks, the Royal African Company persuaded the Privy Council in England to nullify the law. By 1750, Pennsylvania had approximately 11,000 slaves, most of whom were living in Philadelphia.

The New England colonies imported fewer slaves than the Middle or Southern colonies, but African slavery also was a part of their economy and culture. By 1715, there were approximately 2,000 slaves in Massachusetts and 1,500 in Connecticut. During the early 1770s, on the eve of the American Revolution, Rhode Island boasted a slave population of almost 3,800 while New Hampshire had only 654 slaves in a total population of about 62,000.

Unlike voluntary immigrants, Africans did not leave or arrive in family groups. They also had little opportunity to form family groups for several years after their arrival, because a typical cargo included twice as many males as females. Strangers in a foreign land, forced to comprehend a new language spoken by people who looked and behaved so differently from themselves, confronted with racism, sexism, hunger, epidemics, back-breaking work quotas, and harsh corporal punishment, these first few Africans spread thinly throughout the colonies undoubtedly suffered great emotional and physical distress. Slave owners conducted a general "seasoning" aimed at acclimating "outlandish" Africans so they might know their "place" and function appropriately in the system. Slave responses to this process varied tremendously. Even those Africans who lived with numerous other blacks might need anywhere from two years for minimal "seasoning" to four years for learning a functional creole language. For many, it took an entire lifetime or generations to reconcile their African cultural heritage and perspectives with their new lives as slaves in America.

Agricultural labor was not foreign to them. Slaves performed a number of diverse tasks from the very beginning of their presence on the North American mainland, but most were farm workers. Rising early in the morning to the sound of an overseer or driver blowing a horn and working until nightfall for five and one-half to six days a week, slaves planted, grew, harvested, and helped to ready crops for local, domestic, and international markets.

In colonial Virginia and North Carolina, they raised tobacco, corn, wheat, and other grains, grew vegetables, and raised livestock. South Carolina piedmont slaves produced tobacco, corn, and indigo. Those along the coastal plain of that colony and Georgia used their rice-growing skills they brought from their native African societies to reap great fortunes for their owners.

In the Northern and Middle colonies their labor was more diverse because of the shorter growing season. They mostly worked on small farms, dairy farms, and cattle-raising estates. They cultivated vegetables, tended livestock, and served as house slaves. Others worked in shipbuilding and mercantile enterprises and as artisans of one sort or another.

The development of black slavery as an institution and racism as an underlying ideology progressed with little public opposition or even debate until the era of the American Revolution. But this opposition, much of it disparate and disorganized, did yield results and did change the character of slavery by the end of the Revolutionary period. First, and perhaps most important, slavery had become a Southern phenomenon. Slavery was abolished or gradually eliminated through measures created in 1780 in Pennsylvania, in 1783 in Massachusetts, in 1784 in Connecticut and Rhode Island, in 1785 in New York, and in 1786 in New Jersey. In 1787, Congress prohibited slavery in the Northwest Territory. Scores of slaves were freed in the Upper South after the American Revolution, and the colonization of blacks in the Caribbean or West Africa was being entertained as a viable "solution" to the problem of free blacks in a society that embraced black slavery.

Slavery had changed with the American Revolution, but dependence on slave agricultural labor was growing rapidly in the Southern states. The profitable cultivation and ginning of short staple cotton made possible by the cotton gin in 1793, the expansion of U.S. terri-

tory in the Lower South and Southwest and West, and slave labor
fueled an economic boom that lasted until the Civil War. It made an
extremely small portion of Southern society extremely wealthy and
powerful, perhaps more so than any other group in the young nation.

Cotton was king. National production of raw cotton, a major U.S.
export to Europe, increased 921 percent, from 349,000 bales in 1819
to 3.2 million in 1855. This explosion in production led to an insa-
tiable demand for slaves, particularly in the Deep South. Between
1820 and 1860, the number of slaves increased by 257 percent, to nearly
four million. At the same time, the concentration of Southern blacks
was shifting dramatically from the Upper to the Lower South. For instance, the slave population of the Lower South increased 34 percent
from 1850 to 1860 while in the Upper South it rose only 9.7 percent.

The labor that slaves performed greatly influenced the quality of
their lives. With few exceptions, men and women generally did the
same kind of field work. The slave Austin Steward, for example,
noted that on the plantation on which he worked "it was usual for men
and women to work side by side . . . and in many kinds of work, the
women were compelled to do as much as the men."[6] Some males did
perform more physically strenuous work, and few females held super-
visory roles, such as driver, that males routinely occupied. Women,
nonetheless, usually worked longer hours, spinning, weaving, nurs-
ing, and cooking for their owners once their field work was over,
then doing all their own child care and domestic chores in the slave
quarters.

Male slaves fared better materially than their female counterparts.
When distributing food rations, slaveholders rarely gave females as
much meat, meal, or other items as they gave males. Since slave women
usually lived with their children and had to share some of their smaller
portion with them, a mother's food allotment was especially sparse.
Some fathers who lived away from their wives and children may have
put aside part of their food allowance for their families, but owners
did not compel them to do so. Similarly, the long pants, shirts, jack-
ets, and other clothing that masters provided male slaves twice a year

were much more appropriate for bending, stooping, and repelling insects endemic to field labor than the skirts and dresses females had to wear. Slave owners might have expected women to work as hard as men, but they were unwilling to provide women with equal material support. While the vast majority of slaves worked in the fields, up to ten percent of them were occupied otherwise. In urban settings, females worked as waitresses, washerwomen, midwives, domestics, and in factory maintenance. Male slaves had more access to skilled positions and exclusively held the more lucrative and prestigious jobs of blacksmith, cooper, painter, wheelwright, carpenter, tanner, joiner, cobbler, miner, and seaman.

Slaves began working at about age six or sometimes earlier if they seemed physically mature. Boys traditionally learned how to herd and tend livestock, pick up trash and stones, gather moss and other grasses, and carry water. Girls did similar tasks but also helped care for young children and worked in the kitchen. Both boys and girls picked fruit, nuts, and berries, pulled weeds and worms, and occasionally served as companions for their master's young children. Childhood was a time when slaves began to learn not only work routines but work discipline and related punishment.

Slaveholding women usually were in charge of disciplining slave children who worked in and around their master's home. One ex-slave interviewed in 1841 stated that whenever his mistress did not like his work she would hit him with tongs or a shovel, pull his hair, pinch his ears until they bled, or order him to sit in a corner and eat dry bread until he almost choked. George Jackson recalled that his mistress scolded and beat him when he was pulling weeds. "I pulled a cabbage stead of weed," he confessed. "She would jump me and beat me. I can remember cryin'. She told me she had to learn me to be careful."[7] These kinds of "lessons" hardly ceased as a slave matured.

Slaves young and old had to complete their assigned tasks satisfactorily to escape punishment. Such reprisals usually meant verbal abuse for small offenses, but owners, overseers, and drivers did not hesitate to impose severe floggings and public humiliation or even sell those who did not or would not complete tasks or were disrespectful to authority figures. "Beat women! Why sure he beat women," former slave Elizabeth Sparks exclaimed. "Beat women jes' lak men."[8] Slaves were stripped of their clothing, faced against a tree or wall, tied down or made to hang from a beam, their legs roped together with a rail or board between them, and severely beaten. The beatings provided owners and overseers with a vehicle to both chastise and symbolically strip slaves of their personal pride and integrity while invoking terrifying images of the master's power.

For slaves, the worst punishment imaginable was to be sold away from one's family and friends. This phenomenon was tied more to economic variables than the owner's need to punish or chastise "troublesome" slaves. Amanda Edmonds recalled the regret she felt when watching her family's slaves sold to pay off debts after her father's death. "I know servants are very aggravating sometimes and [you] wish they were in Georgia," she confessed in her diary, "but when I see the poor . . . and sometimes faithful, ones torn away so, I cannot help feeling for them."[9]

The dramatic shift in slave concentrations from the Upper to the Lower South and Southwest brought devastating consequences in the domestic lives of slaves. Hundreds of thousands lost husbands, wives, sons, daughters, other kin, and friends to this internal slave trade. Would-be slaveholders regularly attended public sales for slaves that usually were held in a town square, on the front steps of the local courthouse or sometimes at the slave trader's place of business.

Owners who wished to sell slaves usually brought them to town a few days before the auction and temporarily kept them in the county jail as a security precaution. Prospective buyers or their representatives went to the jail to examine slaves, who sat there miserably contemplating their fate and what might happen to family members and friends.

The despair was tremendous. One slave imprisoned in Bruin's jail in Alexandria, Virginia, wrote a desperate plea to her free black mother who worked as a laundress in New York City. "Aunt Sally and all of her children, and Aunt Hagar and all her children are sold, and grandmother is almost crazy," Emily Russel wrote in January 1850, and she, too, would be sold if her mother did not soon raise enough money to purchase her. "O mother! my dear mother! come now and see your distressed and heartbroken daughter once more. Mother! my dear mother! do not forsake me; for I feel desolate! Please come now."[10] The young woman eventually was sold to a long-distance slave trader for $1,200, but she died on the way to the "fancy girl" prostitution market in New Orleans.

Unfortunately, slave owners often benefitted from and thus were willing to instigate or ignore the tragedies that crippled a slave family's emotional and physical well-being. Even the sexual abuse of slave mothers and daughters often meant a financial gain for owners, who could claim as their property the children who might result since slave children derived their status from their mothers. Likewise, the domestic slave trade broke up families and extended kin networks. The loss of spouses and family members came to be so great in the Upper South that many children in the last slave generations grew up without the benefit of their mothers or fathers.

Despite the devastating impact of slave life on black kinship, the family was the slave's most important survival tool. It flourished not so much because of its stability but its flexibility. The extended family of persons related by blood, marriage, and long-standing familial-like contact was its most persistent and essential characteristic. When fathers disappeared in the domestic slave trade, uncles and grandfathers often took on a paternal role for children left behind. Grandmothers and aunts nurtured, fed, and socialized motherless children. Young adults cared for the elderly whose children had been sold away. Extended kin did not replace husbands or wives lost forever to the Deep South but did offer some measure of comfort. Some slaves chose to remarry, and others were compelled by their owners to find another spouse to continue to have children who would become slaves.

Slave marriages were not recognized legally, but the weddings and commitments of African Americans were important events for slave families and communities. Georgianna Gibbs remembered that when the slaves on her farm married they had to "jump over a broom three times" before they actually were considered married.[11] Some owners performed a brief service; others relied on slave or local ministers to officiate. A spirited celebration attended by family and friends usually followed with music, food, and dancing that often lasted most of the night.

Religion, dance, music, and food were vital aspects of the slaves' cultural life and exhibited traits drawn from their ancestral past in West Africa and their experiences in America. While many slaves converted to Christianity, especially as Baptists and Methodists, others held onto their Islamic faith and other religious rituals and beliefs derived from Africa. Like so much of slave culture, the religion in the quarters often was created from both sources. African traditions appeared in their musical instruments, medicines, and domestic wares, such as textiles, baskets, containers, and buttons. African slaves also helped introduce various West African foods like millet, groundnut, benne, gourds, Congo peas, and yams to America. Scholars have documented that the slaves' reliance on their own cultural references often allowed them to control aspects of their lives and withstand the psychological inhumanity of enslavement.

From the perspective of the slave, however, life was not experienced in this scholarly fashion. Slave life meant hard work, poor rations, sometimes brutal beatings, lost families, and illness. It also meant marriage on negotiated terms, but marriage nonetheless, and children who learned how to appreciate their kin, communities of friends, and, between hard times, laughter, pride, romance, song, dance, and God.

NOTES

1. From Olaudah Equiano, *The Interesting Narrative of the Life of Olaudah Equiano, or Gustavus Vassa, the African. Written by Himself, Vol. I.*, 1789, Schomburg Center for Research in Black Culture, New York Public Library.
2. Ibid.
3. Ibid.

4. August Meier and Elliott M. Rudwick, *From Plantation to Ghetto*, 3rd ed. (New York: Macmillan, 1976), p. 38.

5. Brenda E. Stevenson, "Slavery," in *Black Women in America: An Historical Encyclopedia*, vol. 2, Darlene Clark Hine, ed. (New York: Carlson Publishing, 1993).

6. From Austin Steward, *Twenty-Two Years a Slave, and Forty Years a Freeman; Embracing a Correspondence of Several Years, While President of Wilberforce Colony, London, Canada West*, 1857 (Academic Affairs Library, University of North Carolina at Chapel Hill, 1997).

7. Brenda E. Stevenson, *Life in Black and White: Family and Community in the Slave South* (New York: Oxford University Press, 1997), pp. 187–88.

8. Ibid., p. 194.

9. Ibid., p. 213.

10. John W. Blassingame, *Slave Testimony: Two Centuries of Letters, Speeches, Interviews, and Autobiographies* (Baton Rouge: *Louisiana State University* Press, 1977), p. 87.

11. Stevenson, *Life in Black and White*, p. 228.

Bibliography

Aptheker, Herbert. *American Negro Slave Revolts*. New York: Columbia University Press, 1943.

———. *Nat Turner's Slave Rebellion*. New York: Humanities Press, 1966.

Berlin, Ira. "Coming to Terms with Slavery in Twenty-First-Century America." In *Slavery and Public History: The Tough Stuff of American Memory,* James Oliver Horton and Lois E. Horton, eds. New York: New Press, 2006.

———. *Many Thousands Gone: The First Two Centuries of Slavery in North America*. Cambridge, MA: Harvard University Press, 1998.

Boles, John B. *Black Southerners, 1619–1869.* Lexington: University Press of Kentucky, 1984.

Chaplin, Joyce E. "Creating a Cotton South in Georgia and South Carolina, 1760–1815." *Journal of Southern History* 57, no. 2 (May 1991): 171.

Davis, David Brion. *The Problem of Slavery in the Age of Revolution*. New York: Oxford University Press, 1999.

Foner, Eric. *Reconstruction: America's Unfinished Revolution, 1863–1877.* New York: Harper Collins, 1989.

Foner, Philip S. *History of Black Americans: From Africa to the Emergence of the Cotton Kingdom*. Westport, CT: Greenwood Press, 1975.

———. *History of Black Americans: From the Emergence of the Cotton Kingdom to the Eve of the Compromise of 1850*. Westport, CT: Greenwood Press, 1983.

Forbes, Robert Pierce. *The Missouri Compromise and Its Aftermath*. Chapel Hill: University of North Carolina Press, 2007.

Franklin, John Hope, and Alfred A. Moss Jr. *From Slavery to Freedom: A History of African Americans*. New York: Knopf, 2000.

Franklin, John Hope, and Loren Schweninger. *Runaway Slaves: Rebels on the Plantation*. New York: Oxford University Press, 2000.

Genovese, Eugene D. *Roll Jordan Roll: The World Slaves Made*. New York: Vintage, 1976.

Gordon-Reed, Annette. *Thomas Jefferson and Sally Hemings: An American Controversy.* Charlottesville: University of Virginia Press, 1997.

Gross, Ariela. *Double Character: Slavery and Mastery in the Antebellum Southern Courtroom.* Princeton, NJ: Princeton University Press, 2000.

Gutman, Herbert G. *The Black Family in Slavery and Freedom, 1750–1925.* New York: Vintage, 1976.

Hartgrove, W. B. "The Negro Soldier in the American Revolution." *Journal of Negro History* 1 (1916).

Higginbotham, Leon A. *In the Matter of Color: Race and the American Legal Process.* New York: Oxford University Press, 1980.

Horton, James Oliver. "Slavery in American History: An Uncomfortable National Dialogue." In *Slavery and Public History: The Tough Stuff of American Memory,* James Oliver Horton and Lois E. Horton, eds. New York: New Press, 2006.

Horton, James Oliver, and Lois E. Horton. "Introduction." In *Slavery and Public History: The Tough Stuff of American Memory,* James Oliver Horton and Lois E. Horton, eds. New York: New Press, 2006.

Kolchin, Peter. *American Slavery, 1619–1877.* New York: Hill and Wang, 1993.

Levine, Bruce. *Half Slave and Half Free: The Roots of Civil War.* New York: Hill and Wang, 1992.

Miller, Randall M. "Slavery." In *Encyclopedia of African American Culture and History,* Jack Salzman, David Lionel Smith, and Cornel West, eds. New York: Macmillan Library Reference, 1996.

Pierce, Yolanda. "*The Narrative of the Life of J. D. Green, a Runaway Slave:* Some New Thoughts on an Old Form." *ANQ* 14, no. 4 (2001): 15–23.

Pybus, Cassandra. "Jefferson's Faulty Math: The Question of Slave Defections in the American Revolution." *William & Mary Quarterly* 62, no. 2 (2005): 243.

Raboteau, Albert J. *Slave Religion: The "Invisible Institution" in the Antebellum South.* New York: Oxford University Press, 1978.

Reiss, Oscar. *Blacks in Colonial America.* Jefferson, NC: McFarland & Company, 1997.

Robertson, Claire. "Africa into the Americas? Slavery and Women, the Family, and the Gender Division of Labor." In *More Than Chattel: Black Women and Slavery in the Americas,* David Barry Gaspar and Darlene Clark Hine, eds. Bloomington: Indiana University Press, 1996.

Rose, Willie Lee. *A Documentary History of Slavery in North America.* New York: Oxford University Press, 1976.

Smith, Mark M. "Remembering Mary, Shaping Revolt: Reconsidering the Stono Rebellion." *Journal of Southern History* 67, no. 3 (2001): 513–34.

Stevenson, Brenda E. "From Bondage to Freedom: Slavery in America." In *Underground Railroad: An Epic in United States History,* Larry Gara et al. Washington, DC: U.S. Department of the Interior, National Park Service, 1998.

———. *Life in Black and White: Family and Community in the Slave South.* New York: Oxford University Press, 1996.

Sullivan, Ronald S., Jr. "Classical Racialism, Justice Story, and Margaret Morgan's Journey From Freedom to Slavery: The Story of *Prigg v. Pennsylvania*." In *Race Law Stories*, Rachel Moran and Devon Wayne Carbado, eds. New York: Foundation Press, 2008.

Tushnet, Mark. *The American Law of Slavery, 1810–1860: Considerations of Humanity and Interest*. Princeton, NJ: Princeton University Press, 1981.

White, Deborah Gray. *Ar'n't I a Woman? Female Slaves in the Plantation South*. New York: W. W. Norton, 1985.

White, Shane. "Slavery in the North." *OAH [Organization of American Historians] Magazine of History* 17, no. 3 (2003): 18.

Zinn, Howard. *A People's History of the United States: 1492–Present*. New York: Harper Perennial, 1995.

About the Editors

Devon W. Carbado is a professor of law and of African American studies at the University of California at Los Angeles. The former vice dean of the UCLA Law School, he teaches courses in constitutional law, race and the law, critical race theory, and African American studies. He was named Professor of the Year by the UCLA School of Law Classes of 2000 and 2006, was the 2003 recipient of the Rutter Award for Excellence in Teaching, and was recently awarded the University Distinguished Teaching Award, the Eby Award for the Art of Teaching. Carbado is also a recipient of the Fletcher Foundation Fellowship, which, modeled on the Guggenheim Fellowships, is awarded to scholars whose work furthers the goals of *Brown v. Board of Education*. Carbado is the editor of several books, including *Race Law Stories* (with Rachel Moran), and his articles have appeared in the law reviews of UCLA, the University of Michigan, Yale, Cornell, and UC-Berkeley, among others. A board member of the African American Policy Forum and a Jamestown Fellow, Carbado lives in Los Angeles.

Donald Weise is the coeditor (with David Hilliard) of *The Huey P. Newton Reader*, a book of writings by the Black Panther Party founder and chief theoretician. As a writer, Weise was involved with the Huey P. Newton Foundation for ten years and worked with former Black

Panther Party members David Hilliard and Bobby Seale, among others. He is also coeditor (with Devon W. Carbado) of the Lambda Award–winning anthology *Time on Two Crosses: The Collected Writings of Bayard Rustin,* as well as *Black Like Us: A Century of Lesbian, Gay and Bisexual African American Fiction* (with Carbado and Dwight A. McBride). Weise is publisher of Magnus Books, a press specializing in LGBT literature whose list includes notable writers such as Edmund White, Samuel R. Delany, David Mixner, and Rev. Mel White. Weise lives in New York.